LIBEL AND THE FIRST AMENDMENT

LIBEL AND THE FIRST AMENDMENT

Legal History and Practice in Print and Broadcasting

RICHARD LABUNSKI

Transaction Books
New Brunswick (U.S.A.) and Oxford (U.K.)

Copyright © 1987 by Transaction, Inc.
New Brunswick, New Jersey 08903

Library of Congress Catalog Number: 85-24656
ISBN: 0-88738-082-4
Printed in the United States of America

Library of Congress Cataloging in Publication Data

Labunski, Richard E.
  Libel and the First Amendment.

  Includes index.
  1. Libel and slander—United States.   2. Mass media—Law and legislation—United States.   3. Freedom of the press—United States.
I. Title.
KF1266.L3   1986   343.73′099   85-24656
ISBN 0-88738-082-4   347.30399

*To my wife Elisa,
whose help and love
are all that a writer needs*

Contents

1

Journalists in Court:
A Hostile Environment

Of the many troubling issues facing journalists in the 1980s, none is more complicated and potentially damaging to their First Amendment rights than libel. There are indications that the number of lawsuits against media organizations has been increasing at an alarming rate in recent years. The possibility that a single successful lawsuit will put a newspaper or broadcasting station out of business has never been greater. Even meritless suits brought to harass journalists can be costly to defend. The expense and commitment required to fight a libel suit can make even the most courageous editor or news director think more carefully about doing the next controversial story.

Not long ago it could hardly have been imagined that a jury would award $26.5 million to a former Miss Wyoming who claimed that a fictional story in a magazine was actually about her.[1] In the last few years newspapers in large and small cities have lost libel suits in which plaintiffs have been awarded huge sums of money.[2] Several cases have sent shock waves throughout journalism: a newspaper in Illinois lost a $9.2 million suit because of a memo written by two reporters that was never published;[3] a broadcasting company spent $7 million on legal expenses in a case it eventually settled for a reported $1.25 million;[4] and a jury so badly misunderstood a judge's explanation of the applicable libel laws in awarding $2 million to the president of an oil company that the judge had to overturn the verdict.[5]

The impact of such lawsuits, even when journalists are at fault, could significantly affect what people read in newspapers and hear and see on radio and television. A form of self-imposed censorship, the natural hesitancy to do a story that although true might be difficult to prove in court, could deprive readers and viewers of access to important information about their communities and public officials. Such self-imposed censorship is especially ominous because it is virtually immeasurable.[6]

1

The increasing number of libel suits and the size of the monetary awards are only part of the problem. The U.S. Supreme Court, which nationalized libel laws some twenty years ago, has decided a number of major libel cases by adopting standards it has been unable or unwilling to enunciate clearly. No journalist, no matter how schooled in law and judicial process, knows for certain what standard of liability will be applied to a particular case. By adopting several tests that determine if the plaintiff is a public or private figure, or whether the controversy involves a public issue, the Court has failed to provide guidance to even the most perceptive journalist, or to individuals seeking to vindicate their reputation. In a major decision the Court even deviated from a test it had established in the very same opinion.[7] The result has been substantial variance among lower courts in complying with Supreme Court decisions, and much confusion.[8] The disarray of libel laws and recent well-publicized cases in which plaintiffs have won in or out of court large sums of money from news organizations have probably emboldened the subjects of news stories to file lawsuits in what is clearly an already litigious society.

Ever since its landmark decision in *New York Times v. Sullivan*[9] in 1964, the Court has attempted to balance reputational interests with First Amendment press freedoms. Our society legitimately recognizes the right of individuals to be free from the printing or broadcasting of defamatory falsehoods made in reckless disregard for whether they were true or not. Except in the minds of a few individuals, the First Amendment has never been held to be so absolute.[10] Society has a substantial interest in preventing irresponsible journalists from damaging the reputations of public figures and private individuals.

Yet society also has a compelling interest in seeing that the press freedoms granted under the First Amendment allow the media to cover the activities of government and individuals with a reasonable margin of error, and without the responsibility of proving that everything printed or broadcast was true. That protection is necessary for an independent and courageous press, even if individual reputations sometimes suffer. Particularly for journalists producing a daily newspaper or daily newscast, there must be latitude in which they can make mistakes without being held to so strict a standard of liability that innocent errors are severely punished. Although special care must be taken when news stories involve private individuals who, through no effort of their own, are thrust into a public controversy, there must still be sufficient room for error.[11]

In attempting to balance these competing interests, the Supreme Court, in a series of cases from 1964 to 1971, initially added weight to the First Amendment side of the scales.[12] The Court believed that state libel laws, a mixture of English common law and restrictive statutes, provided insufficient protection to the press.[13] After growing increasingly concerned that its rulings had caused a serious imbalance, the Court from 1974 to 1979 tried to recalibrate the scales by adding weight to the reputational side.[14] Rather than delineate rules that provide appropriate protection to each side, the Court's decisions have only obscured the constitutional framework of libel laws and created tests that do not provide the necessary balance.

Applying historical principles of libel law to modern electronic media has proved to be especially difficult. Most libel cases have involved a lawsuit directed at a newspaper. Long before the first broadcasting station went on the air more than half a century ago, newspapers and magazines informed and entertained the public.[15] When the First Amendment became part of the U.S. Constitution in 1791, the Framers could not have imagined television networks broadcasting live pictures of men walking on the moon, or cable systems delivering dozens of channels, or radio and television networks bouncing their signals off satellites orbiting many miles above the earth's surface. Nor could they have conceived the potential that television in particular has to inflict damage to an individual's reputation.

Today broadcasting has assumed a role that could not have been envisioned by even its strongest advocates a few decades ago. Americans in substantial numbers are puttting down their newspapers and turning to television as their primary source of news.[16] The special informing function that broadcasting has assumed makes its vulnerability to libel suits a subject of much importance. How the nature of the journalism practiced by broadcasters makes them susceptible to libel suits is worthy of serious examination.

The special position that the First Amendment is granted in our system is a recognition of the paramount importance of the free exchange of ideas to self-government. Freedom of speech and press provisions of the First Amendment are designed to remove barriers that interfere with the exchange of information citizens need to make intelligent decisions when choosing public officials and shaping policy.

The Constitution, however, protects other rights that sometimes conflict with the First Amendment. The right to a fair trial can be imperiled by an irresponsible press more interested in public curiosity than public interest. Threats to national security may weaken the First Amendment's intolerance for prior restraint. The right to vindicate a damaged reputation predates our own Constitution, and both criminal and civil libel cases were heard by our courts long after the First Amendment became part of the Constitution.

"Balancing" the First Amendment with other societal interests has become immensely difficult but is of no less importance today. Much of the balancing is done in a courtroom, where journalists and others fight to preserve the vitality of the First Amendment. It is, however, a forum journalists are increasingly afraid to enter. And when defending libel suits before juries, they sometimes learn that their "readers" and "viewers" are not entirely happy with the way they do their jobs, and are often unconvinced that the First Amendment grants them special protection.

Journalists in Court

All journalists, whether working for print or electronic media, are facing increasingly hostile courts and a skeptical public that often contend that journalists enjoy only the rights granted to all citizens. Particularly when attempting to cover criminal trials, journalists have found judges to be impatient with First Amendment claims that journalists are entitled, because of their special informing function, to certain privileges not granted to others. In various cases courts have held that the First Amendment does not grant reporters a constitutional right to keep confidential the names of sources;[17] that police can conduct unannounced raids on newsrooms armed only with a search warrant;[18] that a reporter who refuses to name a source of information may be jailed for contempt;[19] and that preliminary hearings, and sometimes trials, can be closed to the press.[20] In libel cases courts have held that a plaintiff may look for the forum most unfriendly to First Amendment interests to file the suit even when neither the plaintiff nor the defendant has any relationship to that state;[21] and some judges have held in libel cases that even if reporters have granted confidentiality, they must reveal the names of sources. If a reporter refuses, the judge assumes there was no source and a default judgment is entered for the plaintiff.[22] Considered together, the cases indicate the increasingly unfriendly environment that journalists are forced to enter when defending libel suits.

Confidential Sources

On June 29, 1972, the Supreme Court issued a decision long awaited by journalists and others. Do news reporters have a constitutional privilege against disclosing sources of information or the information itself? By a 5-4 decision, the Court held that no such constitutional privilege exists, at least when reporters are called before grand juries to testify about criminal activity.[23]

Reporter Paul Branzburg wrote a series of stories in the *Louisville Courier-Journal* about two persons, whom he did not identify, who synthesized hashish from marijuana. Branzburg had personally observed the possession of the drugs and the synthesis process. When he was called before the county grand jury and asked to identify the pair, Branzburg refused on the grounds that the Kentucky shield law and the state and U.S. constitutions granted him a privilege to keep the names of the individuals confidential.[24]

Branzburg moved to quash the subpoena issued by the grand jury because it would entail a drastic "incursion upon First Amendment freedoms in the absence of compelling Commonwealth interest in requiring [Branzburg's] appearance before the grand jury."[25] Branzburg also argued that he must be excused from any appearance before the grand jury because once he "is required to go behind the closed doors of the grand jury room, his effectiveness as a reporter in these cases [use and sale of illegal drugs] is totally destroyed."[26] Justice Byron White, writing for the majority of the Supreme Court in *Branzburg v. Hayes*, said the sole issue is the obligation of reporters to respond to subpoenas as other citizens are required to do and to answer questions relevant to an investigation into the commission of a crime:

> Until now the only testimonial privilege for unofficial witnesses that is rooted in the Federal Constitution is the Fifth Amendment privilege against compelled self-incrimination. We are asked to create another by interpreting the First Amendment to grant newsmen a testimonial privilege that other citizens do not enjoy. This we decline to do.[27]

White indicated that refusing to grant journalists such a privilege would not necessarily interfere with the news-gathering process, but in any event, he believed the public interest in pursuing and prosecuting crimes must take precedence. He noted that none of the traditional types of infringement on press freedom was at issue in the Branzburg case such as prior restraint, a tax on the publication, or denial of access to sources. If grand juries abused their powers, White promised that the courts would intervene. He also argued that the press was far from powerless to protect itself from abuse:

> There is much force in the pragmatic view that the press has at its disposal powerful mechanisms of communication and is far from helpless to protect itself from harassment or substantial harm. . . . Newsgathering is not without its First Amendment protections. . . . Official harassment of the press undertaken not for purposes of law enforcement but to disrupt a reporter's relationship with his news sources would have no justification.[28]

White's "pragmatic" point, that the press is far from helpless to protect itself, overlooks the fact that it is not the "press" but individual journalists who must weigh the prospect of going to jail for defying a grand jury subpoena, as has happened in a considerable number of cases.[29] It is necessary to distinguish between the power of the media as institutions and that of individual reporters who may need to promise confidentiality to uncover information that could be gathered no other way

Dissenting in *Branzburg*, Justice Potter Stewart criticized White's "crabbed view of the First Amendment" that showed, in his words, "a disturbing insensitivity to the critical role of an independent press in our society."[30] Stewart, whose opinion was joined by Justices William Brennan and Thurgood Marshall, believed that "a corollary of the right to publish must be the right to gather news," and "the right to gather news implies, in turn, a right to a confidential relationship between a reporter and his source."[31] Stewart was convinced that the absence of this right would interfere with the news-gathering process:

> It is... obvious that the promise of confidentiality may be a necessary pre-requisite to a productive relationship between a newsman and his informants. An officeholder may fear his superior; a member of the bureaucracy, his associates; a dissident, the scorn of majority opinion. . . . The First Amendment concern must not be with the motives of any particular news source, but rather with the conditions in which informants of all shades of the spectrum may make information available through the press to the public.[32]

Stewart also expressed concern over the self-censorship that would follow in the wake of the majority opinion in *Branzburg*:

> Finally, and most important, when governmental officials possess an unchecked power to compel newsmen to disclose information received in confidence, sources will clearly be deterred from giving information, and reporters will clearly be deterred from publishing it, because uncertainty about exercise of the power will lead to "self-censorship."[33]

As sometimes happens in constitutional law, *Branzburg v. Hayes* was in a number of respects a bad case in which to test the Court's attitude on such an important First Amendment principle. Branzburg actually witnessed the commission of a crime, namely, the manufacture and possession of illegal drugs. When preparing a story, a reporter is often provided information about a crime but does not actually witness it. Justice White considered this to be significant:

> We cannot seriously entertain the notion that the First Amendment protects a newsman's agreement to conceal the criminal conduct of his source, or evidence thereof, on the theory that it is better to write about crime than to do something about it. . . . The crimes of news sources are no less reprehensible and threatening to the public interest when witnessed by a reporter than when they are not.[34]

Unfortunately for those concerned about press freedoms, a fundamental constitutional decision was based on a mostly unrepresentative set of circumstances. Yet *Branzburg* is considered to be the Supreme Court's most authoritative statement on the privilege to keep confidential the names of sources.

The notion that reporters have no First Amendment right to keep confidential the names of sources has encouraged defense and prosecuting attorneys to call reporters as witnesses in criminal trials, and judges to hold them in contempt when they refuse to testify or reveal the names of sources. In 1978, *New York Times* reporter Myron Farber was sentenced to jail for civil and criminal contempt after he refused to identify the source of a story involving a New Jersey doctor accused of murder.[35] The U.S. Supreme Court refused to hear the case.[36] The New Jersey Supreme Court, in upholding the judge's contempt order, held that newspaper reporters are not entitled by the First Amendment to refuse to reveal relevant confidential information and its sources to a trial court in a criminal prosecution:

> In our view the Supreme Court of the United States has clearly rejected this claim and has squarely held that no such First Amendment right exists. . . . Thus we do no weighing or balancing of societal interests in reaching our determination that the First Amendment does not afford appellants the privilege they claim. The weighing and balancing has been done by a higher court . . . the ruling in *Branzburg* is binding upon us . . . the obligation to appear at a criminal trial on behalf of a defendant who is enforcing his Sixth Amendment rights is at least as compelling as the duty to appear before a grand jury.[37]

The court also held that New Jersey's shield law must yield to the provisions of the New Jersey Constitution affording a criminal defendant the right to compel the testimony of witnesses who have relevant information. Despite the fact that New Jersey's shield law was "said to be as strongly worded as any in the country,"[38] the court held it must yield to the defendant's rights to a fair trial under the United States and New Jersey constitutions:

> We interpret [Article 1, Section 10 of the Constitution of the State of New Jersey and the Sixth Amendment to the U.S. Constitution] as affording a defendant in a criminal prosecution the right to compel the attendance of witnesses and the production of documents and other material for which he may have, or may believe he has, a legitimate need in preparing or undertaking his defense.[39]

The penalties for Farber's refusal to identify certain sources were rather harsh. The trial judge imposed a fine of $100,000 on the *New York Times*, and Farber was ordered to jail on a civil contempt charge until he provided the requested information. He was also sentenced to six months in the Bergen County jail for criminal contempt to be served after the civil contempt citation had ended, and ordered to pay a fine of $1,000. In addition, the court, in an effort to compel the *Times* to turn over materials subpoenaed by the defendant, fined the newspaper $5,000 per day "every day that elapsed until compliance with Judge Arnold's order."[40]

The Farber case may been complicated by the fact that he was subpoened by the defense attorney, rather than the more common situtation where a reporter is called as a prosecution witness. But Farber did not refuse to testify; in fact, he spent a substantial number of hours on the witness stand. He refused, citing New Jersey's shield law as authority, to name certain sources.[41] When the defendant was eventually acquitted, the judge released Farber from jail and later set aside the criminal contempt sentence.[42]

The New Jersey Supreme Court agreed with Farber's attorneys that he was entitled to a full hearing on the issues of "relevance, materiality and over-breadth of the subpoena," but it also determined that Farber had "aborted that hearing by refusing to submit the material subpoenaed for an in camera inspection by the court." Allowing the judge to inspect Farber's notes, documents, and other materials was not viewed by the New Jersey Supreme Court as a violation of his rights under the shield law; "rather it is a preliminary step to determine whether, and if so to what extent, the statutory privilege [shield law] must yield to the defendant's constitutional rights."[43]

It is probably accurate to assume that without Farber's investigative work and the articles which the Times ran, no one would have been prosecuted in the case.[44] But Farber himself must have felt that he, too, was on trial.

Search Warrants

Besides the difficulty of convincing nervous sources that a reporter can keep their names confidential, the press today faces a direct disruption of its informing function. Only a few months after the Farber case, the Supreme Court in 1978 held that police armed with only a search warrant could raid and search the offices of a student newspaper at Stanford University to look for evidence and photographs of a clash between police and demonstrators. In *Zurcher v. Stanford Daily*,[45] the Court held by a 6-2 vote (with Justice William Brennan not participating) that a warrant to search for evidence can be issued even if the possessor of the place to be searched is not reasonably suspected of criminal involvement. The Court, which found the issues to be based mainly on the Fourth Amendment's search and seizure provisions, held that the safeguards built into the process of securing a search warrant already consider First Amendment interests:

> Prior cases do no more than insist that the courts apply the warrant requirements with particular exactitude when First Amendment interests would be endangered by the search. As we see it, no more than this is required where the warrant request is for the seizure of criminal evidence reasonably believed to be on the premises occupied by a newspaper. Properly administered, the preconditions for a warrant—probable cause, specificity with respect to the place to be searched and the things to be seized, and overall reasonableness—should afford sufficient protection against the harms that are assertedly threatened by warrants for searching newspaper offices.[46]

A key issue is that a search warrant, as opposed to a subpoena, requires only a *single-party* hearing. Law enforcement officials present evidence of probable cause and the things to be seized to a judge or magistrate; the magistrate then issues or does not issue the search warrant. If law enforcement officials were required to obtain a subpoena for the evidence, the press organization would be able to contest the subpoena in a *two-party* hearing and perhaps prevent an unannounced raid on its facilities. Justice White dismissed the claims of journalists that the issuance of a subpoena would allow them to present persuasive evidence that it should be quashed:

> If the evidence sought by warrant is sufficiently connected with the crime to satisfy the probable-cause requirement, it will very likely be sufficiently relevant to justify a subpoena and to withstand a motion to quash. Further, Fifth Amendment and state shield-law objections that might be asserted in opposition to compliance with a subpoena are largely irrelevant to determining the legality of a search warrant under the Fourth Amendment.[47]

As he had in *Branzburg*, Justice Stewart wrote a vigorous dissent. Joined by Marshall, Stewart argued that police searches of newsrooms not only disrupted the operation of a newspaper for what could be "for an extended period of time" but posed a more serious threat to a free press: "the possibility of disclosure of information received from confidential sources, or of the identity of the sources themselves."[48] Stewart argued that a subpoena would be less harmful to the First Amendment rights of the newspaper:

> A search warrant allows police officers to ransack the files of a newspaper, reading each and every document until they have found the one named in the warrant, while a subpoena would permit the newspaper itself to produce only the specific documents requested. A search, unlike a subpoena, will therefore lead to the needless exposure of confidential information completely unrelated to the purpose of the investigation. The knowledge that police officers can make an unannounced raid on a newsroom is thus bound to have a deterrent effect on the availability of confidential news sources. The end result, wholly inimical to the First Amendment, will be a diminishing flow of potentially important information to the public.[49]

As a result of the *Zurcher* case, police have raided newsrooms on a number of occasions.[50] Reporters must now be more careful than ever that they not leave notes or videotapes lying around the newsroom, particularly if they are related to a criminal investigation. But of even more significance was the lack of understanding of the role of journalists expressed by the majority in *Zurcher*. By dealing with the case on largely Fourth Amendment grounds, the Court relegated the First Amendment issues to secondary status. To journalists already concerned about the legal environment in which they must defend press freedoms, *Zurcher* added additional fears: not only do journalists legitimately worry about defending the First Amendment in judicial proceedings to which they are a party, they also know that courts may grant without their knowledge search warrants to police anxious to ransack their newsroom, and learn only later when the raid begins that the judge and prosecutor have already made in their absence an important decision affecting their rights.

Preliminary Hearings and Trials

Journalists have found that antipress attitudes on the part of those suing the media or demanding information on threat of contempt can make them feel uncomfortable in courtrooms; sometimes they also feel downright unwelcome. In *Gannett v. DePasquale*,[51] a confusing and complicated case, the Supreme Court by a 5-4 ruling held that the press and public could be exluded from pretrial proceedings in which the judge believes prejudicial publicity threatens the defendant's Sixth Amendment rights.

Stated by Justice Stewart, who wrote the majority opinion, the issues sounded deceivingly simple: "The question presented in this case is whether members of the public have an independent constitutional right to insist upon access to a pretrial judicial proceeding, even though the accused, the prosecutor, and the trial judge all have agreed to the closing of that proceeding in order to assure a fair trial."[52] The issues were not, in fact, simple at all, and the case caused so much confusion that the Supreme Court felt compelled to clarify its views one year later.

After reviewing previous Sixth Amendment cases, Stewart concluded that the "constitutional guarantee of a public trial is for the benefit of the defendant."[53] He acknowledged the public's very substantial interest in public trials, but also held that "there is a strong societal interest in other constitutional guarantees extended to the accused as well." Stewart suggested that when First Amendment interests conflict with those guarantees, a balancing follows that, in his view, suggests that Sixth Amendment interests transcend those of the First Amendment:

> The trial court found that the representatives of the press did have a right of access of constitutional dimension, but held, under the circumstances of this case, that this right was outweighed by the defendant's right to a fair trial. In short, the closure decision was based "on an assessment of the competing societal interests involved . . . rather than on any determination that First Amendment freedoms were not implicated."[54]

Such a view fails to recognize sufficiently the importance that public scrutiny plays in guaranteeing a defendant due process rights. This is not to suggest, of course, that the press has always behaved responsibly when covering criminal trials. For present purposes, however, the issue is whether the Supreme Court confers legitimacy on press claims when it cannot witness newsworthy events firsthand, that it has a fiduciary responsibility to represent the public. Not very many people have the opportunity to attend a trial, or a city council meeting, or any other event in which they have some interest. They rely instead, although sometimes reluctantly, on the press to be their "eyes and ears."

Such a notion is central to the argument that the press, in defending libel suits, is not simply covering news events and the activities of individuals for its own sake; it is, instead, acting on behalf of the public. Therefore, the argument goes, the press not only deserves substantial latitude in which it can make mistakes without being severely punished but is entitled occasionally to sacrifice individual reputation for the larger good, namely, the public on whose behalf the press acts. If the courts strip from the media their claim that they enjoy a degree of sovereignty bequeathed by the First Amendment, what is left is an industry that markets communication but is primarily in business to maximize profits. Under such an interpretation the provisions of the First Amendment become statements of general principle, not a consecration to gather information and publish in the name of the people. Although the issues in *Gannett* are partially obscured because both the press and the public were barred from the preliminary hearing, the case reveals judicial impatience with the media that is reflected in a number of important libel cases. If the status conferred by the First Amendment does not gain for the press admission to a preliminary hearing, it may not provide protection from judges and juries who are determined in libel cases to treat the press like any defendant in a civil suit. Deprived to some degree of its measure of "sovereignty" in recent years, the media have found themselves defending libel suits in courtrooms without the full protection of the First Amendment.

Much confusion followed the *Gannett* decision as some judges closed not only preliminary hearings but actual trials. A year later the Supreme Court again attempted to clarify the circumstances under which the press can be barred from judicial proceedings. In *Richmond Newspapers v. Virginia*,[55] the Court, dividing 7-1, did not guarantee that all trials would be open to the press and public, but it did allow for the closing of trials in only the most extraordinary circumstances. The seven justices in the majority could not agree on very much and wrote six different opinions; nevertheless, the case calmed fears that *Gannett* was the beginning of closed trials in this country. The lead opinion, written by Chief Justice Warren Burger and joined by Byron White and John Paul Stevens, concluded that the public and the press are entitled under the First and Fourteenth Amendments to attend criminal trials:

> In guaranteeing freedoms such as those of speech and press, the First Amendment can be read as protecting the right of everyone to attend trials so as to give meaning to those explicit guarantees. . . . In the context of trials . . . the First

Amendment guarantees of speech and press, standing alone, prohibit government from summarily closing courtroom doors which had long been open to the public at the time that Amendment was adopted.[56]

The lead opinion distinguished *Richmond* from *Gannett* by considering whether the Constitution guaranteed a right of access to trials, as in *Richmond*, as opposed to pretrial motions. Burger's opinion sought to limit the scope of *Gannett* by saying it held that the "Sixth Amendment's guarantee to the accused of a public trial gave neither the public nor the press an enforceable right of access to a *pre*trial suppression hearing."[57] It became apparent in *Richmond* that the Court did not intend that actual trials be closed. But the Court did leave open the possibility that trials could be closed in the future:

> Our holding today does not mean that the First Amendment rights of the public and representatives of the press are absolute. Just as a government may impose reasonable time, place, and manner restrictions upon the use of its streets in the interest of such objectives and the free flow of traffic . . . so may a trial judge, in the interest of the fair administration of justice, impose reasonable limitations on access to a trial.[58]

To Justice Stevens, *Richmond* did more than just virtually guarantee that trials will be open:

> This is a watershed case. Until today the Court has accorded virtually absolute protection to the dissemination of information or ideas, but never before has it squarely held that the acquisition of newsworthy matter is entitled to any constitutional protection whatsoever. . . . I agree that the First Amendment protects the public and the press from abridgment of their rights of access to information about the operation of their government, including the Judicial Branch.[59]

Richmond did much to allay fears that the Supreme Court was moving toward allowing trial judges, at the request of the prosecution and defense, to close trials to the press and public. Yet while the decision includes eloquent language extolling the virtues of the First Amendment, it cannot be interpreted as a sudden acceptance by the Court of all claims made under the First Amendment by journalists and others. Public trials had been so deeply rooted in the country's legal tradition that it would have been almost unthinkable that the Supreme Court would routinely allow trials to be closed. The Court clearly recognized the importance of the press in covering trials; it has not been so appreciative in recent years when the press asserts a privilege to keep confidential the names of sources, or argues that the First Amendment allows latitude in which innocent error will not be punished in libel suits.

Justice William Rehnquist, dissenting in *Richmond*, criticized the majority for not granting the states more autonomy over their court procedures. He believed that if the states wanted to close trials under certain circumstances, the Court should be restrained when overruling those decisions. Four years after *Richmond*, he and his brethren had the opportunity to return to the states substantial discretion in a libel case that put national media organizations on notice that they may be forced to defend a libel suit in a distant and hostile forum.

In *Keeton v. Hustler*, the Court held that a libel plaintiff may sue a magazine in a state with which neither the plaintiff nor the publication has any direct relationship. *Hustler* is published in Ohio, and Kathy Keeton, the plaintiff, is a resident of New York. In every state except New Hampshire the statute of limitations had run out. New Hampshire's statute of limitations, six years, is the longest in the nation.[60] The Supreme Court overruled the First Circuit Court of Appeals that had dismissed the suit. About 1 percent of *Hustler*'s circulation is in New Hampshire. Justice Rehnquist, who wrote the unanimous opinion, said that neither Keeton's lack of contact with New Hampshire nor her tactical reason for choosing to sue in that state was relevant. "The tort of libel is generally held to occur wherever the offending material is circulated."[61] To Rehnquist, libelous statements do more than injure the reputation of the victim: "False statements of fact harm both the subject of the falsehood *and* the readers of the statement. New Hampshire may rightly employ its libel laws to discourage the deception of its citizens. There is 'no constitutional value in false statements of fact.'"[62]

Rehnquist, suggesting that national media organizations should defend libel suits in any jurisdiction where they disseminate information, seemed to minimize the importance of residency:

> It is undoubtedly true that the bulk of the harm done to petitioner occurred outside New Hampshire. But that will be true in almost every libel action brought somewhere other than the plaintiff's domicile. There is no justification for restricting libel actions to the plaintiff's home forum. The victim of libel, like the victim of any other tort, may choose to bring suit in any forum in which the defendant has "certain minimum contacts."[63]

Because *Hustler* "continuously and deliberately exploited the New Hampshire market," Rehnquist argued, "there is no unfairness [in requiring Hustler] to answer for the contents of that publication wherever a substantial number of copies are sold and distributed."[64]

Keeton essentially means that any media organization with national circulation can be forced to defend a libel suit in the forum most hostile to First Amendment interests, whether or not the plaintiff or the defendant has any direct relationship to the state.[65] Juries have expressed substantial impatience with media defendants in libel suits. It is difficult to imagine what standards will guide them as they deliberate in cases in which the harm to reputation has been caused in a distant place by a media organization based in another part of the country.

The *Keeton* case may not lead to more jury verdicts against the media in libel suits; that is because plaintiffs, according to a study conducted by the Libel Defense Resource Center, already win 83 percent of the cases decided by juries.[66] The survey, covering the years 1980-83, also revealed that the average award in the eighty libel cases having gone to a verdict was $2.2 million. Even when three megaverdicts of more than $10 million each are excluded, the average award was $871,891. That compares with $785,651 in product-liability suits and $665,764 in medical-malpractice cases.[67]

The cases of *Branzburg*, *Farber*, *Zurcher*, *Gannett*, and *Keeton* indicate the increasingly unfriendly environment that news organizations encounter when dealing with the courts, both at the trial and appellate levels. The trend suggests judicial impatience with First Amendment claims: prosecutors subpoena reporters to testify about what they have seen and heard and to reveal the names of sources they have used; defense attorneys demand that reporters testify if it is believed they have information that could be useful to the attorneys' clients; and judges hold reporters in contempt if they refuse to comply or judges allow police to search newsrooms on the chance they will find information relevant to a criminal investigation. Pretrial proceedings, although rarely trials, can be closed to the press. And those suing media organizations for libel can look for the forum most hostile to First Amendment interests. At each step, the Supreme Court has either held that the First Amendment offers journalists no protections from such actions, or it has refused to disturb lower court decisions making such rulings.

The problems journalists have had in securing First Amendment rights in some of the cases discussed above are significant and can seriously interfere with the news-gathering function, but they do not provide the potentially life-threatening danger posed by a libel suit. Despite the potential for large fines and the jailing of reporters and editors, newspapers, magazines, and radio and television stations can survive a judicial order to reveal confidential sources; they can survive the closing of a preliminary hearing or trial; or a raid on a newsroom by police. They may or may not survive a large libel judgment.

Considered together, these cases suggest not only judicial impatience with the assertions of constitutional privilege by reporters, but public skepticism as well. Nowhere is that skepticism better illustrated than by the public's attitude about broadcasting. The public seems to have almost a love/hate relationship with the industry, particularly television. It seems to understand the very important informing function that broadcasting serves, yet likes to criticize both the news and the way it is presented. When a jury retires to consider a libel verdict against a broadcasting station, it gets the opportunity, if it chooses, to let the messenger know that it is not nice to bring bad news.

Broadcasting and Libel

As mentioned before, television has become the primary source of news for most Americans. It has also been suggested, and will be explored in greater detail, that because of the nature of the journalism practiced by broadcasters, they are particularly vulnerable to libel suits. Television's pervasiveness in American society and its high visibility make it an especially tempting target.

The Supreme Court has also recognized the very significant role played by broadcasting in disseminating information, but is concerned about its potential for harm. In *Federal Communications Commission v. Pacifica Foundation*,[68] the Court reiterated what broadcasters had long understood: "We have long recognized that each medium of expression presents special First Amendment problems. . . . And of all forms of communication, it is broadcasting that has received the most limited First Amendment protection."[69] *Pacifica* involved "indecent language" broadcast in a radio program and was not a libel case; nevertheless, the Court's concern that "the broadcast media have established a uniquely pervasive presence in the lives of all Americans" suggests a keen interest on the part of all courts with the potential of the broadcast media to cause harm to an individual's reputation.

Very little has been written about broadcasting's susceptibility to libel suits. Yet, as the medium of communication by which most Americans learn what is going on in their world, its vulnerability to libel suits becomes a subject of much importance. There are trends in both radio and television that indicate the potential for increased libel activity in the near future. Some of these trends will be introduced now, and will be explored later in greater detail.

One of the most important reasons for the potential for increased libel activity is related to the very nature of the industry: television is a visual medium; it relies on pictures to inform and entertain. Those who work in television know that when it comes to generating high ratings for their news programs, the more "exciting" the pictures, the higher the ratings; that of course translates into larger profits.

When events or people are recorded by a camera to be shown on a news program, there is the potential for mistakes at almost very stage. Beginning with the actual recording of the events, unwitting individuals may have their pictures included in the newscast simply because they happen to be near the person who was the subject of the news story. For example, many newscasts feature individuals leaving or entering a courthouse after being indicted or named in connection with the investigation or prosecution of a crime. A viewer often sees several individuals in the picture, yet the reporter will not always specifically state that "John Doe, who has been indicted for fraud, is the second person from the left." Anyone leaving the courthouse could be mistaken for the person under indictment. The camera records all; the individual who was simply doing other business in the courthouse may claim later that people in the community could have mistaken him or her for the person accused of fraud and that it caused embarrassment or financial harm. This may seem like something that reporters would avoid, yet it is surprising how many times one sees this kind of problem in television news reports.

This kind of problem is also seen in other contexts. In what could be called the "generic-picture" syndrome, a reporter does a story about alcoholism or drunk driving. As with any television news story, pictures of some kind are needed. The reporter goes to the the nearest bar, and without fully explaining to the patrons what the story is about, gets generic shots of people drinking. Then, when the story is put on the air, the narration is about alcoholism, or people who drink too much and get behind the wheel of a car, all with pictures that show people drinking. Only when the report is shown on the air do the people at the bar realize the context in which they are appearing. Again, it seems remarkable that this would still be shown on the news, but it seems to happen with alarming frequency. It is easy then for a bar patron to contact a lawyer and talk about a libel or invasion-of-privacy suit.

With the development of small, very portable cameras that record videotape, it is possible for a television news crew to record several stories in the same day. When that is multiplied by the number of crews at each station and the many hundreds of stations that do daily newscasts, there is at least the mathematical potential for many libel problems to arise.

Technological development of video equipment has not ended. Cameras are becoming even smaller and require less and less lighting. A station of almost any size has the equipment to record videotape virtually without being noticed. Most television stations also have wireless microphones that can be concealed by reporters who then question unwitting subjects. In some cases technical skills seem to exceed knowledge of state law that may, for example, require that all parties be informed before conversations are recorded.

In addition, the editing of videotape allows tremendous flexibility. For example, after someone has been interviewed, question A can be matched with answer B, or comment A can be combined with comment C, and with a quick cutaway (usually a shot of the reporter listening to the interviewee), the audience has no way of knowing that audio was cut out. Broadcasters may learn later that they have several days on the witness stand to explain to the jury why they were being clever in the editing room or used statements out of context.

While the recession of the early 1980s was hard on the budgets of news departments, indications are that more and more stations are experimenting with "investigative reporting," particularly smaller stations that a few years ago would not have made a commitment to that type of reporting. Many stations are hiring or designating news personnel as investigative reporters.[70]

Investigative reporting by its very nature involves the portrayal of evil, often committed by individuals. For a number of reasons, television investigative reporting takes special skills that are highly rewarded in the larger stations.[71] The reporters in the largest cities also have the benefit of full-time producers, high visibility, and access to legal advice. Their counterparts in smaller markets, some of whom will be experimenting with investigative reporting for the first time, are not nearly as experienced, and they may find highly paid lawyers less accessible. In addition, they will often find that investigative work must be squeezed in between daily assignments. Most investigative reporters in large television markets work on those types of stories full-time. Even the most thorough investigative reporters in the largest markets can get sued; in the smaller and medium markets, the circumstances add up to potential legal trouble.

There is, in the view of some, a growing trend in investigative television reporting to use what is sometimes called ambush journalism or the confrontation interview. A reporter, after catching an individual doing something wrong, leaps out from behind the bushes, shoves a microphone in the face of the suspected wrongdoer, and with lights blaring and camera whirring, asks why the person did it. (A reporter will sometimes choose the ambush interview even without asking the subject of the story if he or she would sit down for an interview.) For even the most innocent individual, such an experience can be traumatizing. If the suspected villain does not want to talk and walks away, the reporter follows, asking questions. The entire episode is then shown on the news. It is difficult in an ambush interview *not* to look guilty or sinister. Confrontation interviews may be on the decline, but they are still popular with a number of television reporters, even though they are sometimes dangerous. A reporter and cameraman for a Grand Rapids, Michigan, television station were beaten by a man they were investigating for real estate fraud while a second camera from the station captured the grisly event and showed it as part of the story. In the same series, the subject of the investigation tried to run the reporter down with his car while the second camera recorded the entire episode.[72] It must be said that there are occasions when an ambush interview is absolutely necessary. In the Michigan story, for example, the investigation involved corruption of public officials and the principals involved repeatedly refused to be interviewed. Particularly where the public trust or the expenditure of public money is involved, a reporter is entitled to a comment or reaction from those charged with public responsibilities. However, some reporters do abuse the confrontation interview.

When doing investigative reports, the pressure on stations to use the stories once produced are substantial. The reporters and producers who prepared the reports become their strongest advocates; they vigorously lobby nervous news directors and general managers while lawyers try to mediate. Particularly at smaller stations where legal advice may seem like a large expense, the lawyer may be brought in *after* the report is completed but before it is shown on the air. Unlike in newspaper journalism where a video display terminal can change words in a moment, changing the recorded part of a television story is often difficult and time consuming. The reporter must rerecord his or her part of the story, which may involve shooting again on location, and a cameraperson or editor must refit the pictures to go with the new copy. Because of what is required to make changes, the reporter and producer may try to convince the news director to go with the story as it is, rather than tie up precious resources. In smaller stations, it may pose hardships to spare the reporter or cameraperson while they reshoot and reedit. The result can be a libel suit that may be difficult to defend before a jury that does not care about the technical requirements of broadcast news.

Few industries can claim a more transient work force than broadcasting. In radio and television news, careers are developed by moving from a smaller to a larger city and in the process, from a smaller to a larger broadcast station. The incentives are clear: with few exceptions, larger broadcasting stations pay higher salaries, have better equipment, more personnel to cover the news, more opportunity for newspeople to cover areas of individual interest, and other opportunities not offered by smaller stations. That is not to suggest that everyone leaps to a larger radio or television market after a brief apprenticeship in a smaller city. Many broadcasters spend their entire careers in a medium- or small-market station, although they make some sacrifices to do so. [73] In television, for example, salaries vary significantly between small and large markets, and often take a huge jump in the nation's top twenty-five cities. In a major city an anchor for a television station can earn well over half a million dollars a year. Even a sportscaster or weathercaster can earn hundreds of thousands of dollars. It is not unusual for an anchor in a medium-sized city to make over $100,000 annually. Obviously with the possibility of large salaries urging them on, ambitious young journalists may find the larger markets inviting.

The effect on news coverage and the station's vulnerability to libel suits can be significant. People who work in a television station in a small or moderate-sized city who know in advance they will soon be moving on to a larger town and more money may feel little commitment to the station and community where they are currently working. It can take several years to learn the key issues in a local community. One can attend a city council meeting and merely report what was said around the table; but it takes some time before one can report with any perspective or sense of history, and few issues considered at the local level are brand new. The result can often be shallow coverage of important community issues by news reporters who may have greater interest in preparing an audition tape for the next station than in learning complex zoning, urban development, or educational issues that do not provide "exciting" pictures anyway.[74] Simple mistakes can easily be made in any of these routine stories, especially by a reporter who is newly assigned to a local beat but may not feel much of a stake in the community.

Perhaps even more important than the relative youthfulness and lack of experience of many newspeople in smaller stations is the emphasis in television on what can be politely called "cosmetics." To make a profit, stations must attract large enough audiences to their newscasts that they can charge enough for their local commercial time. Because the stations do not share that revenue with the networks, the income can account for a substantial portion of the stations' profits. In the last decade, the public has demonstrated a special affection for news programs that feature attractive anchors and reporters, and viewers seem sometimes not to care whether the individuals covering problems in their community have even fundamental journalistic skills. Even the best journalists, print or broadcast, can be sued for libel. When those lacking in journalistic skills take to the airwaves, there is the potential for serious libel trouble.

A basic tenet of journalism also provides the potential for libel problems. Reporters in the print and electronic media must struggle against one of the profession's most seductive characteristics: the more sinister someone appears, the better the story. Particularly in television, where personalities become central to a story because the *issues* are difficult to explain in the limited time available, there is a temptation to make someone look as sinister as possible, whether a member of the city council, an appointed official, head of the local political party, or a private individual involved in some public controversy. Because a television camera records gestures and expressions and transmits emotion, it is a powerful tool and gives substantial discretion to those who use it to present the subjects of news stories in either favorable or unfavorable light.

It is important to distinguish between the networks and local stations because each faces somewhat different circumstances when doing reports that could lead to libel suits. One might think, for example, that the networks, with the ability to attract the most professional and experienced newspeople, would be relatively free of libel suits. That has not been the case in recent years. Their high visibility and sometimes courageous coverage of controversial issues have been both a blessing and a curse. Networks appear to be in a stronger position to defend libel actions. They can afford to hire expensive legal counsel, can bring public opinion to bear, and often seem committed to fighting such suits to prevent the setting of precedents that could be used against other broadcasters. Yet that has not deterred individuals from filing libel suits against some of the largest broadcasting companies and pursuing those lawsuits for many years.

Local stations, on the other hand, seem to be both less willing and less able to fight a libel suit. For a number of reasons they may be more susceptible to libel suits arising out of mistakes made in routine stories, as well as investigative reports, while it appears that networks are more likely to be sued over "hard-hitting" investigative pieces. For reasons cited above and to be discussed in detail, local stations will continue to be the object of libel suits and those lawsuits will have an impact at all levels of industry.

Radio and television journalists, because of the nature of the electronic media, are tempted to "hype" or exaggerate their stories to pique audience interest. Yet the courts have sometimes been most unconvinced that such hype was necessary or appropriate.[75] In *Rosenbloom v. Metromedia*, for example, an over-exuberant radio newscaster almost cost his company three-quarters of a million dollars in a libel suit after describing a man arrested for selling obscene literature as a "smut peddler."[76]

Radio is also undergoing significant changes that could affect the amount of libel litigation. Long-established AM stations are turning to news and information formats, and away from music, as a way to survive in the rapidly changing environment of the 1980s. Combined profits of the nation's 4,600 AM radio stations fell about $42 million in 1980 from $172 million in 1978. In the same period, the net income of the 3,200 FM stations climbed to $91 million from $24 million. Because of FM stereo and better fidelity, the trend toward more talk and news on AM and more music on FM will probably continue, even if AM stereo, which has been discussed for years, becomes a reality.[77] As more and more AM stations turn to information and news formats, there is at least the possibility of more controversy, more personal attacks on individuals, and more litigation arising from those programs.[78]

It is television, however, that is involved in more controversy and is more likely to be the object of libel suits. It is interesting that broadcasters have been lobbying for deregulation of their industry when at least one of the policies, the right to reply to personal attacks, could be helpful in libel suits. Although the Supreme Court in *Miami Herald v. Tornillo*[79] said the First Amendment does not permit a government-mandated right to reply for the print media, it has held such a requirement for broadcasters to be constitutional.[80] The role right-to-reply or retraction rules should play in libel suits will be explored in the final chapter.

The Supreme Court has provided some national standards in libel, but it has still left to the states substantial discretion over how libel standards are to be applied. In some states, for example, plaintiffs have been limited to compensatory damages if a retraction or reply has been published or broadcast. Newspapers resent such intrusions as a violation of their First Amendment rights, yet there are some advantages to a right-to-reply policy. Broadcasters have more experience with personal attacks and the right to reply that goes with them. In broadcasting, where conversation is not always read from a prepared script, there is always the possibility that statements could be made that are damaging to an individual's reputation.[81]

Defending a libel suit can be especially difficult for a broadcaster because the allegedly libelous statement is sometimes not the only issue. Particularly in television, libel is often mixed with other issues such as the right to privacy, access to private property or place of business, and deceptive explanations given by reporters as to why they want to do the story in the first place. Obviously some stories cannot be covered if reporters are completely candid about why they want to film or tape activity in a private place or do interviews with certain individuals. A television investigative reporter who announces to a sweatshop owner that a story is being done about workers who are paid less than minimum wage and are toiling under inhumane conditions will never be granted permission by the owner to film on the premises. A reporter who wants to do a story about a night club that seats too many people and creates a fire hazard gains entrance only by saying that it is the entertainment that is being covered. Lawyers must then argue whether the deception that gained the consent to enter the premises makes the station more liable for damages if there is a lawsuit, even if the story could be covered in no other way.[82] There are difficult ethical questions as to whether a reporter should impersonate someone to gain entrance to a place that would otherwise be closed to him or her. In recent years print and broadcast reporters have impersonated illegal aliens, workers in nursing homes, members of the KKK, and others to carry out their investigations. Some believe the fact that certain stories could not be covered in a more straightforward fashion justifies the deception.[83]

Before exploring modern libel issues, it is important to understand the detailed, often perplexing history of defamation. The evolution of libel law, from the common law in England to today when courts are attempting to balance reputational and First Amendment interests, is considered in chapter 2. This examination helps to explain why it has been difficult to find an appropriate accommodation of these vital interests. Chapter 3 considers Supreme Court efforts to establish national standards in libel, beginning with *New York Times v. Sullivan* in 1964. In these early decisions, the Court provided substantial protection to the media when covering the activities of public officials. Chapter 4 examines the extension of this protection to reporting on the activities of "public figures," those who do not hold official position but nevertheless play a prominent role in society or in an issue in which the public has an interest.

The Supreme Court became concerned in 1974 that its previous rulings had unfairly favored the media and made it impossible for individuals to be compensated for harm to reputation. Chapter 5 considers its efforts from 1974 to 1979 to protect reputational interests further. The Court did leave substantial discretion to the states to determine appropriate standards in libel cases, particularly those involving "private persons." Chapter 6 examines in detail the nature of broadcast journalism and its relationship to libel. Finally, chapter 7 suggests ways to get out of the libel morass in which neither media organizations nor individuals seeking to vindicate damaged reputations are well served.

Notes

1. Apparently even the judge found the damages to be excessive; he reduced the $26.5 million awarded by the jury to $14 million. In November, 1982, the United States Court of Appeals for the 10th Circuit in Denver overturned the award by a 2-1 vote, saying that although the article was "gross, unpleasant and crude," and had "no redeeming features whatever," it was "pure fantasy" and not libelous. *Pring v. Penthouse*, 8 Med. L. Rptr. 2409 (1982) at 2412. The trial judge had determined that the former Miss Wyoming was a "private person" for purposes of her libel suit against *Penthouse* and had dismissed the magazine's motion for summary judgment. 7 Med. L. Rptr. 1101 (1981). See also William G. Blair, "Libel Lawyer Says Penthouse Ruling Aids Writers," *New York Times*, 7 November 1982, p. 41.
2. A number of these cases will be discussed in this and later chapters. Several sources provide information about libel cases around the country. The Libel Defense Resource Center in New York City publishes a quarterly bulletin that tracks state and federal cases, and a yearly survey of libel laws in all fifty states. The Reporters Committee for Freedom of the Press in Washington, D.C. publishes a quarterly journal, *The News Media and the Law*, that always includes an examination of recent libel cases. Among newspapers, the *New York Times* probably has the most comprehensive coverage of libel cases at the state and federal level.
3. *Green v. Alton Telegraph* (1982) involved a confidential memo sent by two reporters at the paper to federal law enforcement officials with the eventual result that a local builder's credit was cut off and he was forced out of business. Even though the memo was never published, a court found in the builder's favor. Because the paper was unable to post the necessary appeal bond, it declared bankruptcy to protect its assets and eventually settled with the builder for $1.4 million. "*Alton Telegraph* Case Settled, Paper Reportedly to Pay $1.4M," The *News Media and the Law* (June-July, 1982): 20. In *Green v. Alton Telegraph*, 8 Med. L. Rptr. 1345 (1982), the Illinois Appellate Court for the Fifth District held that it lacked jurisdiction to hear the paper's appeal because it had filed for corporate reorganization under chapter 11 of the Bankruptcy Reform Act, and thus federal bankruptcy court had jurisdiction.
4. After defending a $42 million libel suit against Synanon Foundation, KGO-TV, the ABC-owned and operated television station in San Francisco, decided to settle out of court in June 1982, after five months of testimony before the jury. Pretrial

motions, discovery proceedings, and other legal maneuvering had prolonged the case for four years. As part of the agreement, Synanon agreed to drop a second suit pending against ABC. *New York Times*, 4 June 1982, p. A21. See also Charles P. Wallace, "ABC Payoff: Unanswered Questions," *Los Angeles Times*, 3 July 1982, p. 1.

5. *Tavoulareas v. Washington Post* (1983). The judge, in overturning the jury's verdict, said, "'There is no evidence in the record' to support the jury's apparent finding that the article 'contained knowing lies or statements made in reckless disregard of the truth.'" William Tavoulareas, the president of Mobil Oil, and his son Peter had sued the *Washington Post* over an article published in 1979 accusing the father of "setting up his son" as a partner in a shipping company that obtained contracts from Mobil. Stuart Taylor, Jr., "Libel Law: A Tough Puzzle for Trial Jury," *New York Times*, 5 May 1983, p. B15. See also C.T. Hanson, "What Went Wrong at *The Washington Post*," *Columbia Journalism Review* (January/February 1983): 31-37.

6. In the wake of the *Green v. Alton Telegraph* case, Stephen A. Cousley, the editor and publisher of the paper, was quoted as saying, "All the ideals and principles in the world don't mean a damn when it comes down to hard economics." When someone called with a tip about misconduct in the sheriff's office, Cousley decided against investigating. "Let someone else stick their neck out this time," he was quoted as saying by a reporter who heard him talking to an editor. When asked about the remark, he responded, "I probably said that." John Curley, "How Libel Suit Sapped the Crusading Spirit of a Small Newspaper," *Wall Street Journal*, 29 September 1983, p. 1.

7. *Time, Inc. v. Firestone*, 424 U.S. 448 (1976), will be discussed in detail in chapter 5. In the case the Court asserted it based its decision on a public-figure/private-person test, but it seemed to decide the case based on the public interest test it had discredited in *Gertz v. Welch*, 418 U.S. 323 (1974).

8. John Gruhl, "The Supreme Court's Impact on the Law of Libel: Compliance by Lower Federal Courts," 33 *Western Political Quarterly* 502 (December 1980).

9. 376 U.S. 254.

10. Most constitutional scholars agree that the "purest" of the First Amendment absolutists was Justice Hugo L. Black who served on the U.S. Supreme Court from 1937 to 1971. He summarized his view in 1959 in *Smith v. California*, 361 U.S. 147, at 157-59:

> I read "no law abridging" to mean *no law abridging*. The First Amendment, which is the supreme law of the land, has thus fixed its own value on freedom of speech and press by putting these freedoms wholly "beyond the reach" of *federal* power to abridge. No other provision of the Constitution purports to dilute the scope of these unequivocal commands of the First Amendment. Consequently, I do not believe that any federal agencies, including Congress and this Court, have power or authority to subordinate speech and press to what they think are "more important interests."

Justice William O. Douglas, another strong advocate of the First Amendment and who served on the Court from 1939 to 1975, was not quite the absolutist that Black was. Douglas conceded, although reluctantly, that there were circumstances under which the First Amendment must yield to other interests.

The question of the responsibility of the states under the First Amendment will be discussed in chapter 2.

11. In a series of cases from 1974 to 1979, the Court attempted to distinguish between public figures and private individuals in deciding the appropriate standard of liability in libel cases. As will be seen, the Court has had a difficult time enunciating clear standards.

12. *New York Times v. Sullivan*, 376 U.S. 254 (1964); *Curtis Publishing Company v. Butts*, 388 U.S. 130 (1967); *Associated Press v. Walker*, 388 U.S. 130 (1967); *St. Amant v. Thompson*, 390 U.S. 727 (1968); and *Rosenbloom v. Metromedia*, 403 U.S. 29 (1971). These and other cases expanding First Amendment protection to media defendants in libel suits will be discussed in detail.

13. Clifton O. Lawhorne, *Defamation and Public Officials: The Evolving Law of Libel* (Carbondale: Southern Illinois University Press, 1971). Lawhorne traces the evolution of state libel laws and thoroughly analyzes their development.

14. *Gertz v. Welch*, 418 U.S. 323 (1974); *Time, Inc. v. Firestone*, 424 U.S. 448 (1976); *Herbert v. Lando*, 441 U.S. 153 (1979); *Hutchinson v. Proxmire*, 443 U.S. 111 (1979); and *Wolston v. Reader's Digest*, 443 U.S. 157 (1979).

15. It is significant that the constitutional history of the electronic media is a relatively recent phenomenon, while our experience with print media is significantly longer. The First Amendment was framed out of experience with print media and that may explain to some extent why courts have afforded substantially greater First Amendment protection to print as opposed to electronic media. For a discussion of the First Amendment and broadcast regulation, see Richard E. Labunski, *The First Amendment Under Siege: The Politics of Broadcast Regulation* (Westport, Conn.: Greenwood Press, 1982).

16. A Roper Survey conducted in November 1980 reported that 64 percent of the respondents named television as their primary source of news. *Broadcasting* magazine, 13 April 1981, p. 84. Other surveys have reinforced the Roper findings.

17. *Branzburg v. Hayes*, 408 U.S. 665 (1972).

18. *Zurcher v. Stanford Daily*, 436 U.S. 547 (1978).

19. *In re Farber*, 78 N.J. 259, 392 A. 2d 330 (1978).

20. *Gannett Company v. DePasquale*, 443 U.S. 368 (1979); *Richmond Newspapers v. Virginia*, 448 U.S. 555 (1980).

21. *Keeton v. Hustler*, 104 S. Ct. 1473 (1984).

22. *Plotkin v. Daily News* (1982). When two reporters for the *Daily News* in Los Angeles refused to name the sources of a story about Jerry Plotkin, a civilian who was held hostage in the Iranian embassy, Judge Sara Radin granted a default judgment and temporarily ordered the paper to pay him the $60 million in damages sought. The article had said Plotkin was being investigated for involvement in drug dealing. Judge Radin eventually reversed the default judgment. Robert Lindsay, "Paper Orders Reporters to Identify Source Accusing Ex-Iran Hostage," *New York Times*, 24 December 1982, p. A8.

23. *Branzburg* was joined with two other cases, *In re Pappas* and *U.S. v. Caldwell*.

24. By 1982 twenty-six states had shield laws that were intended to prevent reporters from being held in contempt for refusing to divulge the identities of their sources. Some shield laws protected all types of information, such as notes and outtakes, while others protected just the identity of confidential sources. In some states, courts have on occasion granted reporters some limited constitutional protection in the absence of an explicit shield law. *The News Media and the Law* (February-March 1982): 24.

25. 408 U.S. at 669-70 n. 5.
26. Ibid.
27. Ibid. at 689-90.
28. Ibid. at 706-08.
29. C. Herman Pritchett, *The American Constitution*, 3d ed. (New York: McGraw-Hill, 1977), p. 341.
30. 408 U.S. at 725.
31. Ibid. at 727-28.
32. Ibid. at 729-30.
33. Ibid. at 731.
34. Ibid. at 692.
35. *In re Farber*, 394 A. 2d 330 (1978). See also Myron Farber, *Somebody Is Lying* (Garden City, N.Y.: Doubleday, 1982). The doctor, Mario E. Jascalevich, was eventually acquitted.
36. Cert. denied, 439 U.S. 997.
37. 394 A. 2d at 333-34.
38. Ibid. at 335.
39. Ibid. at 337. In another case, *In re Walter Roche*, a Boston television reporter was found in contempt and sentenced to jail for refusing to disclose the sources of a story alleging misconduct by a local judge. In January 1979, Roche broadcast the story and was subpoenaed by the State Commission on Judicial Disability. He refused to comply and appealed to the Massachusetts Supreme Judicial Circuit. But Justice William Brennan of the U.S. Supreme Court stayed the contempt order and the judge who was the subject of the news story resigned before the Supreme Court decided whether to review the case. *The News Media and the Law* (February-March 1982): 25.
40. 394 A. 2d at 332. Farber eventually spent forty days in jail and the *New York Times* paid $286,000 in fines. In January 1982, Governor Brendan Byrne of New Jersey pardoned the *Times* and Farber of their convictions for criminal contempt and returned $101,000 to the paper, which, according to Farber, was the full amount Byrne was empowered to give back. Farber, *Somebody Is Lying*, pp. 350, 356-57.
41. See Farber, *Somebody Is Lying*, pp. 270-72, for the explanation he gave to the court for refusing to turn over certain notes, documents, and other materials that would reveal sources to whom he had promised confidentiality. As a kind of corollary to state shield laws, the Department of Justice has adopted rules that define the conditions under which a U.S. attorney can obtain a subpoena against a working reporter. See Don. R. Pember, *Mass Media Law*, 3d ed. (Dubuque: Wm. C. Brown Publishers, 1984), p. 305.
42. Farber, *Somebody Is Lying*, p. 350.
43. 394 A. 2d at 338.
44. Farber, *Somebody Is Lying*, pp. 3-32.
45. 436 U.S. 547 (1978).
46. Ibid. at 565.
47. Ibid. at 567.
48. Ibid. at 571.
49. 436 U.S. 573. Stewart noted that the *Stanford Daily* itself had experienced problems gaining the confidence of sources in the wake of the search of its premises: "The record in this case included affidavits not only from members of the staff of the Stanford Daily but also from many professional journalists and editors, attesting to precisely such personal experience. . . . According to these uncontradicted

affidavits, when it becomes known that a newsman cannot guarantee confidentiality, potential sources of information often become unavailable. Moreover, efforts are sometimes made, occasionally by force, to prevent reporters and photographers from covering newsworthy events, because of fear that the police will seize the newsman's notes or photographs as evidence. The affidavits of the members of the staff of the Stanford Daily give examples of how this very search produced such an impact on the Daily's own journalistic functions.'' 436 U.S. at 573-74 n. 8.

50. According to *New York Times* columnist Anthony Lewis, prior to the search of the *Stanford Daily* in 1971, there had been only fifteen police searches of newsrooms in this country ever. In the ten years following the search, nearly twenty newsroom searches were conducted. Pember, *Mass Media Law*, pp. 307-08. Justice White, in his majority opinion in *Zurcher*, did not think searches of newsrooms were a serious problem: ''The fact is that respondents and *amici* have pointed to only a very few instances in the entire United States since 1971 involving the issuance of warrants for searching newspaper premises. This reality hardly suggests abuse; and if abuse occurs, there will be time enough to deal with it.'' 436 U.S. at 566.

   After a riot at the Idaho State Penitentiary in July 1980, a county prosecutor and the police searched the newsroom of KBCI-TV in Boise looking for videotape shot inside the prison. Inmates had invited the managing editor of the station to hear their grievances. The prosecutor obtained the search warrant on the grounds that he wanted to prosecute inmates for damaging the prison. After ninety minutes of what was described as ''heavy-handed'' searching, the tapes were found and confiscated. A district court, citing *Zurcher*, later dismissed the station's petition asking that the search be declared illegal and to get an injunction preventing future searches. Pember, *Mass Media Law*, p. 308.

51. 443 U.S. 368 (1979).

52. Ibid. at 370-71.

53. Ibid. at 381.

54. Ibid. at 393 quoting *Saxbe v. Washington Post*, 417 U.S. 843, at 860; Justice Powell dissenting.

55. 448 U.S. 555 (1980).

56. Ibid. at 575-76.

57. Ibid. at 563; emphasis in original.

58. Ibid. at 581 n. 18.

59. Ibid. at 583-84.

60. Linda Greenhouse, ''High Court Rules Libel Suits May Be Filed in Distant Jurisdictions,'' *New York Times*, 21 March 1984, p. A18.

61. No. 82-485 (decided 20 March 1984) at 6. (Slip Opinion.)

62. Ibid. at 5; emphasis in original.

63. Ibid. at 9-10.

64. Ibid. at 10.

65. On the same day the Court decided the *Keeton* case, it handed down its unanimous decision in *Calder v. Jones*, 104 S. Ct. 1482 (1984). The Court ruled that two reporters for the *National Enquirer* must defend, as individual employees, a libel suit brought by actress Shirley Jones, a resident of California. There was never any question that the *Enquirer* would have to defend the libel suit in California, for the article ''concerned the California activities of a California resident.'' The issue decided by the Court was whether the reporters, as individuals, also had to go to California to defend the suit. Justice Rehnquist held that they were ''primary

participants in the alleged wrongdoing" and must defend the suit in California. No. 82-1401 at 7. (Slip Opinion.)

66. Jonathan Friendly, "Libel Awards Found to Exceed 2 Other Groups," *New York Times*, 10 March 1984, p. 29.
67. Ibid.
68. 438 U.S. 726 (1978).
69. Ibid. at 748.
70. See Charles Burke, "Sleuthing on Local TV: How Much? How Good?" *Columbia Journalism Review* (January/February 1984): 43-45.
71. Investigative reporters in the largest cities can make between $50,000 and $100,000 per year, with several making more. Network investigative reporters make even larger salaries.
72. The reporter, Mark Lagerkvist of WZZM-TV in Grand Rapids, was not seriously injured in the beating and successfully got out of the way of the car.
73. A related trend has developed in the last decade. Network reporters, tired of traveling, being on the air infrequently, and other aspects of their trade, have been seeking and getting jobs as anchors at local television stations in the largest markets, often at very attractive salaries. It is no longer true that all broadcast journalists see the network as the pinnacle of their careers.
74. Broadcast reporters sometimes rely on their print counterparts, who have often covered the activities of local government for a longer period of time, to supply needed information. A television reporter may be covering several stories in the same day and can stay only long enough to get tape of the meeting. While the camera operator gets pictures of the proceedings, the broadcast reporter huddles with a newspaper colleague and learns enough to put together a minute-and-a-half report. It is ironic that the television reporter is instantly recognized when arriving at a city council meeting while the print counterpart, who may possess greater knowledge of the issues, goes unnoticed.
75. Examples of legal problems caused by such programming will be discussed.
76. 403 U.S. at 33.
77. Paul Richter, "AM Radio Turns Down the Volume," *Los Angeles Times*, 14 April 1982, p. 1.
78. The substantial cost of of talk and information formats may discourage some AM broadcasters from going that route. The expense of full-time AM stations with news-talk formats averaged $1.7 million in 1980, compared with average expenses of $449,000 for all full-time AM stations, according to the National Association of Broadcasters. Yet those formats have often been successful, particularly in large cities. Ibid.
79. 418 U.S. 241 (1974).
80. *Red Lion Broadcasting v. FCC*, 395 U.S. 367 (1969).
81. Some shows, such as call-in programs on radio stations, are done live, and although the producer or host can stop something from being broadcast because the program is usually aired with a slight delay, they are most likely on the alert for indecent language, not attacks on someone's reputation. Live chatter among newspeople, which is sometimes encouraged by television stations as a way to get the viewers to feel they "know" their newspeople, presents the potential for problems.
82. These questions and how they relate to libel suits will be explored later. Most states have not addressed in statutory or case law the question of whether a repor-

ter must be completely candid with the subject of a news story, although the jury is free to consider such deception when deciding a libel case.

83. On 23 January 1982 CBS News broadcast a documentary entitled, "The Uncounted Enemy: A Vietnam Deception." The report accused General William Westmoreland and others of conspiracy to deceive the president, Congress, and the American people by underreporting the size and strength of the enemy. Westmoreland, in a *TV Guide* article, said he had been misled by the producer of the documentary as to what subjects would be discussed. On the list of topics for the interview sent to Westmoreland, enemy strength estimates was fourth. Don Kowet and Sally Bedell, "Anatomy of a Smear," *TV Guide*, 29 May 1982, p. 10.

2

The Evolution of Libel Laws: Complexity and Inconsistency

The era is long past when an individual vindicated what he considered to be a damaged reputation by challenging the miscreant publisher of the defamation to a duel. Such physical retaliation was accepted as a way to avenge wounded feelings of honor. Today the battlegrounds are courtrooms where litigants joust not with swords or pistols but with immensely complicated libel statutes, case law, and customs that have developed over several centuries. Although the participants are concerned with the case at hand, their actions affect how some of society's most compelling interests are to be balanced.

In few areas of jurisprudence is U.S. legal experience more directly connected to English practice than in libel. Much of the case law and many of the statutes that have developed in the United States have English antecedents. That has meant the development of some principles sympathetic to freedom of the press, such as an intolerance for prior restraint, but it has also meant that we have imported some of the least desirable characteristics of the English common law of libel. In this country the influence of English doctrine led to the jailing and fining of publishers, and it allowed an interpretation of the First Amendment that permitted such practices. The Sedition Act of 1798,[1] for example, enacted just a few years after ratification of the First Amendment, indicated the willingness of the new government to punish what it considered to be defamatory statements about public institutions and officials.[2]

In a discussion of modern libel law in this country, it is of limited value to consider its emergence in a purely chronological fashion. Libel laws, the province of the states for so much of our history, reflect the inconsistent, often contradictory attitudes, customs, and styles of the various states. While such an examination clearly holds historical interest, the Supreme Court's efforts in the past twenty years to provide "national" standards have drastically altered the previously uninterrupted development of libel standards by the states.[3] For that reason a discussion of the evolution of libel laws necessarily involves a blending of the old and the new, old standards incorporated into modern legal doctrine. It also requires at the outset a preliminary definition of libel that will be expanded when the libel cases themselves are considered in detail.

In its simplest form, libel is the publishing or broadcasting of defamatory falsehoods.[4] Such a definition applies now; the path that led to those simple phrases was crooked and broken, and people who went to prison for publishing the truth would envy the protection at least theoretically provided by those words. In addition, broadcasting's inclusion reflects modern electronic communication. Defamation by audio or visual presentation, such as radio and television, is usually governed by libel laws. Slander, defamation by oral communication, invokes different legal issues and is now largely confined to spoken communication not transmitted over radio or television stations.[5] Most courts have held that in cases of defamation by broadcasters, libel statutes and case law are controlling.[6]

Several elements must be present before a statement can be libelous, although those elements require elaboration through the cases that gave them content.

1. The statement must actually be defamatory, meaning that it harmed someone's reputation. Standards and definitions vary somewhat, but a defamatory statement subjects an individual to ridicule or scorn or the contempt of those who come into contact with the individual. It also causes third parties to refuse to associate with the victim of the libelous statement, causes financial harm, or damages the victim's general reputation or good name.[7] Not all the above elements need be proved to demonstrate that a statement is defamatory. However, no longer does a plaintiff merely have to show that a critical statement was published; it must be proved that it was damaging to the plaintiff's reputation.

Although the difference is somewhat blurred today, courts have divided defamatory statements into two categories: libel *per se* and libel *per quod*. Words libelous *per se* are libelous on their face; no additional context is required. Words such as coward, liar, thief, murderer, rapist, communist, or Marxist are libelous per se. If the publication or broadcast accuses a person of professional incompetence, of a serious crime, or immorality, or possessing some serious disease, it can be considered defamatory.[8]

Some words may not be defamatory in themselves, but when one understands additional facts associated with the statement, they can be interpreted as defamatory, as libelous *per quod*. A plaintiff would normally have to convince a jury that those who read or heard the defamation were aware of the additional facts and therefore of the defamatory nature of the statement. If a newspaper runs a picture of a couple eating dinner at a new restaurant with the caption "young lovers enjoying opening night at new eatery," that is not defamatory *per se*. However, if the woman is not the man's wife and people who know him thereby assume he is having an affair, the caption can be defamatory *per quod*.

The distinction between libel per se and per quod is less significant today because the Supreme Court, in establishing "national" standards for libel laws, prohibited "presumed" damages.[9] Under previous laws and cases, juries could automatically assume that words libelous *per se* did in fact harm one's reputation; the plaintiff did not have to prove actual damages. Under the standards enunciated in the 1974 case *Gertz v. Welch*,[10] a plaintiff must now demonstrate the suffering of actual damages unless he or she can also prove that the statement was published with "actual malice," a very strict standard to be discussed later in detail.[11]

2. The statement must actually have been communicated to be libelous. In other words, someone other than the victim of the defamation must have read or heard it. The courts have relatively liberal rules in this area. Once the statement is published or broadcast, it clearly has been communicated to third parties. Although the actual requirement of communication is technically satisfied whenever a third party is exposed to the statement, a plaintiff would have a difficult time convincing a jury of a damaged reputation if only a few individuals had been exposed to the defamatory statement.[12] The Court in *Gertz v. Welch* required the demonstration of actual damages, and proving such injury may be difficult if only a few persons read or heard the statement. Nevertheless, the communication of defamation to a third party constitutes publication.

It is important to note that anyone who contributes to the dissemination of the defamatory statement can be sued for libel. A plaintiff can sue not only the reporter or editor as well as the newspaper that published the story but any other media organization that used the story. The media must be careful even if they accurately and fairly report a defamatory statement made by one individual against another unless it is covered by one of several constitutional privileges.[13]

The issue of communication to third parties arose when the Alton Telegraph in Illinois lost a \$9.2 million libel suit in 1982 for a memo written by two reporters that had not been published but ended up in the hands of federal officials who cut off a builder's credit.[14] The case created much controversy because of the size of the judgment—several times the total assets of the family-owned newspaper—and also because the memo had never been published.[15]

There are some related issues in broadcasting that so far have not been the subject of litigation but could presumably present problems. A videotaped report done for television normally requires the cooperation of several persons. If there is controversy associated with the report, it may be shown to the producer, news director, general manager, or the station's lawyers. Such a showing may constitute a broadcast or publication and satisfy the communication requirement for a libel suit. It is conceivable that a report that may never have been aired could have the effect of causing third parties to refuse to associate with the individual defamed in it. For example, a member of a city council is accused in a report of taking kickbacks. It is shown around the station both because that kind of report often creates substantial curiosity and also so management can decide if it should run.[16] Even if the report is never broadcast, if fellow reporters and managers assume the council member is corrupt, they may not want to associate with that individual. Other reporters, upon hearing about the report, may choose not to interview the council member when seeking comments on public issues. In the case of a politician whose tenure in office and reelection may depend on exposure, the reporters' "blackout" of statements or activities can create substantial problems for the officeholder. Moreover, city hall reporters often know one another well. It would be possible that a reporter from television station "X" would tell a reporter from station "Y" that council member Jones is corrupt, but "X" is not airing the story. The point is that the communication requirement of a libel suit is easily satisfied, and persons preparing controversial reports must be extremely careful.[17]

3. The statement must identify a victim of defamation either by name or by some designation that third parties will understand to refer to that individual.[18] When a person's name is used, there is usually little disagreement over to whom the statement refers. But when a defamatory statement is made that does not refer to an individual by name, the courts have had to determine if the reference was direct enough to constitute libel.

Interestingly, *New York Times v. Sullivan*, the Supreme Court's first major libel case, arose after a civil rights group placed an advertisement in the *New York Times* that criticized the police treatment of blacks in Montgomery, Alabama.[19] City Commissioner L.B. Sullivan, who was not mentioned by name in the advertisement, claimed that because he had authority over the police department, it was understood to refer to him. The Supreme Court expressed doubt that the advertisement referred to him or had injured his reputation.[20]

Other problems arise when defamatory stories can be interpreted as referring to more than one person. For a time the Supreme Court embraced the concept of group libel,[21] later rejecting it as too close to seditious libel.[22] If a newspaper or broadcast station defames a group small enough for individuals to suffer, they can pursue a libel suit. The statement "all members of the city council are corrupt" refers to an identifiable group whose members could suffer from such a statement. On the other hand, "all voters are stupid" does not refer to a small enough group for any one of its members to bring a libel suit.

4. In addition to the requirements that the statement must be defamatory, must be communicated, and must name an identifiable victim or group, the Supreme Court has ruled that there must be at least some element of fault. This requirement will be discussed later in detail. In *Gertz v. Welch*, the 1974 case that revised the libel laws of all fifty states, the Court ruled that the First Amendment does not permit a libel suit against a media defendant unless it can be demonstrated that there was a degree of fault on the part of the defendant beyond just the publishing or broadcasting of an untrue statement.[23] As will be seen, this essentially overruled the concept of "strict liability" that for decades automatically assumed that the disseminator must accept responsibility regardless of whether there was fault involved.[24] Two standards of liability or fault, negligence and actual malice, have developed (although some states have adopted variations of the two). Both terms have long histories in English and American jurisprudence, although their definitions have been changed from their traditional meaning in the area of libel law. The Court has left to the states discretion to determine the standard of liability, negligence, maliciousness, or some combination applicable in cases involving private individuals who sue media defendants.[25] The Court, however, does require that public officials and public figures must continue to meet the stricter standard of "actual malice."[26]

5. The final element of libel is a mixture of standards of liability and damage awards. The Court, in *Gertz v. Welch*, determined that the First Amendment cannot tolerate the continuation of "presumed" damages, where courts could assume that the publication of a defamatory statement automatically resulted in reputational injury that should be compensated.[27] The Court tied the negligence and malice standard to damages by ruling that only those who prove actual malice can be compensated beyond the loss of income or damage to reputation.[28] Only those who prove that the media defendant acted with actual malice are entitled to punitive damages.[29] Under the *Gertz* ruling, some proof of damaged reputation must be offered before monetary compensation is awarded. Juries have sometimes been greatly confused over this issue, but the Court does require the stricter standard of malice before punitive damages are awarded.[30]

Libel suits today are civil cases, but for many years our importation of English common law included the criminal prosecution of publishers for seditious libel, defamation of the government and its officials.[31] The theory of a criminal prosecution is that libel is an offense against the peace and good order of the community, and is likely to incite acts of physical retaliation.[32] Criminal punishment for libel provided a lawful means of redress and was designed to avert the possibility that libelous statements would provoke the enraged victim to breach of the peace.

Once libel laws were constituted to prevent breaches of the peace, it was not difficult to move to the next stage, where libel of the government or public officials was criminally punishable, as in the Sedition Act of 1798.[33] The English law of seditious libel permitted punishment for publications tending to bring into hatred or contempt, or to excite disaffection against, the king, the government, Parliament, or the administration of justice.[34] The English law of libel was initially developed by the Star Chamber, which did not bother with such inconveniences as a jury.[35] After the Star Chamber was abolished in 1641, judges permitted a limited role for juries, such as simply finding facts as to authorship or publication, while reserving for the bench the question of whether the facts constituted libel. A long series of oppressive libel prosecutions finally led to Fox's Libel Act in 1792, which allowed jurors to determine both the fact and the law.[36]

English methods of dealing with the publishers of newspapers, handbills, or books considered to be seditious and defamatory were sometimes barbaric. Punishment of those who had the temerity to publish criticism of the king was severe. Such was the fate of John Twyn in 1663. Twyn was indicted and tried for printing *A Treatise on the Execution of Justice*. The book, whose author Twyn refused to identify, suggested that the ruler is accountable to the people, and "that the people may take up arms against a king and his family and put the king to death if he refuses accountability."[37] The court's vengeance was demonstrated in the sentence:

> The judgment is that you be led back to the place from whence you came and from thence to be drawn upon an hurdle to the place of execution; and there you shall be hanged by the neck, and being alive, shall be cut down, and your privy-members shall be cut off, your entrails shall be taken out of your body, and you living, the same to be burnt before your eyes; your head to be cut off, your body to be divided into four quarters and your head and quarters to be disposed of at the pleasure of the king's majesty. And the Lord have mercy upon your soul.[38]

Twyn was actually charged with treason, it being alleged that he plotted and imagined the king's death, but the overt act outlined in the indictment against him was the printing of a "seditious, poisonous and scandalous book." In effect Twyn was executed for committing treason through seditious libel.[39]

Some years earlier, in 1637, William Prynn was severely punished for writing a book that was interpreted to be critical of the queen. He was fined, given life imprisonment, pilloried, and had his ears cropped off.[40] Two other men were also found guilty of publishing "seditious, schismatical and libelous" books. They were fined, had their cheeks burned and their ears cut off, and were banished to prisons on islands at sea.[41] In 1641, when the Star Chamber was abolished, all three were pardoned, and they returned to England in triumph.[42]

The colonists were not as barbaric as their counterparts in the mother country in punishing the publishers of defamation and were in fact, becoming enlightened about the need for comment on public issues. The most significant feature of that evolution was the increasingly important role of the jury. Beginning with the trial in 1692 of William Bradford, a Philadelphia printer, a jury was allowed to determine if a publication was libelous, and Bradford's codefendant was allowed to introduce evidence of truth as a justification of the libel charged against him.[43] Out of the early prosecutions, two trends developed: libel is justified by truth; and juries should determine whether libel actually was involved.[44]

It was not until the trial of a New York newspaperman, John Peter Zenger, in 1735, that juries were recognized as the appropriate body to determine if a libel had been committed on the basis of truth or falsity. Zenger's was the first trial in the colonies in which a newspaperman was accused of publishing articles that libeled a public official. The case attracted substantial attention and he was found not guilty.[45] But the break from English common law was incomplete, for criminal libel was still a very potent tool for punishing or attempting to silence those who published statements that government officials found offensive. Proof that the legacy persisted was evident in the Sedition Act of 1798.[46]

The Sedition Act, enacted when the ink of the First Amendment was barely dry, made it a crime punishable by a $5,000 fine and five years in prison "if any person shall write, print, utter or publish . . . any false, scandalous and malicious writing or writings against the government of the United States, or either house of the Congress . . ., or the President . . ., with intent to defame . . . or to bring them, or either of them, into contempt or disrepute; or to excite against them, or either or any of them, the hatred of the good people of the United States."[47] Although the act was broad enough to make criminal virtually any criticism of the government, it did allow the defendant the defense of truth, and provided that the jury was to be judge both of the law and the facts.[48] Despite these qualifications, the law did not provide very much protection to publishers. Fourteen indictments were brought under it, all against Republican newspapermen and publicists, and all fourteen resulted in convictions.[49] A relatively mild criticism of the president, certainly by today's standards, resulted in the jailing and fining of Representative Mathew Lyon. He suggested that under President Adams the executive branch showed "an unbounded thirst for ridiculous pomp, foolish adulation, and selfish avarice," and that the public welfare was "swallowed up in a continual grasp for power."[50] Lyon's sentence was four months in jail and a fine of $1,000.[51] A publisher who wrote in Lyon's defense while he was in jail was fined $200 and sentenced to prison for two months.[52]

The Sedition Act expired by its terms in 1801 and no case testing its constitutionality was brought to the Supreme Court.[53] It had been widely condemned as patently unconstitutional and an affront to the First Amendment. James Madison vigorously denounced it on the basis that the government established by the Constitution was powerless to impose sanctions for criticism of government and government officials.[54] In *New York Times v. Sullivan*, Justice William Brennan devoted particular attention to Madison's views in the Virginia Resolutions of 1798. The Court stated:

> His premise was that the Constitution created a form of government under which "The people, not the government, possess the absolute sovereignty." The structure of the government dispersed power in reflection of the people's distrust of concentrated power, and of power itself at all levels. This form of government was "altogether different" from the British form, under which the Crown was sovereign and the people were subjects. "Is it not natural and necessary, under such different circumstances," he asked, "that a different degree of freedom in the use of the press should be contemplated?" Earlier, in a debate in the House of Representatives, Madison had said: "If we advert to the nature of Republican Government, we shall find that the censorial power is in the people over the Government, and not in the Government over the people." 4 Annals of Congress, p. 934 (1794). Of the exercise of that power by the press, his Report said: "In every state, probably, in the Union, the press has exerted a freedom in canvassing the merits and measures of public men, of every description, which has not been confined to the strict limits of common law. On this footing the freedom of the press has stood; on this foundation it yet stands. . . ." 4 Elliot's Debates, p. 570. The right of free public discussion of the stewardship of public officials was thus, in Madison's view, a fundamental principle of the American form of government.[55]

There is some disagreement among scholars about whether the First Amendment was intended to abolish the law of seditious libel. In his influential book *Free Speech in the United States*, Zechariah Chafee wrote:

> The framers of the First Amendment make it plain that they regarded freedom of speech as very important; "absolutely necessary" is Luther Martin's phrase. But they say very little about its exact meaning. . . . Therefore, it was not until the Sedition Law of 1798 made the limits of liberty of the press a concrete and burning issue that we get much helpful expression of opinion on our problem. Before that time, however, we have a few important pieces of evidence to show that the words were used in the Constitution in a wide and liberal sense.[56]

Despite Madison's eloquent argument that government officials were agents and servants of the people and not their superiors, Chafee contends that such a view did not prevail during the final years of the eighteenth century, culminating in the Sedition Act of 1798. The law of seditious libel sprang from the view that the people could not criticize their rulers in newspapers and pamphlets but only through their lawful representatives in the legislature, who might be petitioned in an orderly manner. Seditious libel, according to

Chafee, was defined as "the intentional publication, without lawful excuse or justification, of written blame of any public men, or of the law, or of any institution established by law."[57] It was clear that under such a restrictive law, freedom of the press, as Chafee indicated, was nothing more than the absence of censorship, the type of narrow view suggested by Blackstone. To Chafee, however, there existed throughout the eighteenth century a definite popular meaning of freedom of the press that transcended the legal meaning of liberty of the press: the right of unrestricted discussion of public affairs. In Chafee's words, "There can be no doubt that this was in a general way what freedom of speech meant to the framers of the Constitution."[58] Chafee quoted Professor Henry Schofield, who wrote in 1914, "One of the objects of the Revolution was to get rid of the English common law on liberty of speech and of the press. . . . Liberty of the press as declared in the First Amendment, and the English common-law crime of sedition, cannot co-exist."[59]

Others, such as Leonard Levy, argue that it was not until after the adoption of the Act of 1798 that opinion crystallized against seditious libel.[60]

Having survived the Sedition Act of 1798, the First Amendment's role in the development of libel law was uncertain. Its words proudly proclaimed the freedom to speak and publish, yet the common law of libel continued to grow in complexity, rigidity, and inconsistency. The states applied varying attitudes, doctrines, and practices in defamation actions, and most, if not all, demonstrated a zealous interest in preventing and redressing attacks by the press upon the reputations of their citizens. Emerging from the various state doctrines was the so-called rule of strict liability. Until 1964, when the Supreme Court became alarmed that libel law had grown to favor reputational interests at the expense of First Amendment press freedom, states were free to establish restrictive standards that warned publishers that they printed materials susceptible of defamatory meaning at their own peril. So limited were the privileges afforded the press, that the American Law Institute's *Restatement of Torts*, published in 1938, listed truth,[61] consent,[62] and a very narrow conditional privilege based upon a limited interpretation of the public interest[63] as the only defense to the publication of defamatory material. *Restatement* made it clear that the conditional privilege applied only when a substantial interest of the public, such as the prevention of a crime or the apprehension of criminals, was threatened. It specifically stated that the rule "does not afford a privilege to publish false defamatory statements of fact about public officers or candidates for office"[64] and "is not intended to constitute an all-inclusive category of public interests which may be protected."[65]

The rule of strict liability was viewed by many as too restrictive and not sufficiently sensitive to the special role of the First Amendment. As the law of defamation evolved into the standard of strict liability, various writers and judges developed interpretations of its relationship to the First Amendment and suggested methods by which the competing interests could be accommodated.

Three prominent thinkers reacted to what they considered to be inappropriate encroachment on fragile First Amendment guarantees. In a number of significant cases, Justice Hugo L. Black, who served on the Supreme Court from 1937 to 1971, advanced the view that the language of the First Amendment is to be given literal effect. Known as an "absolutist" interpretation, Justice Black read the words "Congress shall make no law . . . abridging freedom of speech, or of the press"[66] as applying without qualification to Congress under the First Amendment and to the states through the Fourteenth Amendment.[67] In Justice Black's view, the First Amendment completely eliminates the law of libel.

Black's "absolute" view of the First Amendment has never commanded a majority of the Supreme Court, yet it has influenced the Court in many of its First Amendment decisions by providing a standard against which other approaches to the First Amendment can be considered. Such a view, argued persuasively by Black for many years, claimed that because libel and obscenity are forms of speech, laws punishing either are unconstitutional.[68] Black did not suggest that the First Amendment denies government the power to regulate the manner and conditions under which speech protected by it is exercised. Black made the point that some restrictions are permissible:

> The First and Fourteenth Amendments, I think, take away from government, state and federal, all power to restrict freedom of speech, press, and assembly *where people have a right to be for such purposes*. This does not mean, however, that these amendments also grant a constitutional right to engage in the conduct of picketing or patrolling, whether on publicly owned streets or on privately owned property. . . . Were the law otherwise, people on the streets, in their homes and anywhere else could be compelled to listen against their will to speakers they did not want to hear [emphasis in original].[69]

Black believed that while speech itself may be under the protection of the First Amendment, the manner of its exercise or "its collateral aspects" may fall beyond the scope of the amendment. Government has some power to regulate how and where freedoms are to be exercised; it is not powerless to say that one cannot blare a political message by loudspeaker in the middle of the night, or litter the streets with copies of a handbill.[70] The disagreements have been over whether and to what extent government may regulate or suppress speech at places where the speaker has a right to be.[71]

Those disagreements have been accentuated by a number of tests that were developed to limit the scope of the First Amendment. Justice Oliver Wendell Holmes, in a case appealing a conviction under the Sedition Act of 1918, wrote: "The question in every case is whether the words used are used in such circumstances and are of such a nature as to create a clear and present danger that will bring about the substantive evils that Congress has a right to prevent. It is a question of proximity and degree.''[72] The clear and present danger test, finally discarded by the Court in free speech cases some years later,[73] was rewritten by Judge Learned Hand in a case involving prosecution of the leaders of the Communist party, *Dennis v. United States*, and the Supreme Court adopted Hand's modification: ''In each case [courts] . . . must ask whether the gravity of the 'evil,' discounted by its improbability, justifies such invasion of free speech as is necessary to avoid the danger.''[74] The clear and present danger test had been applied in the very troublesome area of punishment in criminal contempt for publications critical of courts and judges. The Court has held that the free press guarantee of the First Amendment bars punishment in criminal contempt in the absence of a showing of a clear and present danger of the obstruction of justice.[75]

The Court also developed another test, primarily for use in the area of obscenity. The Court has held that speech that is ''utterly without redeeming social value'' is not entitled to First Amendment protection.[76] Justice William Brennan, writing the opinion of the Court in *Roth v. United States*, explained that such speech has never enjoyed constitutional protection:

> All ideas having even the slightest redeeming social importance—unorthodox ideas, controversial ideas, even ideas hateful to the prevailing climate of opinion—have the full protection of the guaranties, unless excludable because they encroach upon the limited area of more important interests. But implicit in the history of the First Amendment is the rejection of obscenity as utterly without redeeming social importance. . . . We hold that obscenity is not within the area of constitutionally protected speech or press.[77]

Some years earlier, Justice Frank Murphy, as devoted a civil libertarian as ever sat on the Court,[78] wrote for a unanimous Court in *Chaplinsky v. New Hampshire*:

> There are certain well-defined and narrowly limited classes of speech, the prevention and punishment of which has never been thought to raise any Constitutional problem. These include the lewd and the obscene, the profane, the libelous, and the insulting or ''fighting'' words—those which by their very utterance inflict injury or tend to incite an immediate breach of the peace. It has been well observed that such utterances are no essential part of any exposition of ideas, and are of such slight social value as a step to truth that any benefit that may be derived from them is clearly outweighed by the social interest in order and morality.[79]

The notion that only speech that has social value is protected by the First Amendment solved some short-term problems for the Court, but certainly raised larger questions about the types of speech entitled to First Amendment protection.

The absolutist view of Justice Black, the clear and present danger test of Justice Holmes, and the redeeming social value test in obscenity have been overshadowed by the so-called balancing test that has dominated constitutional interpretation of the First Amendment. One of its most vocal and influential proponents, Justice John M. Harlan, discussed the balancing of societal interests in a case that challenged the validity of a state's refusal to admit an applicant to the practice of law. The applicant, on First Amendment grounds, refused to answer any question pertaining to membership in the Communist party. There was no proof that he was in fact a party member. In an opinion upholding the state's refusal to admit him to practice law, Justice Harlan wrote:

> General regulatory statutes, not intended to control the content of speech but incidentally limiting its unfettered exercise, have not been regarded as the type of law the First or Fourteenth Amendment forbade Congress or the States to pass, when they have been found justified by subordinating valid governmental interests, a prerequisite to constitutionality which has necessarily involved a weighing of the governmental interest involved. . . . It is in the latter class of cases that this Court has always placed rules compelling disclosure of prior association as an incident of the informed exercise of a valid governmental function. . . . Whenever, in such context, these constitutional protections are asserted against the exercise of valid governmental powers a reconciliation must be effected, and that perforce requires an appropriate weighing of the respective interests involved. . . . With more particular reference to the present context of a state decision as to character qualifications, it is difficult, indeed, to imagine a view of the constitutional protections of speech and association which would automatically and without consideration of the extent of the deterrence of speech and association and of the importance of the state function, exclude all reference to prior speech or association on such issues as character, purpose, credibility or intent.[80]

The balancing approach to the First Amendment has received substantial attention by academics as well. Professor Thomas I. Emerson of Yale, in his seminal essay "Toward a General Theory of the First Amendment," defined the balancing test: "The formula is that the court must, in each case, balance the individual and social interest in freedom of expression against the societal interest sought by the regulation which restricts expression."[81] Emerson is sometimes misunderstood to advocate that the balancing approach is the best method by which to protect First Amendment and other societal interests. He is, in fact, extremely critical of the balancing test, claiming that the principal difficulty with an "ad hoc balancing" test is that "it frames the issues in such a broad and undefined way, is in effect so unstructured, that it can hardly be described as a rule of law at all. As a legal doctrine for affording judicial protection to a system of freedom of expression, it is not tenable."[82]

Emerson asserted that a court is "cast loose in a vast space, embracing the broadest possible range of issues, to strike a general balance in the light of its own best judgment."[83] Not only does the test allow a court to reach either conclusion in almost every case, said Emerson, the "lack of structure makes it realistically impossible for a court to perform its difficult function of applying accepted and impartial rules to hold in check the unruly forces that seek to destroy a system of free expression."[84]

Emerson was concerned that such a balancing test left the freedoms of expression and press insufficiently protected: "The test gives no real meaning to the First Amendment. As Mr. Justice Black has justifiably protested, it amounts to no more than a statement that the legislature may restrict expression whenever it finds it reasonable to do so."[85] Moreover, "the test is unworkable from the viewpoint of judicial administration, requiring for ultimate decision an ad hoc resolution by the highest tribunal in each case. . . . The test is wholly incapable of coping with the dynamic forces evoked by governmental efforts at limitation of expression."[86]

Unlike the absolutist interpretation of the First Amendment, the clear and present danger, redeeming social value, and balancing tests recognize some governmental power to inhibit speech. But none of these limitations has been given an across-the-board application. Each has been primarily utilized to sustain government regulation in particular contexts: the clear and present danger test primarily in regulation of subversive activity and of the publication of materials thought to obstruct justice; the redeeming social value test primarily in obscenity cases; and the balancing test primarily in the case of regulations not intended to directly condemn the content of the speech but incidentally limiting its exercise.[87]

There was always the danger that one or all of the tests may be employed more generally to permit government regulation of speech. That concern was addressed by Alexander Meiklejohn, who developed a broader theory of the First Amendment that prevented what he considered to be a fundamental departure from the very form of government created by the Framers of the Constitution. Meiklejohn argued that the people created a form of government under which they granted only some powers to the federal and state instruments they established; they reserved very significant powers of government to themselves. This was, in Meiklejohn's view, because their basic decision was to govern themselves rather than to be governed by others. It was a fundamental departure from the English and other existing forms of government and was this country's great contribution to the science of government.[88] To Meiklejohn, the First Amendment is the repository of these self-governing powers that, because they are exclusively reserved to the people, are immune from regulations by the agencies, federal and state, that are established as the people's servants.[89]

These reserved powers, which Meiklejohn called of "governing importance,'' are concerned not with a private right but with a public power, a governmental responsibility.[90] Freedom of expression in areas of public affairs is an absolute: "Public discussion of public issues, together with the spreading of information and opinion bearing on those issues, must have a freedom unabridged by our agents. Though they govern us, we, in a deeper sense, govern them. Over our governing, they have no power. Over their governing, we have sovereign power."[91]

In describing the importance of granting protection to speech relating to self-government, Meiklejohn wrote that the Bill of Rights is actually misnamed:

> For the understanding of these principles it is essential to keep clear the crucial difference between "the rights" of the governed and "the powers" of the governors. And at this point, the title "Bill of Rights" is lamentably inaccurate as a designation of the first ten amendments. They are not a "Bill of Rights" but a "Bill of Powers and Rights." The Second through Ninth Amendments limit the powers of the subordinate agencies in order that due regard shall be paid to the private "rights of the governed." The First and Tenth Amendments protect the governing "powers" of the people from abridgment by the agencies which are established as their servants. In the field of our governing "powers," the notion of "due process" is irrelevant.[92]

Meiklejohn concluded, "The First Amendment does not protect a 'freedom to speak.' It protects the freedom of those activities of thought and communication by which we 'govern.'" In other words, Meiklejohn would avoid the balancing approach, which, in his view, gives insufficient protection to speech of governing importance. He would not prohibit laws that require the speaker to conform to the necessities of the community with respect to time, place, circumstance, and manner of procedure, as long as these were not mere covers for attempts to suppress speech he classified as having "governing importance."[93] It is within the categories of governing importance that, Meiklejohn believed, the First Amendment gives unqualified protection.

First among those activities is the freedom to vote, what Meiklejohn calls the "official expression of a self-governing man's judgment on issues of public policy."[94] He also included a vast range of thought and expression by which voters might equip themselves to exercise a proper judgment in casting their ballots. "Education, in all its phases, is the attempt to so inform and cultivate the mind and will of a citizen that he shall have the wisdom, the independence, and therefore, the dignity of a governing citizen. Freedom of education is, thus... a basic postulate in the planning of a free society."[95] The achievements of "philosophy and the sciences, literature and the arts, are all within the subjects of 'governing importance' that the First Amendment absolutely protects from abridgement."[96]

Because freedom of speech and press are essential for self-government, the First Amendment has been given in our society a special place in constitutional interpretation. While "legislative reasonableness" may deter the Supreme Court in cases from interfering with the decisions of elected legislatures, such a reasonableness test does not apply where the basic freedoms of the First Amendment are at issue. It has been argued that the courts and legislatures must observe a higher standard because of the "preferred position" that the Constitution gives to First Amendment freedoms. Stated in an extreme form, the argument is that any law touching communication is "infected with presumptive invalidity." A more moderate statement is that "because First Amendment values are so essential to a free society, legislative action infringing those values must be shown to be not only 'reasonably' adapted to the attaining of valid social goals but justified by overwhelmingly conclusive considerations."[97]

The development of the preferred position view may be found in Justice Benjamin N. Cardozo's statement in a 1937 case that First Amendment liberties were on "a different plane of social and moral values."[98] Freedom of thought and speech is "the matrix, the indispensable condition, of nearly every other form of freedom."[99] "Neither liberty nor justice would exist if they were sacrificed."[100] But the credit for creating the preferred position view of the First Amendment is usually given to Justice Harlan F. Stone.

Stone, in a footnote he attached to a 1938 decision, was rehearsing familiar arguments that legislative action should be sustained by the courts if there is any basis on which "a reasonable man" could have reached the same conclusion as the legislature.[101] After reciting the legislative reasonableness standard, Stone followed with one of the most famous and important footnotes ever included in a Supreme Court case:

> There may be narrower scope for operation of the presumption of constitutionality when legislation appears on its face to be within a specific prohibition of the Constitution, such as those of the first ten amendments, which are deemed equally specific when held to be embraced within the Fourteenth. . . . It is unnecessary to consider now whether legislation which restricts those political processes which can ordinarily be expected to bring about repeal of undesirable legislation, is to be subjected to more exacting judicial scrutiny under the general prohibitions of the Fourteenth Amendment than are most other types of legislation. . . . Nor need we enquire . . . whether prejudice against discrete and insular minorities may be a special condition, which tends seriously to curtail the operation of those political processes ordinarily to be relied upon to protect minorities, and which may call for a correspondingly more searching judicial inquiry.[102]

While admittedly a tentative and qualified pronouncement, Stone's footnote began the process by which the Court granted special protection to First

Amendment freedoms. Cases in which those freedoms were being challenged by other societal interests arrived at the Court with increasing presumption of unconstitutionality.[103] The development of the preferred position of the First Amendment eventually attracted a majority of the members of the Supreme Court, although it was some years before the phrase "preferred position" found its way into constitutional language. In dissenting in *Jones v. Opelika*, Stone, by then chief justice, disagreed with the majority, which upheld municipal license taxes on booksellers as applied to Jehovah's Witnesses, and cited the fact that these were general tax ordinances, not taxes aimed at this particular group. Stone observed:

> The First Amendment is not confined to safeguarding freedom of speech and freedom of religion against discriminatory attempts to wipe them out. On the contrary, the Constitution, by virtue of the First and Fourteenth Amendments, has put those freedoms in a preferred position. Their commands are not restricted to cases where the protected privilege is sought out for attack. They extend at least to every form of taxation which, because it is a condition of the exercise of the privilege, is capable of being used to control or suppress it.[104]

One year later Justice Douglas restated the preferred position doctrine, this time for a Court majority, in *Murdock v. Pennsylvania*, which overruled *Jones v. Opelika*: "Freedom of press, freedom of speech, freedom of religion are in a preferred position."[105]

It was Justice Wiley B. Rutledge, in *Thomas v. Collins* in 1945, who made perhaps the strongest statement supporting the special position of the First Amendment:

> Any attempt to restrict those liberties must be justified by clear public interest, threatened not doubtfully or remotely, but by clear and present danger. The rational connection between the remedy provided and the evil to be curbed, which in other contexts might support legislation against attack on due process grounds, will not suffice. These rights rest on firmer foundation. Accordingly, whatever occasion would restrain orderly discussion and persuasion, at appropriate time and place, must have clear support in public danger, actual or impending. Only the gravest abuses, endangering paramount interests, give occasion for permissible limitation.[106]

The development of the preferred position doctrine parallels Meiklejohn's theory that the First Amendment grants special protection to communication of governing importance. Both preferred position theorists and Meiklejohn recognize the role of the First Amendment in removing barriers that interfere with the exchange of information needed to make intelligent decisions as citizens and voters. Meiklejohn's views would have led him to decide against the government in many if not most of the cases applying the clear and present danger and balancing tests. His views also led him to differ with Justice

Black's absolutist view of the First Amendment. Clearly, the First Amendment protects the press in covering news events, the primary method by which citizens inform themselves about public issues. Yet when Meiklejohn applies his theory of governing importance to libel laws, it becomes a narrower interpretation than would be expected if in fact the First Amendment is held in a preferred position:

> The principle here at stake can be seen in our libel laws. In cases of private defamation, one individual does damage to another by tongue or pen; the person so injured in reputation or property may sue for damages. But in that case, the First Amendment gives no protection to the person sued. His verbal attack has no relation to the business of governing. If, however, the same verbal attack is made in order to show the unfitness of a candidate for governmental office, the act is properly regarded as a citizen's participation in government. It is, therefore, protected by the First Amendment. And the same principle holds good if a citizen attacks, by words of disapproval and condemnation, the policies of the government, or even the structure of the Constitution. These are "public" issues concerning which, under our form of government, he has authority, and is assumed to have competence, to judge. Though private libel is subject to legislative control, political or seditious libel is not.[107]

As will be seen in the ensuing discussion of libel cases, the Court, while influenced by Meiklejohn's "governing importance" principle and his distinction between private and public libel, has often adopted a broader view of the role of the press that has allowed greater First Amendment protection than would be available under the Meiklejohn theory. For example, his theory fails to appreciate the very significant role that private individuals play in public affairs. A citizen need not hold an official government position to be influential in politics and government, and in a way that affects the ability of citizens to learn what their government is doing and to retire from office those who do not serve the public's interest. It is, in fact, difficult to determine what is a public issue or a public controversy and who is a public or private figure. The point at which a discussion becomes a matter of governing importance or public and not private libel is blurred when those being portrayed in news stories do not hold an official government position but have, nevertheless, assumed a role of importance in influencing public affairs. Meiklejohn's theory would provide insufficient protection to the media when they cover individuals who are clearly not public officials and may not be "public figures," yet may exert greater influence over public affairs than those who are. Exposing their role is especially important because they are unelected and therefore not responsible to the public. Moreover, the Meiklejohn thesis gives scant attention to the latitude the media must have if they are going to be free from severe punishments that come from errors in judgment. The media should be careful when doing stories about purely private individuals who, through no fault of their own, are thrust into a public controversy, but the media must enjoy at least some margin of error. If not, the self-censorship that would result from punishing with libel suits and huge judgments even innocent errors would certainly inhibit coverage of public issues even if they come squarely under Meiklejohn's definition of governing importance.

Clearly, when the Supreme Court decided *New York Times v. Sullivan* a few years after Meiklejohn's essay was published, it was influenced by his writing. The case was a classic example of an activity that falls within the powers reserved to the people and made invulnerable, in Meiklejohn's view, to sanctions imposed by their "agency-government."[108]

Although Meiklejohn could distinguish between those forms of speech relating to the governing process and those that are private or nonpolitical, Zechariah Chafee was not as comfortable with the idea that only some speech is entitled to First Amendment protection: "The question whether such perplexing cases are within the First Amendment or not cannot be solved by the multiplication of obvious examples, but only by the development of rational principle to mark the limits of constitutional protection."[109] Chafee was concerned with providing appropriate balance to governmental and speech interests and looked for principles that, although not open to exceptions, are also subject to interpretation, to change, or to abolition, as the necessities of a precarious world may require.[110] In his book Chafee summarized his support for a balancing approach: "There are individual interests and social interests, which must be balanced against each other, if they conflict, in order to determine which interest shall be sacrificed under the circumstances and which shall be protected and become the foundation of a legal right."[111] There appears to be conflict between Chafee's obvious support for balancing and his absolutist demand for a "rational principle," but he did express concern that the argument itself may transcend the issues involved:

> It must never be forgotten that the balancing cannot be properly done unless all the interests involved are adequately ascertained, and the great evil of all this talk about rights is that each side is so busy denying the other's claim to rights that it entirely overlooks the human desires and needs behind that claim.[112]

Finally, Chafee describes the First Amendment's role in protecting speech:

> The First Amendment protects two kinds of interests in free speech. There is an individual interest, the need of many men to express their opinions on matters vital to them if life is to be worth living, and a social interest in the attainment of truth, so that the country may not only adopt the wisest course of action but carry it out in the wisest way.[113]

If the First Amendment is narrowly interpreted to protect only the rights of those exercising freedom of speech and the press, and not those to whom the communication is directed, then libel laws that provide substantial protection to reputational interests, even at the expense of the First Amendment, would be acceptable. But clearly, the First Amendment is not so passive. It is designed not just to protect the rights of the speaker or publisher, but to serve as a powerful force in society to remove barriers that interfere with the exchange of information. In a self-governing society, access to information becomes an indispensable prerequisite to the expression of preference for public officials or public policy. Even the most repulsive ideas are entitled to a full hearing before the court of public opinion. At a minimum the First Amendment speaks to the right to receive information as well as the right to disseminate it. It is necessary, therefore, to consider libel laws in light of their effect on the ability of citizens to gain access to information about their community and nation. Libel laws do not simply involve the victim of the alleged defamation and the media organization that disseminated it; libel laws speak directly to the information *process*. Although the First Amendment has evolved through a balancing process, successful weighing of interests cannot be done until it is understood which parties are perched on the scale. The scale holds not only the victim of defamation and the publisher or broadcaster who disseminated the alleged libel, but the interests of the public at large that are, in fact, so paramount, that they may transcend the immediate issues. That is not to suggest, of course, that reputational interests are unimportant or that individuals should be left unprotected from irresponsible reporting that unfairly damages their reputations. What it does suggest is that the press, the one institution in the Bill of Rights singled out for special protection, preciously guards not only the right to publish or broadcast, but the right of the public to be informed. With the special protection granted the press under the First Amendment goes the special responsibility of serving as a conduit of information about issues, officials, and policies so that citizens can make informed decisions as they govern themselves.

The evolution of modern libel laws and how various societal interests have been incorporated in them become a matter of great importance. Because the mass media have assumed the primary responsibility for effecting the mandate of the First Amendment to inform, the legal environment in which that exchange of information takes places is worth careful examination.

The Emergence of Modern Libel Law

The First Amendment has been a part of the Constitution for almost two hundred years, but the Supreme Court's concern with its significance is a product only of the last half-century. Fifty years is not a long time in the history of constitutional interpretation; nor is it long enough to conclude that the Court has spoken the final word about its provisions. As remarkable as it may seem, it was not until 1925 that the Supreme Court held that the freedom of speech and press provisions of the First Amendment are applicable to the states through the Fourteenth Amendment. In one of the strangest developments in constitutional law, the First Amendment became part of modern jurisprudence by way of an almost offhand remark.

There are many reasons that the First Amendment lay largely dormant for 135 years until being called upon to determine in the aftermath of World War I whether certain forms of speech came within its protection. Some have argued that it was only fifty years ago that a number of issues concerning First Amendment rights emerged that could be decided by the Supreme Court. William Brennan wrote that "in our frontier days, not so much problems of individual liberty as problems of respective domains of federal and state power incident to territorial expansion and economic growth came to the surface."[114] Issues of individual liberty and the relationship of the citizen to government waited "in the wings pending the events of this century that brought them to the fore."[115]

Even more significant was the governmental structure of the new republic itself. As far back as 1833 the Supreme Court had declared that the provisions of the Bill of Rights were limitations only on Congress and federal power, and of course the First Amendment specifically states that "Congress shall make no law . . . abridging freedom of speech, or of the press." Thus infringements on speech and press freedoms at the state level, where they were most likely to occur, would not be subject to review by federal courts. As late as 1922 the Court emphatically stated that "neither the 14th Amendment nor any other provision of the Constitution of the United States imposes upon the States any restrictions about 'freedom of speech.'"[116]

The Framers of the Constitution were aware that state governments could deny their citizens constitutional rights, but the Framers thought that state and local governments, which were theoretically "closer" to the people, were not likely to be the sources of political repression. It was the new federal government, established so far away, that needed to be controlled. It was also assumed that state constitutions, about half of which included a bill of rights in their provisions,[117] would provide sufficient protection to the citizens of the states. The concern was that the central government might grow in such a way as to deprive citizens of certain fundamental rights.

Shortly after the ratification of the first ten amendments to the Constitution, differences of opinion arose as to whether the provisions of the Bill of Rights, and more particularly the first eight amendments, were applicable to the federal government alone, or whether they also affected the states. It may seem surprising that doubt on such a fundamental point could have been left in the drafting of the amendments, but the fact is that only two of the amendments are specifically stated as restraints upon the United States.[118] They are the

First Amendment, which is by its terms made applicable only to Congress, and one clause of the Seventh, which provides that "no fact tried by jury, shall be otherwise reexamined in any court of the United States, than according to the rules of the common law." All other amendments, from the Second through the Eighth, state general libertarian principles, with no indication that their protective effect is against only federal action.[119]

The 1833 case *Barron v. Baltimore*[120] provided an opportunity for Chief Justice John Marshall to confirm that the due process clause of the Fifth Amendment,[121] and by application the entire Bill of Rights, did not apply to the states, Marshall said the issue did not present any problems for the Court:

> The constitution was ordained and established by the people of the United States for themselves, for their own government, and not for the government of the individual States. Each State established a constitution for itself, and in that constitution provided such limitations and restrictions on the powers of its particular government as its judgment dictated. The people of the United States framed such a government for the United States as they supposed best adapted to their situation, and best calculated to promote their interests. The powers they conferred on this government were to be exercised by itself; and the limitations on power, if expressed in general terms, are naturally, and, we think, necessarily applicable to the government created by the instrument. They are limitations of power granted in the instrument itself; not of distinct governments, framed by different persons and for different purposes.[122]

Marshall then recalled the debate that surrounded ratification of the Constitution: "In almost every convention by which the constitution was adopted, amendments to guard against the abuse of power were recommended. These amendments demanded security against the apprehended encroachments of the general government—not against those of the local governments."[123] He explained that nothing in the words of the first ten amendments indicated an intention to apply them to state governments, and that the Court cannot, therefore, so apply them.

It was after the Civil War that the demand rose for national protection against the abusive exercise of state power. This led to the adoption of the Fourteenth Amendment with its prohibitions against state abridgment of the privileges and immunities of citizens of the United States against *state*[124] deprivation of life, liberty, or property without due process of law, and against denial to any person within its jurisdiction of the equal protection of the laws.[125]

It is one of the great tragedies of our constitutional history that the Fourteenth Amendment, adopted to protect the rights of newly freed blacks and other citizens from encroachment of constitutional rights by states would not, for so many decades, be used for that purpose. In fact, in many cases from the first to be considered after ratification of the Fourteenth Amendment in 1868 until 1937, the Supreme Court used the due process clause of the Fourteenth Amendment to protect corporations and businesses from state passed minimum wage laws, laws regulating working conditions, and other laws intended to protect the health and welfare of working people.[126]

Nevertheless, the Court's announcement in the *Prudential* case in 1922 that the First Amendment does not apply to the states made all the more astounding a concession made by one of the Court's most conservative members in *Gitlow v. New York*[127] in 1925. In writing the majority opinion upholding the conviction of a prominent Communist under the New York criminal anarchy statute, Justice Edward T. Sanford wrote: "We may and do assume that freedom of speech and of the press—which are protected by the First Amendment from abridgment by Congress—are among the fundamental personal rights and 'liberties' protected by the due process clause of the Fourteenth Amendment from impairment by the States."[128] The issue had not been argued before the Court, and it was not essential to the decision to uphold Benjamin Gitlow's conviction.[129] It was in this offhand manner that the historic decision was made that enormously enlarged the coverage of the First Amendment and the jurisdiction of the Supreme Court to guarantee the freedom of speech and the press against state or local action as well as against Congress.[130]

As a result of the *Gitlow* decision, from 1925 forward competing societal interests would be balanced with the First Amendment to the U.S. Constitution and not just with state constitutional provisions and common law doctrine as interpreted by state judges. The aura of the First Amendment had influenced constitutional debate, but its impact until the first quarter of the twentieth century had been largely symbolic. Its inclusion in constitutional doctrine as applied to the states made it a formidable weight on the proexpression side of the scales.

The effect of adding the First Amendment to our case law had a more practical consequence. Federal judges, by virtue of lifetime tenure and other factors,[131] are largely insulated from partisan politics and, if they choose, from passions of the moment. They are often in a stronger position than appointed or elected state judges to make unpopular, proexpression decisions without fear that they will be removed from office. The exercise of free speech often evokes powerful opposition that may inhibit state judges whose tenure depends on political favor. Particularly when unpopular groups or individuals offering dissenting views are involved, the federal courts have often responded by upholding the freedom of speech side even in the face of majority opposition.[132]

The decision in *Gitlow* to incorporate freedom of speech and press clauses of the First Amendment into the Fourteenth Amendment came just in time. Six years after *Gitlow*, in *Near v. Minnesota*,[133] the First Amendment was called upon to prevent governmental exercise of prior restraint. The case also provided an opportunity for the Court to remind the country that subsequent punishment for publication, namely, libel suits, are available and the Court all but encouraged their use.[134]

In *Near* the Court by a single vote struck down a Minnesota law providing for the abating, as a public nuisance, "malicious, scandalous and defamatory newspapers and periodicals and the enjoining of anyone maintaining such a nuisance."[135] Chief Justice Charles Evans Hughes, in his majority opinion, confirmed what the Court had suggested for the first time six years before: "It is no longer open to doubt that the liberty of the press, and of speech, is within the liberty safeguarded by the due process clause of the Fourteenth Amendment from invasion by state action."[136] And Hughes added, "It was found impossible to conclude that this essential personal liberty of the citizen was left unprotected by the general guaranty of fundamental rights of person and property."[137] In six years, then, a tiny speck of time in the struggle of people to win the right of free speech, the First Amendment had gone from Justice Sanford's "We may and do assume that freedom of speech and of the press . . . are among the fundamental . . . rights . . ." to Chief Justice Hughes's "It is no longer open to doubt that the liberty of the press, and of speech, is within the liberty safeguarded. . . ."

Chief Justice Hughes made it clear in *Near* that while the circumstances under which a newspaper could be enjoined from publishing were very limited,[138] protection from previous restraint did not limit the ability of those defamed to sue for libel. Quoting Blackstone, he wrote:

> The liberty of the press is indeed essential to the nature of a free state; but this consists in laying no *previous* restraints upon publications, and not in freedom from censure for criminal matter when published. Every freeman has an undoubted right to lay what sentiments he pleases before the public; to forbid this, is to destroy the freedom of the press; but if he publishes what is improper, mischievous or illegal, he must take the consequences of his own temerity.[139]

Hughes recognized the important role of the press in exposing official corruption, but he also recognized the harm that newspapers can do by making untrue, defamatory charges:

> While reckless assaults upon public men, and efforts to bring obloquy upon those who are endeavoring faithfully to discharge official duties, exert a baleful influence and deserve the severest condemnation in public opinion, it cannot be said that this abuse is greater, and it is believed to be less, than that which characterized the period in which the institutions took shape. . . . The fact that the liberty of the press may be abused by miscreant purveyors of scandal does not make any the less necessary the immunity of the press from previous restraint in dealing with official misconduct. Subsequent punishment for such abuses as may exist is the appropriate remedy, consistent with constitutional privilege.[140]

The number of instances of prior restraint has been very limited in the years since *Near*. Certainly, the Court's strong and eloquent denunciation of previous restraint established that such governmental efforts to prevent publication are antithetical to a self-governing society. But as Hughes indicated, subsequent punishment is the appropriate remedy when journalists are irresponsible and civil libel suits have been the vehicles by which publishers and broadcasters are made to suffer the consequences of "their own temerity."

While greatly enlarging the scope of the First Amendment's protection, the decisions in *Gitlow* and *Near* did not change the fundamental structure of our federal system. A basic tenet of that system is that certain areas of the law are left to the states to develop their own standards. The federal system provides both an institutional and social explanation for such an arrangement. The Constitution specifically mandates that powers not granted to the federal government are reserved for the people: "The powers not delegated to the United States by the Constitution, nor prohibited by it to the States, are reserved to the States respectively, or to the people."[141] In many areas of constitutional law, the states developed statutes, ordinances, regulations and case law to suit local preference. Many customs and laws were in place before the adoption of the Fourteenth Amendment and the subsequent twentieth-century application of many of the provisions of the Bill of Rights to the states.

Social considerations also suggested that certain issues were more likely to be considered at the state or local level. For much of our history, states had been left to decide how published defamatory statements were to be redressed. Based on local sentiment and influenced by early days of statehood, as well as adaptation of English common law, the states developed libel laws that often provided insufficient protection to First Amendment interests by weighing heavily on the reputational side of the scale. It was not until 1964 that state abuse became so flagrant and so obviously threatening to freedom of the press that the Supreme Court was forced to intervene to begin the process of "nationalizing" libel laws. The Court faced no simple task. For decades, states had developed complex, often rigid and inconsistent libel laws that were unencumbered by the general language of the First Amendment. Synthesizing so many different laws into national standards proved to be very difficult as the Supreme Court became increasingly divided over what standards should be adopted.

The Court recognized that the Constitution did not forbid punishment after publication. As the Court had said in *Near*, subsequent punishment was the appropriate remedy "so long as it was consistent with constitutional privilege." Although the Court did not explain what privileges were consistent with the Constitution, it did warn that society has a substantial interest in punishing those who would abuse freedom of the press:

It is recognized that punishment for the abuse of liberty accorded to the press is essential to the protection of the public, and that the common law rules that subject the libeler to responsibility for the public offense, as well as for the private injury, are not abolished by the protection extended in our constitution.[142]

The Supreme Court had spoken. Not only did each state have the right to punish those who published scandalous and defamatory matter, all of them did.[143] Every state had libel laws, either based on legislative enactment or court decisions.

Definition and Synthesis of *Libel*

At the midpoint of the twentieth century, the Supreme Court had a chance to review the evolution of state libel laws in a case dealing with the now largely discredited concept of *group libel*. In *Beauharnais v. Illinois*,[144] decided in 1952 by a 5-4 vote, the Court upheld the conviction of Joseph Beauharnais for distributing on the streets of Chicago anti-Black leaflets in violation of Illinois law.[145] Although *group libel* was later undermined by court decisions as too close to seditious libel, the case did give the Court an opportunity to trace the development of state libel laws.

The Court found that actual statutory definitions of libel did not vary much from state to state. Eleven jurisdictions had accepted, with some variation, the following statutory version of libel:

> A libel is a malicious defamation, expressed either by printing, or by signs or pictures, or the like, tending to blacken the memory of one who is dead, or to impeach the honesty, integrity, virtue or reputation or publish the natural defects of one who is alive, and thereby to expose him to public hatred, contempt, ridicule, or financial injury.[146]

Another definition of libel, with minor variations, had been adopted in another twelve jurisdictions:

> A libel is a malicious defamation of a person, made public by any printing, writing, sign, picture, representation or effigy, tending to provoke him to wrath or expose him to public hatred, contempt, or ridicule, or to deprive him of the benefits of public confidence and social intercourse; or any malicious defamation, made public as aforesaid, designed to blacken and vilify the memory of one who is dead, and tending to scandalize or provoke his surviving relatives or friends.[147]

Still another twenty jurisdictions followed common law precedents that, in some instances, defined libel as aroused *scorn* or *obloquy* and that impeached *virtue* or that held individuals up to public ridicule. The remaining nine jurisdictions, the Supreme Court found, had definitions that did not fall into common patterns.

The relative uniformity of definitions of libel cited above belie the mosaic of confused, often inconsistent and restrictive libel laws and practices developed by the states. The laws varied not only from state to state, but often from case to case within the same state. Discussing in detail the evolution of state libel laws in the fifty states would be an exhaustive task, and in view of the Supreme Court's effort to provide national standards in the last twenty years, somewhat unproductive.[148] Most state statutes have been changed, in one way or the other, to accommodate the Court's modern interpretation of libel laws, albeit sometimes without much success. There is, nevertheless, value in briefly tracing the development of libel laws leading up to recent efforts to bring some uniformity of standards.

In the period following the adoption of the Constitution and the ratification of the First Amendment, the freedom that newspapers had enjoyed during the post-Revolutionary period had led to what many considered to be excessive criticism of government and public officials. Many persons believed that in the new United States there could no longer be libel against the government, that the old English common law of seditious libel had not been transplanted. Colonial juries had rejected in trial after trial the English doctrine that publications "promoting an ill opinion of government or officials, whether true or false, constituted criminal libel." Yet although the colonial concept was that truthful statements about public officials were not libelous, it soon became clear that the common law of seditious libel was not dead and within fifteen years after independence, criticism of public officials became a crime in the United States.[149]

Some question did exist about the continued viability and applicability of English law. In a case involving the publisher of the *Independent Gazeteer* in Philadelphia, Pennsylvania Chief Justice McKean commented in 1788 that nothing in the Pennsylvania Constitution changed the common law of England regarding liberty of the press.[150] Yet a year later, in 1789, Chief Justice William Cushing of the Massachusetts Supreme Court wrote in a letter that "falsity must be a necessary ingredient in a libel."[151] Cushing, as chief justice in Massachusetts, never had the chance to place his views into case law; he was appointed as one of the first members of the U.S. Supreme Court.[152] A case in Massachusetts a few years later made it clear, however, that judges sitting on its highest bench still believed a publisher could express personal views as long as they were kept them "within the bounds of truth." The majority of judges, in charging the jury in the case, held that the English common law of criminal libel had not been altered by the state constitution.[153] The publisher was found not guilty by the jury. Ironically, the old English common law of criminal libel had been revived only to be rejected by the jurors.

Pennsylvania went further than Massachusetts and other states in protecting freedom of the press. Constitutional reforms in 1790 provided that "citizens were free to investigate public officials in their public capacities."[154] Another provision provided that publications "proper for public information could be justified by truth" in all prosecutions for criminal libel.[155] Pennsylvania was the first state to include this guarantee in a constitution, although it was followed soon by Delaware, Kentucky, and Tennessee. Despite the constitutional provisions, judges in Pennsylvania were left substantial discretion to punish criminal libel because the constitution left unresolved a standard for determining what publications were proper for public information.[156]

During the period following ratification of the U.S. Constitution, there was little uniformity among the states concerning newspaper prosecutions, other than the fact that such prosecutions were sanctioned.[157] Judges and juries were often in disagreement over the extent to which English common law was enforceable in this country. Prosecutions were expanded to the federal courts by the Sedition Act of 1798. The act largely adopted the old English common law with the reservation that truth was a legal defense to libel and that jurors could determine the law as well as fact.[158] Although some judges during this period took tentative steps toward recognizing truth as a defense, it was still clear that publications promoting an "ill opinion of government or public officials were, under the common law, still a crime."[159]

The period before the Civil War saw some liberalizing trends favoring newspapers in libel prosecutions in some jurisdictions. But the press had been granted privilege only for truthful reports and comment on the conduct of elected officials and candidates.[160] This privilege allowed considerably more freedom than existed at the beginning of the century, but the privilege of discussion was tarnished by the English doctrine that "any publication promoting an ill opinion of government or its officials was criminally libelous."

Yet the shift toward greater protection for the press had begun. The English doctrine was altered by a series of court decisions, new laws, and constitutional reforms in various states. In New York, for example, some years earlier, the case of *People v. Croswell* had led to a statute providing that a libelous publication could be defended if it "were true and printed with good motives for justifiable ends."[161] Yet in some ways, the trend was not particularly progressive. Truth alone no longer constituted a defense for libel; motives as well as truth were at issue. During this period, court decisions in some states indicated that under constitutions and at common law, the requirements of good motives and justifiable ends were met if "publishers had an honest intent to inform citizens about their government and elected officials."[162] It also became clear that newspapers could comment on candidates for office with the same freedom that they could comment about officials already in office, although that protection in some cases did not extend to appointed officials.[163]

A key development in the question of federal prosecution took place during this period. In 1812, the U.S. Supreme Court held that the federal government had no common law jurisdiction to prosecute libel cases:[164]

> The only question which this case presents is, whether the circuit courts of the United States can exercise a common law jurisdiction in criminal cases. We state it thus broadly because a decision on a case of libel will apply to every case in which jurisdiction is not vested in those courts by statute.[165]

The Court had no trouble reaching a conclusion:

> Although this question is brought up now for the first time to be decided by this court, we consider it as having been long since settled in public opinion. In no other case for many years has this jurisdiction been asserted; and the general acquiescence of legal men shows the prevalence of opinion in favor of the negative.[166]

And in light of the experience of the Sedition Act of 1798, it was unlikely that Congress would pass another criminal libel statute. As a result criminal libel statutes became the exclusive domain of the states.

In the period preceding the Civil War, another important development took place. There was the beginning of a shift from criminal to civil libel suits and with that trend, increased variety of state libel statutes and case law. By turning to civil libel suits, public officials were moving into an "untried but inviting area" of litigation.[167] Although it was getting to the point where it was no longer a crime to comment truthfully on the character or conduct of public officials, that did not mean that officials were prohibited from collecting damages in civil suits for such comments. This was especially true where the private reputations of officials were involved.[168]

Despite some positive trends, there were few special privileges for the press in discussing public officials. Some courts, such as those in New York, held that there was no privilege to impute crime to an official or even to discuss the public character and qualifications of candidates or officials unless the statement were true.

Throughout many of the formative years of libel law, truth was the focus of much of the debate. Though it was emphasized by courts that elected officials had a right to be protected from attacks in the press, it was gradually recognized that the people had a right to know the truth about their officials' public conduct, character, and qualifications.

During the last half of the nineteenth century, truth continued to be the primary justification for libel against public officials and candidates. But judges in state after state during this period began to recognize that libelous statements made in good faith against officials and candidates could be defended regardless of truth or falsity. The view that a publisher should not be held accountable for the exact truth of articles concerning public officials, although not accepted by all states, did begin to take form.[169]

Between the end of the Civil War and the 1880s, some type of privilege was recognized in twenty-five of twenty-eight jurisdictions in which appellate court decisions in public official libel suits were recorded. Even in jurisdictions where privilege was allowed, there was no uniformity. Judgments differed based on what the privilege included.[170]

Overall, there was much greater privilege of discussion concerning government officials and candidates for office during the last half of the nineteenth century than during the previous fifty years. Newspaper publishers were in some cases able to defend libel suits or mitigate damages by proving that even false articles were published in good faith. Despite widespread variance in individual state policies of privilege, the broad confines offering greater protection for discussion of public affairs had been established by the turn of the century.

In the early part of the twentieth century, as discussed in *Near v. Minnesota*, libel laws were held to be constitutional and did not impair liberty of the press. People had the liberty to place their views before the public without restraint, but they needed to be wary of punishment that awaited the exercise of such liberty. During this period it became apparent that the definition of libel and the culpability of publishers depended on how the published words were interpreted. And often, the meanings of the words were in dispute. The Supreme Court in a 1913 case, *Baker v. Warner*,[171] ruled in effect that it was for the "jury and not the court to determine the meaning of ambiguous language in any publication."[172] Guidelines to help jurors make that determination were developed on a state-by-state basis but were often similar. In a number of states, the "plain and natural" import of the words became the guiding principle.[173] In other states, words were interpreted in accordance with their "ordinary meaning as understood by readers." Several states adopted the "ordinary understanding" standard to indicate that courts would yield to the interpretation that average or ordinary readers would give to the published words. States also required that the articles be considered as a whole and that words were not to be taken out of context. Jurors had such discretion to interpret words and determine whether libel had been committed when the words were ambiguous, as suggested in *Baker v. Warner*.

In some cases, words were libelous *per se*, or libelous on their face and no context was necessary to determine if they were defamatory. But jurors also had to consider libel *per quod*, where the words were not libelous in themselves but were libelous when considered in a larger context.[174] In many states, judges and not jurors determined whether the words were libelous *per se*.[175] But if the words were unclear or could be interpreted in more than one way, it was the responsibility of the jury, in finding fact, to determine if they constituted libel *per quod*. For the most part, however, publishers could defend libel suits on the basis of truth, or possibly truth with good motives, or suits could be defended on the basis of fair comment or privilege.

From 150 years of evolution of libel came relatively clear patterns. Through the first half of the twentieth century, the development of the law of libel was primarily centered on the extent of privilege. It was generally recognized in most states that the freedom to discuss public officials was somewhat broader than the freedom to discuss private citizens. As a result standards developed that allowed ordinarily libelous statements about public officials. The issue of who is a public figure and who is a private citizen is a debate that rages today.[176]

Lawhorne describes these standards of privilege as falling into two broad categories. The narrow rule, that privilege was confined to comment and criticism based on actual facts, eventually was adopted by the largest single group of state courts. It became known as the majority view. The more liberal rule, that privilege extended to misstatements of fact when made without malice, was adopted by the second largest group of state courts. It was referred to as the minority view. Judges had a difficult time applying the formulas to cover all libel cases, but most state courts had adopted one of the views by the end of World War II.

From 1900 to 1945 the narrow rule of privilege was adopted in twenty-one states and the territory of Hawaii. Those jurisdictions had rejected the doctrine that privilege extended to false statements made without malice in the belief they were true. Instead, those courts held to the standard of truth for statements of fact, allowing a limited privilege for fair comment and criticism concerning the acts and conduct of public officials. Lawhorne includes the following states and jurisdictions in this category: Alabama, Arkansas, Florida, Hawaii, Illinois, Kentucky, Louisiana, Maine, Maryland, Massachusetts, Mississippi, New Jersey, New York, North Dakota, Ohio, Oregon, South Carolina, Tennessee, Vermont, Virginia, Washington, and Wisconsin.[177]

Courts in sixteen states adopted the liberal rule of privilege before the end of World War II. They excused false statements about officials that ordinarily would be libelous, provided the statements were published without malice and with probable cause for believing them to be true. Lawhorne includes the following states in this category: Arizona, California, Colorado, Connecticut, Iowa, Kansas, Michigan, Minnesota, Montana, Nebraska, New Hampshire, North Carolina, Pennsylvania, South Dakota, Utah, and West Virginia.[178]

Following a key Supreme Court decision in 1938, federal courts applied *state* law in all cases other than those involving constitutional issues or acts of Congress. In *Erie Railroad v. Thompkins*,[179] Justice Louis Brandeis wrote for the majority:

> Except in matters governed by the Federal Constitution or by Acts of Congress, the law to be applied in any case is the law of the State. And whether the law of the State shall be declared by its Legislature in a statute or by its highest court in

a decision is not a matter of federal concern. There is no federal general common law.[180]

The issue is extremely important in libel cases. In an era when media organizations are national in scope, where and under whose laws they are sued become matters of much significance. The Constitution requires that when citizens of different states sue each other, the case be heard in federal courts under their "diversity jurisdiction." Recently, however, state courts have accepted jurisdiction in libel cases even when nationally distributed media have little direct connection to that state. Lawyers have found shopping for the forum most unfriendly to First Amendment interests to be an important part of bringing a libel suit.[181] At least for the time being, the U.S. Supreme Court seems willing to accept the exercise of such jurisdiction.

It is necessary to point out that the Court did become dissatisfied with the holding in *Erie Railroad*, eventually recognizing "countervailing factors" that reflect a federal interest in diversity litigation, and where these are deemed to be of overriding importance, to apply federal policy rather than state law.[182] Today, federal judges attempt to apply the various doctrines of privilege in states where the publication or broadcast originated, sometimes with conflicting results.[183]

In the period before *New York Times v. Sullivan* in 1964, several more states adopted the liberal rule of privilege, allowing increased immunity from libel suits for misstatement of fact about the public lives of officials and candidates. Idaho, Georgia, Nevada, and Virginia, by issuing liberal rule decisions, increased the number of states that followed the so-called minority view. Yet, it was no longer accurate or appropriate to describe states as being in the majority view. Some in the majority, the less liberal camp, were beginning to allow more freedom with facts. In addition, some in the minority view were becoming even more liberal.

If nothing else, the preceding discussion indicates the lack of uniformity of libel laws. The law as it pertained to libeling public officials and candidates was being applied differently in one part of the country than in another. Although there was movement toward liberalism and greater appreciation for the role of the First Amendment, there was a need for uniform administration and application of libel laws. And some states continued to display an astonishing lack of appreciation for the role of the First Amendment in protecting discussion of public officials and public issues. Such was the case in Alabama, which gave the Supreme Court the opportunity to revolutionize and modernize libel laws.

Notes

1. I. Stat. 596 (1798).

2. In a sense, the Sedition Act of 1798 was an ''indirect'' importation of English common law because in the early years of the new nation it had been settled that the federal government had no common law jurisdiction in criminal cases. *United States v. Hudson and Goodwin*, 7 Cranch 32 (1812), is discussed later in this chapter.

3. With *New York Times v. Sullivan*, 376 U.S. 254 (1964), the Supreme Court began the process of ''nationalizing'' libel laws, although during the following two decades, the Court left to the states substantial discretion to decide the standard of liability in certain types of libel cases. The major cases will be discussed in chapters 3, 4 and 5.

4. Any definition of libel must consider the court cases that give it content; therefore, a complete definition must await a discussion of the cases themselves. Although there are circumstances that may be considered exceptions, a statement must be both defamatory and false before it can be considered libelous.

5. Historically, libel suits have been based on written defamatory statements; slander suits spoken defamation. Some court decisions suggested that if a statement was *read* from a script over a radio or television station, it was libel, but if it was spoken extemporaneously or without a script, it was slander. Today most courts consider any communication that is broadcast over radio or television to be controlled by libel laws.

6. Some states, however, treat broadcast defamation as slander, as does California. Civil Code, sec. 46; *Arno v. Stewart*, 245 Cal. App. 2d 955, 961; 54 Cal. Rptr. 392 (1966). The difference may be more in the name than in substance. California courts have adopted many of the standards enunciated by the Supreme Court in *libel* cases.

7. In the wake of *Gertz v. Welch*, 418 U.S. 323 (1974), it is somewhat unclear how much proof must be offered that someone's general reputation was actually damaged. Justice Lewis Powell, writing the opinion of the Court, said the Constitution does not permit recovery for ''presumed damages'':

> We hold that the States may not permit recovery of presumed or punitive damages, at least when liability is not based on a showing of knowledge or falsity or reckless disregard for the truth.

> The common law of defamation is an oddity of tort law, for it allows recovery of purportedly compensatory damages without evidence of actual loss. . . . The largely uncontrolled discretion of juries to award damages where there is no loss unnecessarily compounds the potential of any system of liability for defamatory falsehood to inhibit vigorous exercise of First Amendment freedoms. Additionally, the doctrine of presumed damages invites juries to punish unpopular opinion rather than to compensate individuals for injury sustained by the publication of the false fact. [Ibid. at 349.]

Powell then turned to the issue of ''actual injury'':

> It is . . . appropriate to require that state remedies for defamatory falsehood reach no farther than is necessary to protect the legitimate interest involved. It is necessary to restrict defamation plaintiffs who do not prove knowledge of falsity or reckless disregard for the truth to compensation for actual injury. We need not define actual injury, as trial courts have wide experience in framing appropriate jury instructions in tort actions. Suffice it to say that actual injury is not limited to out-of-pocket loss. Indeed, the more customary types of actual harm inflicted

by defamatory falsehood include impairment of reputation and standing in the community, personal humiliation, and mental anguish and suffering. Of course, juries must be limited by appropriate instructions, and all awards must be supported by competent evidence concerning the injury, although there need be no evidence which assigns an actual dollar value to the injury. [Ibid. at 349-50].

8. Even true statements can be considered defamatory, although not libelous. Media organizations face an additional problem with invasion of privacy suits that can result from even accurate and truthful reports. In privacy cases, discussed later, the issue is the "invasion" and not necessarily the publication or broadcast itself.

9. See *Gertz v. Welch*, 418 U.S. 323.

10. Ibid. at 348-50.

11. Ibid. at 349. The actual malice standard in libel cases, first enunciated in *New York Times v. Sullivan*, will be discussed in detail.

12. Yet, depending on the action taken by those exposed to the defamation, there are circumstances under which an individual can suffer injury to reputation when only a few persons have read or heard the statement. The *Alton Telegraph* case, mentioned below and discussed in detail later, is an example.

13. The media enjoy a qualified privilege to report statements made at public and official meetings. The privilege is conditional, and applies only to reports that are a fair and accurate or truthful summary of what occurred at a meeting. Privilege to report such statements is virtually absolute. It is highly unlikely a successful libel suit could be brought against a news organization that accurately portrayed the activities and statements of those at public meetings. The media are granted substantial protection to report on legislatures, courts, and other governmental bodies, but to be covered by such immunity, they must report on matters related to official business. The accurate reporting of, say, libelous statements made by a city council member about a private person that have nothing to do with city business could still lead to a libel suit. Reporters *may* also enjoy a limited privilege to report charges made against public and private figures if the charges are made by responsible parties and the reporting of them adds to public debate on an issue of importance. See Don Pember, *Mass Media Law* (Dubuque: Wm. C. Brown Publishers, 1984), pp. 164-65 for a discussion of "neutral reportage."

14. The memo, written by reporters Joseph Melosi and William Lhotka, was forwarded without their knowledge to the Federal Loan Bank Board by a U.S. attorney who was investigating labor racketeering and criminal activity in East St. Louis, Illinois. The board found no Mafia connection with the developer, James Green, but discovered what it considered to be alleged irregularities in a bank's dealings with him. The bank eventually restricted further credit to Green and his businesses collapsed. *"Alton Telegraph* Case Settled, Paper Reportedly to Pay $1.4M," *The News Media and the Law*, June/July 1982: 20.

15. Because a settlement was eventually reached for a reported $1.4 million—further legal actions were withdrawn by both parties, and the trial court's ruling was therefore vacated—the case will technically not serve as a precedent for holding a newspaper liable for an unpublished memo written by its reporters. Nevertheless, the decision and the size of the judgment alarmed many of those concerned about the effect of libel suits on news-gathering. Ibid.

16. Which managers see a controversial report before it is aired is a matter of individual station policy. Some broadcast stations give the news director sole discretion; in other stations the general manager must also give prior approval.

17. Reporters and editors have also learned, sometimes the hard way, that any comments made by them during the preparation of a story could conceivably come out during the pretrial and discovery process and be exposed to the jury. During the trial in which the *Washington Post* lost a $2.05 million suit to the president of Mobil Oil in July, 1982, a reporter had to explain what he meant by a comment made to a colleague working with him on the story that "it isn't every day that you knock off one of the Seven Sisters [oil companies]." "What Went Wrong at the *Washington Post?*" *Columbia Journalism Review* (January/February 1983): 33. As a jury struggles to determine the state of mind of the reporter as the story was being prepared, such comments could be interpreted as evidence of malice or reckless disregard of the truth.

18. If a libelous statement does not refer explicitly to an individual, the plaintiff must convince the jury that the defamatory words referred to him or her. One of the most difficult questions is whether a group that has been libeled is small enough that individuals within the group could have suffered injury. If the group is a city council with five members and the local newspaper reports that all members of the council are corrupt, that is probably a small enough group for individuals to bring a lawsuit. If, on the other hand, a campus newspaper says that all students at a university smoke marijuana, that is probably too large a group for any individual to claim he or she suffered injury. In between are such groups as athletic teams. In one case, some individuals on a sixty-member football team successfully sued a magazine when it reported that some members of the team used drugs.

19. 376 U.S. 254. The advertisement ran on 29 March 1960.

20. Ibid. at 257-60.

21. *Beauharnais v. Illinois*, 343 U.S. 250 (1952).

22. C. Herman Pritchett, *The American Constitution* (New York: McGraw-Hill, 1977), p. 370. When Illinois revised its criminal code in 1961, the three criminal libel laws on the books were merged into a single statute keyed to breach of the peace, apparently in recognition that group libel laws punish the act of discussion itself and that breach of the peace laws are less constitutionally intrusive.

In a concurring opinion that Justice Black joined, Justice William O. Douglas wrote in *Garrison v. Louisiana* that "*Beauharnais*, a case decided by the narrowest of margins, should be overruled as a misfit in our constitutional system and as out of line with the dictates of the First Amendment." 379 U.S. 64 (1964) at 82.

23. The concept of "fault" has created some confusion. In *Gertz*, the Court said:

> We hold that, so long as they do not impose liability without fault, the States may define for themselves the appropriate standard of liability for a publisher or broadcaster of a defamatory falsehood injurious to a private individual. This approach provides a more equitable boundary between the competing concerns involved here. It recognizes the strength of the legitimate state interest in compensating private individuals for wrongful injury to reputation, yet shields the press and broadcast media from the rigors of strict liability for defamation. [418 U.S. at 347-48.]

24. Justice Powell, writing the opinion of the Court, recognized that this point was one of the main reasons that Justice White bitterly dissented. Powell, in interpreting White, said,

> He would hold that a publisher or broadcaster may be required to prove the truth of a defamatory statement concerning a private individual

and, failing such proof, that the publisher or broadcaster may be held liable for defamation even though he took every conceivable precaution to ensure the accuracy of the offending statement prior to its dissemination. Ibid. at 388-92. In Mr. Justice White's view, one who publishes a statement that later turns out to be inaccurate can never be "without fault" in any meaningful sense, for "it is he who circulated a falsehood that he was not required to publish." [Ibid. at 347.]

A majority of the Supreme Court has been hesitant to punish what could be called "innocent errors" even if they involve private individuals. But determining where innocent error ends and irresponsible reporting begins is very difficult. Ensuing chapters will deal with this and related issues.

25. Some states, such as New York, have blended various standards of liability. For example, a private individual who was involved in a matter of public interest has to meet a standard in New York that is sometimes described as "gross negligence," falling somewhere between "actual malice" and mere negligence. The plaintiff in such a case has to establish "by a preponderance of evidence that the publication was made in a grossly irresponsible manner without due regard for the standards of information gathering and dissemination ordinarily followed by responsible parties." *Chapadeau v. Utica Observer-Dispatch*, 341 N.E. 2d 569, 1 Med. L. Rptr. 1693 (1975).

26. *Curtis Publishing Company v. Butts*, 388 U.S. 130 (1967); *Associated Press v. Walker*, 388 U.S. 130 (1967); *Rosenbloom v. Metromedia*, 403 U.S. 29 (1971); *Gertz v. Welch*, 418 U.S. 323 (1974); *Time, Inc. v. Firestone*, 424 U.S. 448 (1976).

27. 418 U.S. at 348-50. The Court seemed to say that "presumed damages" would still be permitted if the plaintiff demonstrated actual malice on the part of the media defendant.

28. Ibid. at 349-50.

29. Ibid. at 350.

30. In a number of important cases in recent years that requirement has not deterred juries that are determined to award substantial monetary damages to plaintiffs. Juries in some of those cases, not satisfied simply to award compensatory damages, appeared to hold that the actual malice requirement had been met so it could award the substantially larger punitive damages. Trial judges and appellate courts later ruled that there was no showing of reckless disregard for the truth and overturned many of the verdicts.

31. A subject of much debate among scholars, to be discussed later in this chapter, has been whether the First Amendment was meant by the Framers to put an end to prosecution for seditious libel. The Supreme Court, in *New York Times v. Sullivan*, seemed to suggest that such prosecutions have no place in a society that places value on free expression:

> Although the Sedition Act [of 1798] was never tested in this Court, the attack upon its validity has carried the day in the court of history. . . . These views reflect a broad consensus that the Act, because of the restraint it imposed upon criticism of government and public officials, was inconsistent with the First Amendment. [376 U.S. at 276.] What a State may not constitutionally bring about by means of a criminal statute is likewise beyond the reach of its civil law of libel. The fear of damage awards under a rule such as that invoked by the Alabama courts here may be markedly more inhibiting than the fear of prosecution under a criminal statute. [Ibid. at 277.]

32. Pritchett, *The American Constitution*, p. 362.
33. I. Stat. 596 (1798).
34. Pritchett, *The American Constitution*, pp. 362-63.
35. The Star Chamber also had a less-than-progressive view about what was permissible criticism of government. As early as 1606 its justices declared that it was immaterial whether libels were true or false. The decision in *Case de Libellis Famosis* was considered the formal beginning of libel prosecutions in England. Clifton O. Lawhorne, *Defamation and Public Officials: The Evolving Law of Libel* (Carbondale: Southern Illinois University Press, 1971), p. 266.
36. Pritchett, *The American Constitution*, p. 363.
37. Harold L. Nelson and Dwight L. Teeter, Jr., *Law of Mass Communications: Freedom and Control of Print and Broadcast Media* (Mineola, N.Y.: The Foundation Press, 1978), p. 21.
38. 6 Howell's State Trials 513 (1663).
39. Treason in England had been defined by law since 1352. It included "compassing" or imagining the king's death, levying war against the king, or giving aid and comfort to his enemies. Writing was included as part of compassing the king's death. Nelson and Teeter, *Law of Mass Communications*, p. 21. Lawhorne claimed that Twyn's sentence was the worst ever imposed on someone for the printing of a book in England. Lawhorne, *Defamation and Public Officials*, p. 7.
40. Nelson and Teeter, *Law of Mass Communications*, p. 21.
41. Lawhorne, *Defamation and Public Officials*, p. 6.
42. Ibid.
43. Ibid., p. 23.
44. Ibid.
45. Zenger's lawyer, Andrew Hamilton, urged the jury to recognize truth as a defense, and argued that the jury should decide "the law"—the libelousness of the words—as well as the fact of printing. Although blocked by the judge from pursuing this argument, he made an impassioned plea that liberty itself was on trial in that courtroom.
46. See note 31 above.
47. I. Stat. 596 (1798).
48. 376 U.S. at 274.
49. Nelson and Teeter, *Law of Mass Communications*, p. 26.
50. Ibid.
51. Ibid.
52. Ibid.
53. 376 U.S. at 276.
54. William J. Brennan, Jr., "The Supreme Court and the Meiklejohn Interpretation of the First Amendment," 79 *Harvard Law Review* 1 (November 1965): 15.
55. 376 U.S. at 274-75.
56. Zechariah Chafee, Jr., *Free Speech in the United States* (Cambridge: Harvard University Press, 1941), p. 16.
57. Ibid., p. 19.
58. Ibid.
59. Ibid., p. 20.
60. Pritchett, *The American Constitution*, p. 363. See Leonard W. Levy, *Legacy of Suppression: Freedom of Speech and Press in Early American History* (Cambridge: Harvard University Press, 1964).
61. *Restatement of Torts*, sec. 582 (1938).

62. Ibid., sec. 583.
63. Ibid., sec. 598.
64. Ibid., comment a.
65. Ibid., comment b.
66. First Amendment to U.S. Constitution.
67. For a discussion of how provisions of the Bill of Rights became applicable to the states through the Fourteenth Amendment, see Pritchett, *The American Constitution*, pp. 285-97, 412-82.
68. This quotation, from Justice Brennan's *Harvard Law Review* article cited above, refers the reader to *Roth v. United States* 354 U.S. 476 (1957) at 514. Black joined Douglas's dissent in *Roth*, but that particular page does not include a passage on Black's absolutist views of the First Amendment. A better source is perhaps a conversation that Black had with Edmond Cahn in 1962 about his views:

    > Professor Cahn: Do you make an exception [that the press should never be censored] in freedom of speech and press for the law of defamation? That is, are you willing to allow people to sue for damages when they are subjected to libel or slander?

    > Justice Black: My view of the First Amendment, as originally ratified, is that it said Congress should pass none of these kinds of laws. As written at that time, the Amendment applied only to Congress. I have no doubt myself that the provision, as written and adopted, intended that there should be no libel or defamation law in the United States under the United States Government, just absolutely none so far as I am concerned. . . . My belief is that the First Amendment was made applicable to the states by the Fourteenth. I do not hesitate, so far as my own view is concerned, as to what should be and what I hope will sometime be the constitutional doctrine that just as it was not intended to authorize damage suits for mere words as distinguished from conduct as far as the Federal Government is concerned, the same rule should apply to the states. . . . I believe with Jefferson that it is time enough for government to step in to regulate people when they *do* something, not when they *say* something, and I do not believe myself that there is *any* halfway ground if you enforce the protections of the First Amendment. [Irving Dilliard, ed., *One Man's Stand for Freedom* (New York: Knopf, 1963), pp. 476-77; emphasis in original.]

69. *Cox v. Louisiana*, 379 U.S. 559 (1964) at 578.
70. *Kovacs v. Cooper*, 336 U.S. 77 (1949); *Breard v. City of Alexandria*, 341 U.S. 622 (1951).
71. Brennan, "The Supreme Court and the Meiklejohn Interpretation of the First Amendment," p. 5.
72. *Schenck v. United States*, 249 U.S. 47 (1919) at 52.
73. Although the expression "clear and present danger" continues to be used today in a number of contexts, it has been mostly discontinued as a test in free speech and association cases since *Brandenburg v. Ohio*, 395 U.S. 444 (1969).
74. 183 F. 2d 201 at 212 (2d Circuit), affirmed, 341 U.S. 494 (1951) at 510.
75. *Craig v. Harney*, 331 U.S. 367 (1947); *Pennekamp v. Florida*, 328 U.S. 331 (1946); *Bridges v. California*, 314 U.S. 252 (1941); *Wood v. Georgia*, 370 U.S. 375 (1962).
76. *Roth v. United States*, 354 U.S. 476 (1957) at 484.
77. Ibid. at 484-85.

78. Pritchett, *The American Constitution*, p. 309.
79. 315 U.S. 568 (1942) at 571-72.
80. *Konigsberg v. State Bar*, 366 U.S. 36 (1961) at 50-51.
81. Thomas I. Emerson, "Toward a General Theory of the First Amendment," 72 *Yale Law Journal* 5 (April 1963): 912.
82. Ibid.
83. Ibid., p. 913.
84. Ibid.
85. Ibid.
86. Ibid., pp. 913-14.
87. Brennan, "The Supreme Court and the Meiklejohn Interpretation of the First Amendment," p. 11.
88. Ibid.
89. Alexander Meiklejohn, "The First Amendment Is an Absolute," *The Supreme Court Review* (1961): 253-54.
90. Ibid., p. 255.
91. Ibid., p. 257.
92. Ibid., p. 254.
93. Brennan, "The Supreme Court and the Meiklejohn Interpretation of the First Amendment," p. 13.
94. Meiklejohn, "The First Amendment Is an Absolute," p. 256.
95. Ibid., p. 257.
96. Ibid.
97. Pritchett, *The American Constitution*, p. 305.
98. *Palko v. Connecticut*, 302 U.S. 319 (1937) at 326.
99. Ibid. at 327.
100. Ibid. at 326.
101. Pritchett, *The American Constitution*, p. 305.
102. *United States v. Carolene Products Co.*, 304 U.S. 144 (1938) at 152-53.
103. Pritchett, *The American Constitution*, p. 306.
104. *Jones v. Opelika*, 316 U.S. 584 (1942), Stone, C.J., dissenting at 608.
105. 319 U.S. 105 (1943) at 115.
106. 323 U.S. 516 (1945) at 530.
107. Meiklejohn, "The First Amendment Is an Absolute," p. 259.
108. After the *New York Times* decision was announced, Meiklejohn told Professor Harry Kalven that "it is an occasion for dancing in the streets." Harry Kalven, Jr., "The *New York Times* Case: A Note on 'The Central Meaning of the First Amendment'" *The Supreme Court Review* (1964): 221 n. 125.
109. Chafee, *Free Speech in the United States*, p. 109.
110. Meiklejohn, "The First Amendment Is an Absolute," p. 253.
111. Chafee, Free Speech in the United States, p. 32.
112. Ibid.
113. Ibid., p. 33.
114. Brennan, "The Supreme Court and the Meiklejohn Interpretation of the First Amendment," p. 2.
115. Ibid.
116. *Prudential Insurance Co. of America v. Cheek*, 259 U.S. 530 (1922) at 543.
117. Pritchett, *The American Constitution*, p. 288.
118. Ibid.
119. Ibid.
120. 7 Pet. 243 (1833).

121. The due process clause of the Fifth Amendment to the U.S. Constitution reads: "Nor shall any person . . . be deprived of life, liberty, or property, without due process of law; nor shall private property be taken for public use, without just compensation."
122. 7 Pet. 243 (1833) at 247.
123. Ibid. at 250.
124. Author's emphasis.
125. The Fourteenth Amendment was adopted in 1868.
126. See Pritchett, *The American Constitution*, pp. 518-34.
127. 268 U.S. 652.
128. Ibid. at 666. Interestingly, Justice Sanford began this famous phrase with the words "for present purposes," as if to suggest that freedom of speech and the press were applicable to the states through the Fourteenth Amendment in the *Gitlow* case only. If that was his intention, it was lost on other jurists, who ruled as early as six years later that those freedoms had in fact been absorbed into the due process clause of the Fourteenth Amendment. Because history must judge by the words placed into law in the Court's decision, there is no way of knowing his exact meaning. Nevertheless, he must have known that the principle of *stare decisis* would likely compel future judges to hold that First Amendment freedoms had now become applicable to the states regardless of any "for present purposes" prefix.
129. Pritchett, *The American Constitution*, p. 301.
130. Ibid.
131. Article III, section 1 of the U.S. Constitution says:
     The judicial Power of the United States, shall be vested in one supreme Court and in such inferior Courts as the Congress may from time to time ordain and establish. The Judges, both of the supreme and inferior Courts, shall hold their Offices during good Behaviour, and shall, at stated Times, receive for their Services, a Compensation, which shall not be diminished during their Continuance in Office.
     "Good behaviour" has been interpreted to mean lifetime tenure. A federal judge can be removed from office only by impeachment and conviction.
132. This is not to suggest that state judges have not on occasion shown substantial courage in defending unpopular groups, but for the most part, federal judges, who usually enjoy greater insulation from popular pressure than state judges, who often must be reelected or reappointed, are in a stronger position to protect unpopular groups in society.
133. 283 U.S. 697 (1931).
134. Chief Justice Hughes, in the opinion of the Court, wrote that "public officers, whose character and conduct remain open to debate and free discussion in the press, find their remedies for false accusations in actions under libel laws providing for redress and punishment, and not in proceedings to restrain the publication of newspapers and periodicals." 283 U.S. at 718-19.
135. Ibid. at 701-03.
136. Ibid. at 707.
137. Ibid.
138. Ibid. at 715-16.
139. Ibid. at 713-14; emphasis in original.
140. Ibid. at 719-20.
141. Tenth Amendment to the U.S. Constitution.
142. 283 U.S. at 715.

143. Lawhorne, *Defamation and Public Officials*, p. 115.
144. 343 U.S. 250.
145. Ibid. at 251.
146. Ibid. at 255-56 n. 5. The question of whether someone dead can be libeled is un-settled at the moment. In the view of some, it had been settled in the common law that reputation is a personal rather than a property interest that cannot be passed on to heirs or family. But on 13 January 1983 a federal judge in New Jer-sey ruled that the family of a deceased individual who was the target of the "Abscam" investigation could sue Time, Inc. for libel to clear his name. Judge H. Lee Sarokin said that if an individual had a valid claim of libel, "there is no just reason why it should not survive his death." "Court Allows Libel Suit De-spite Plaintiff's Death," *New York Times*, 14 January 1983, p. A10. See also Timothy F. Bannon, "Libel After Death?" *New York Times*, 21 March 1983, p. A15.
147. 343 U.S. at 256 n. 5.
148. This is not a criticism of, for example, Lawhorne's book, which has been most helpful in tracing the development of libel laws. But because of the Supreme Court's efforts in the last twenty years to "nationalize" libel standards, and state reaction to such efforts, a discussion of the evolution of libel laws becomes somewhat outdated unless combined with more recent developments.
149. See earlier discussion of Sedition Act of 1798.
150. Lawhorne, *Defamation and Public Officials*, p. 40.
151. Ibid.
152. William Cushing, appointed by President George Washington to the Supreme Court, served from 1789 to 1810.
153. One member of the majority, Justice Sumner, rejected such a notion and, quoting the Massachusetts Bill of Rights, said a publisher had a right to express his views as long as he kept them "within the bounds of truth." Lawhorne, *Defamation and Public Officials*, p. 41.
154. Ibid., p. 42.
155. Ibid.
156. Ibid.
157. Ibid., p. 55.
158. In some cases, defendants were prohibited from calling witnesses who could have verified the truth of their statements, thus depriving them of any practical opportunity to use truth as a defense. Some lawyers, in defending their clients, also suggested that people must have an unrestricted right of discussion, separate from the issue of truth. Nelson and Teeter, *Law of Mass Communications*, p. 27.
159. Lawhorne, *Defamation and Public Officials*, p. 56.
160. Ibid., p. 67.
161. Ibid., p. 68. Truth is an absolute defense to a libel suit today, and if a statement is truthful, a media defendant does not have to demonstrate that it was published or broadcast for justifiable ends. On the other hand, invasion of privacy suits can be successful whether or not the statement turns out to be true. Privacy, an issue that poses some serious problems for journalists, will be discussed later.
162. Ibid.
163. Ibid.
164. *United States v. Hudson and Goodwin*, 7 Cranch 32 (1812).
165. 7 Cranch at 32.
166. Ibid.
167. Lawhorne, *Defamation and Public Officials*, p. 70.

168. It has always been very difficult for courts and journalists to determine where private reputations end and the "official duties" of an elected or appointed official begin. Journalists are called upon to make difficult determinations as to when private activities or characteristics begin to affect performance of public responsibilities. These issues will be considered later. Some persons believe that recent libel decisions grant the media too much protection to cover the private lives of public officials and public figures, and that the "public" activities of private citizens get less attention because of the relative ease with which they can sue for libel.

169. Lawhorne, *Defamation and Public Officials*, p. 108.

170. Ibid., p. 109.

171. 231 U.S. 588.

172. Ibid. at 594.

173. Lawhorne, *Defamation and Public Officials*, p. 117.

174. Ibid., pp. 118-19. See discussion of libel *per quod* in earlier section of this chapter.

175. See notes 7 and 27, supra.

176. The public-figure/private-person standard, one of the most important and controversial isses in libel litigation, will be discussed in detail.

177. Lawhorne, *Defamation and Public Officials*, p. 129.

178. Some states adopted a middle ground where they left room for a more liberal interpretation of privilege but did not extend such privilege to falsehoods. Lawhorne includes Delaware, the District of Columbia, Georgia, Indiana, Missouri, Oklahoma, Texas, and Wyoming. Ibid., pp. 142-43.

179. 304 U.S. 64 (1938).

180. Ibid. at 78.

181. A number of states have developed reputations over the past few years for having laws and juries that are particularly hostile to media defendants. In those states, for example, media organizations often pay a substantially higher premium for libel insurance than do media organizations in neighboring states.

182. Pritchett, *The American Constitution*, pp. 114-15.

183. In *Steaks Unlimited v. Deaner*, 6 Med. L. Rptr. 1129 (1980), for example, a case involving WTAE-TV in Pittsburgh, which broadcasts to several states, the United States Court of Appeals for the Third Circuit, which was handling the case as a diversity action, wrote,

> Inasmuch as Pennsylvania has an interest in the outcome of this litigation—and the allegedly defamatory acts as well as the subject of the disputed broadcast occurred in Pennsylvania—there is no cause for this Court, sua sponte, to challenge the parties' consensual choice of law. Accordingly, we turn to the determination of how a Pennsylvania court would be expected to resolve the substantive questions presented by this appeal. [At 1132.]

3

The Nationalization of Libel Laws:
The Search for Standards

The Framers of the Constitution, while recognizing the importance of state autonomy over some areas of the law, did not intend for the United States to be governed under fifty different First Amendments. The states had enjoyed for more than a century and a half substantial discretion over how much protection the First Amendment should grant to media organizations in defending libel suits. But the potential for abuse, and the serious threats that such abuse posed for the vitality of the First Amendment forced the Supreme Court to begin in 1964 the process of providing national standards in libel cases. Although the Court has had a difficult time enunciating clear standards that provide an appropriate balance between First Amendment and reputational interests, it was clear that it could not stand by as some states ignored or abused the First Amendment rights of media defendants. Whether governed by loyalty to the principles of federalism, or a fear of entering the complicated libel morass, the Court had waited far too long before acting. Beginning in 1964 the Court began a twenty-year journey that would prove very trying for it and troublesome for individuals attempting to vindicate their damaged reputations and journalists trying to do their jobs.

Supreme Court efforts to apply First Amendment principles in libel cases can be considered from a number of perspectives, the two most obvious being a chronological examination and one dividing court cases into several subjects. A chronological examination perhaps provides more continuity, but the nature of libel decisions lends itself to an examination based more on issues than chronology. In the next three chapters, the Supreme Court's most important libel cases are considered by means of several key issues. Some attention is paid to the chronology of the cases; however, the focus is on the parallel development of major themes and how they evolved into legal doctrine.

Beginning with *New York Times v. Sullivan* in 1964, the Court considered a series of cases in which public officials were the *subject* of defamatory statements made by individuals ranging from a district attorney to a newspaper columnist to a candidate for the United State Senate. The statements all became the subjects of libel suits when reported by media organizations. In these important decisions the Court explicitly granted the press First Amendment freedoms it had never before enjoyed.

This chapter will also examine defamatory statements made *by* public officials. In a self-governing society that is committed to a free exchange of ideas, public officials must be provided some latitude in making statements about their public responsibilities without having constantly to defend in a court of law the truthfulness of those statements. It may seem at times that the privilege granted to public officials to make defamatory statements about co-workers, members of the public, or the way individuals spend public money is abused, yet the privilege is necessary if communication between the public and its servants is to be two-way.

The vehicle that the Supreme Court used to provide unprecedented freedom to discuss the fitness and activities of public officials was the *actual malice* rule. After it was first enunciated in *New York Times*, the Court found itself faced with the task of not only trying to fill in the details of a test it had sketched in 1964, but explaining over and over again to unconvinced judges and juries the basic requirements of the test. This chapter traces the initial efforts of the Court to mold a new standard that would allow maximum latitude to discuss the activities of government, yet still provide some method by which reputations damaged by reckless or irresponsible reporting could be vindicated.

Libel *of* Public Officials

When the Supreme Court finally entered the libel arena, it did so not with small, tentative steps but with broad and eloquent phrases that would shape First Amendment interpretation for the next twenty years. *New York Times v. Sullivan*,[1] decided unanimously in 1964, gave new meaning to the First Amendment, changing its largely symbolic role in libel to more active policy directives.

On March 29, 1960 a civil rights group ran a full page advertisement in the *New York Times* with the headline, "Heed Their Rising Voices." The text began this way: "As the whole world knows by now, thousands of Southern Negro students are engaged in widespread non-violent demonstrations in positive affirmation of the right to live in human dignity as guaranteed by the U.S. Constitution and the Bill of Rights."[2]

Over sixty people, many of them well known for their activities in public affairs, religion, unions, and performing arts, signed the advertisement.[3]

Below those names and under a line reading, "We in the south who are struggling daily for dignity and freedom warmly endorse this appeal," appeared the names of twenty other persons, most of whom were clergymen in various southern cities.[4] The advertisement was signed at the bottom by the "Committee to Defend Martin Luther King and the Struggle for Freedom in the South."

L.B. Sullivan, one of three elected commissioners of the city of Montgomery, Alabama, sued the *New York Times*, claiming that as the commissioner of public affairs, whose duties included supervision of the police department, he had been injured by the advertisement.[5] Sullivan cited two paragraphs as the basis of his suit. The third paragraph read:

> In Montgomery, Alabama, after students sang "My Country, 'Tis of Thee" on the State Capitol steps, their leaders were expelled from school, and truckloads of police armed with shotguns and tear-gas ringed the Alabama State College Campus. When the entire student body protested to state authorities by refusing to re-register, their dining hall was padlocked in an attempt to starve them into submission.[6]

The sixth paragraph read, in part:

> Again and again the Southern violators have answered Dr. King's peaceful protests with intimidation and violence. They have bombed his home almost killing his wife and child. They have assaulted his person. They have arrested him seven times—for "speeding," "loitering," and similar "offenses." And now they have charged him with "perjury"—a *felony* under which they could imprison him for *ten years* . . . .[7]

Although none of the statements in the advertisement referred to Sullivan by name, he asserted that the word *police* in the third paragraph was understood to refer to him as the commissioner who had supervision over the Montgomery police department. He claimed that the statement accusing the police, and thus him as well, of trying to starve the students into submission damaged his reputation. As to the sixth paragraph, he said that because police ordinarily make arrests, "they have arrested [King] seven times" was interpreted as referring to an action of his. Thus, the paragraph accused the police, and therefore Sullivan, of answering King's protests with "intimidation and violence," bombing his home, assaulting his person, and charging him with perjury.[8]

The advertisement did contain some errors. The students had staged a demonstration at the state capitol, but had sung the national anthem and not "My Country, 'Tis of Thee." Further, although nine students had been expelled by the State Board of Education, it was not for leading the demonstration at the capitol, but for demanding service at a lunch counter in the Montgomery

County Courthouse on another day. There were other inaccuracies as well. Most, but not all, of the student body had protested the expulsion, not by refusing to register, but by boycotting classes on a single day. Virtually all students did register for the ensuing semester.[9] The campus dining hall was not padlocked on any occasion, and the students who were prevented from eating there had not signed preregistration applications or requested temporary meal tickets.

Perhaps even more significant were other misstatements. The police had been deployed near the campus in large numbers on several occasions, but they did not "ring" the campus and they were not called there in connection with the demonstration on the state capitol steps, as the third paragraph implied.[10] King had been arrested not seven times but four; and although he claimed to have been assaulted some years earlier in connection with his arrest for loitering, one of the arresting officers denied that there had been such an assault.

Alabama law required a public official to make a written demand for a public retraction before he or she can recover punitive damages in a libel action resulting from a statement concerning official conduct. The *New York Times* did not publish a retraction and Sullivan filed his suit a few days later.[11] A jury in the Circuit Court of Montgomery County awarded Sullivan $500,000, the full amount claimed, and the Supreme Court of Alabama upheld the award.[12]

The trial judge instructed the jury that the statements in the advertisement were libelous *per se*.[13] Thus, compensatory damages could be awarded if it found that the *Times* had actually published the statements and if they were made "of and concerning" Sullivan. The judge said that because the statements were libelous *per se*, the law assumes the plaintiff suffered injury from just the fact that the statements were published. He did not have to prove any actual damage to his reputation.

The judge's instructions concerning punitive damages were substantially more confusing. Under Alabama law in force at the time, a plaintiff apparently had to prove actual malice and not just mere negligence or carelessness.[14] But the judge refused to charge that the jury must be "convinced" of malice, in the sense of "actual intent" to harm or "gross negligence and recklessness," to make an award of punitive damages. He also refused to order the jury to distinguish between compensatory and punitive damages and rejected the pleas of the *Times* lawyer that his rulings violated the freedoms of speech and press guaranteed by the First and Fourteenth Amendments.

The Alabama Supreme Court sustained the trial judge's rulings and instructions in all respects. It found that the advertisement could be interpreted as referring to Sullivan and that the *Times* had been irresponsible in printing it. Interestingly, the Alabama Supreme Court said that the *Times* had in its own files articles already published that would have demonstrated the falsity of the allegations in the advertisement.[15] The Alabama Supreme Court also mentioned the failure of the *Times* to retract the advertisement's statements for Sullivan, but that it did so at the request of the governor. It concluded by saying, "The First Amendment of the U.S. Constitution does not protect libelous publications" and "The Fourteenth Amendment is directed against State action and not private action."[16]

The Supreme Court, in reversing the verdict against the *Times*, wrote eloquently about the role of the First Amendment in a free society and the need to allow the press freedom to discuss the conduct of public officials. Justice William Brennan, in describing the role of the press in a self-governing society, placed into law phrases that would be repeated in various contexts for the next two decades.

The Court at the outset rejected Alabama's claim that this was a private dispute and therefore outside the jurisdiction of the Supreme Court. Brennan said:

> That proposition has no application to this case. Although this is a civil lawsuit between private parties, the Alabama courts have applied a state rule of law which petitioners claim to impose invalid restrictions on their constitutional freedoms of speech and press. It matters not that the law has been applied in a civil action.[17]

The Court also rejected the notion that constitutional guarantees of freedom of speech and press did not apply because the statements were contained in a paid, commercial advertisement. The Court denied that a commercial speech case decided in 1942, *Valentine v. Chrestensen*,[18] in which commercial and business advertisements were denied First Amendment protection, was relevant or binding. It held "the reliance [on *Chrestensen*] is wholly misplaced."[19] In that case, the handbill was "purely commercial advertising" and the portion of it devoted to protesting public policy was added only to evade a littering ordinance.

Brennan discussed the differences between the handbill at issue in *Chrestensen* and the advertisement in the *New York Times*:

> The ad here . . . communicated information, expressed opinion, recited grievances, protested claimed abuses, and sought financial support on behalf of a movement whose existence and objectives are matters of the highest public interest and concern. That the *Times* was paid for publishing the advertisement is as immaterial in this connection as is the fact that newspapers and books are sold. Any other conclusion would discourage newspapers from carrying "editorial advertisements" of this type, and so might shut off an important outlet for the promulgation of information and ideas by persons who do not themselves have access to publishing facilities—who wish to exercise their freedom of speech even though they are not members of the press.[20]

Brennan expressed concern that such efforts would prevent the First Amendment from fostering "the widest possible dissemination of information from diverse and antagonistic sources." He said that statements in the press do not forfeit constitutional protection because they were published in the form of paid advertisement.[21]

Having decided the issue of jurisdiction and whether statements in a commercial advertisement qualified for First Amendment protection, the Court then turned to the key issues raised by the case. The Court was concerned that the standard of liability used by Alabama in the case abridged the freedom of speech and press guaranteed by the First and Fourteenth Amendments. The Alabama courts had determined that statements libelous *per se* allowed the jury to presume that damage to reputation had in fact taken place, and that a plaintiff did not to have prove intent to injure to collect punitive damages. In addition, the Alabama courts held that the statements were published "of and concerning" the plaintiff.

Brennan, in tracing the historical role of free discussion and the need for a self-governing society to hear a multitude of viewpoints, answered the lower courts with phrases that were to be become a permanent part the vocabulary of First Amendment thinkers:

> Thus we consider this case against the background of a profound national commitment to the principle that debate on public issues should be uninhibited, robust, and wide-open, and that it may well include vehement, caustic, and sometimes unpleasantly sharp attacks on government and public officials. The present advertisement as an expression of grievance and protest on one of the major public issues of our time, would seem clearly to qualify for the constitutional protection.[22]

The question of whether the advertisement should be deprived of constitutional protection because it contained false statements was directly addressed by the Court and answered in a way that was to provide the press with a substantial degree of latitude for at least the next ten years. The Court wrote: "erroneous statement is inevitable in free debate, and . . . it must be protected if the freedoms of expression are to have the 'breathing space' that they need to survive."[23] And Brennan added:

> A rule compelling the critic of official conduct to guarantee the truth of all his factual assertions—and to do so on pain of libel judgments virtually unlimited in amount—leads to a comparable "self-censorship." Allowance of the defense of truth, with the burden of proving it on the defendant, does not mean that only false speech will be deterred. . . . Under such a rule, would-be critics of official conduct may be deterred from voicing their criticism, even though it is believed to be true and even though it is in fact true, because of doubt whether it can be proved in court or fear of the expense of having to do so. . . . The rule thus dam-

pens the vigor and limits the variety of public debate. It is inconsistent with the First and Fourteenth Amendments.[24]

After so many years of state autonomy over libel decisions and the concomitant inconsistency, rigidity, and failure to appreciate the special role of the First Amendment, the Supreme Court began the process of establishing national standards in libel cases with these words:

> The constitutional guarantees require, we think, a federal rule that prohibits a public official from recovering damages for a defamatory falsehood relating to his official conduct unless he proves that the statement was made with "actual malice"—that is, with knowledge that it was false or with reckless disregard of whether it was false or not.[25]

The debate over what the Court meant by those phrases has raged ever since. "Actual malice," as defined by the Court in the *New York Times* case, seems to refer to a state of mind. The Court appeared to say that in order for a public official, and later a public figure as well,[26] to collect damages from a media defendant, he or she must prove that the publisher or broadcaster either knew in advance that the statement was untrue, or was so irresponsible in not following standard practices of journalism, that the behavior constituted reckless disregard. The Court chose this very strict standard to provide media organizations with what it called "breathing space." It recognized that those publishing a daily newspaper or broadcasting daily news programs make mistakes, and that tolerance for errors is necessary in a society with an independent press; but in doing so, it placed a substantial obstacle in the way of public officials who attempt to vindicate reputations that have been injured by what they feel to be irresponsible reporting.

The *New York Times* decision placed a substantial weight on the First Amendment side of the scales. Perhaps in reaction to state abuse of the First Amendment as demonstrated by the Alabama courts,[27] and perhaps because of eagerness after so long a wait on the sidelines, the Court entered the libel arena with much aggressiveness. It explicitly granted constitutional protection to the citizen-critic, whether it is a media organization or speaker at a town meeting, when making statements concerning the conduct of public officials. And the Court specifically stated that even false statements enjoyed constitutional protection, unless made with knowing falsehood or reckless disregard of the truth: "Raising as it does the possibility that a good-faith critic of government will be penalized for his criticism, the proposition relied on by the Alabama courts strikes at the very center of the constitutionally protected area of free expression."[28]

To those who in earlier years had gone to jail or were fined for daring to publish the truth, the granting of constitutional protection to even false statements would have seemed remarkable. After only occasional involvement in libel for so many years, the Supreme Court, finding the right case, unleashed its First Amendment theories with such force it would have an effect on libel and other First Amendment cases for years to come. Yet, there were those who felt the Court had not gone far enough, among them Justice Hugo Black, with whom Justice William Douglas agreed. In their concurring opinion in the *New York Times* case, Black wrote: ''I based my vote to reverse [the half-million-dollar judgment] on the belief that the First and Fourteenth Amendments not merely 'delimit' a State's power to award damages to 'public officials against critics of their official conduct' but completely prohibit a state from exercising such a power.''[29] Black then restated his commitment to the notion that the First Amendment means what it says:

> The requirement that malice be proved provides at best an evanescent protection for the right critically to discuss public affairs and certainly does not measure up to the sturdy safeguard embodied in the First Amendment. Unlike the Court, therefore, I vote to reverse exclusively on the ground that the *Times* and the individual defendants had an absolute, unconditional constitutional right to publish in the *Times* advertisement their criticisms of the Montgomery agencies and officials.[30]

Black also expressed concern that a second half-million- dollar libel verdict against the *Times* based on the same advertisement had already been awarded to another commissioner:

> There is no reason to believe that there are not more such huge verdicts lurking just around the corner for the *Times* or any other newspaper or broadcaster which might dare to criticize public officials. In fact, briefs before us show that in Alabama there are now pending eleven libel suits by local and state officials against the *Times* seeking $5,600,000, and five such suits against the Columbia Broadcasting System seeking $1,700,000.[31]

Black argued that the federal Constitution granted the press an absolute immunity for criticism of the way public officials do their public duty. And he concluded by suggesting that the country could survive without libel laws when relating to criticism of public officials:

> This Nation, I suspect, can live in peace without libel suits based on public discussions of public affairs and public officials. But I doubt that a country can live in freedom where its people can be made to suffer physically or financially for criticizing their government, its actions, or its officials. . . . An unconditional right to say what one pleases about public affairs is what I consider to be the minimum guarantee of the First Amendment. . . . I regret that the Court has stopped short of this holding indispensable to preserve our free press from destruction.[32]

In adopting the *actual malice* standard, the Court also determined that proof of malice must be demonstrated with "convincing clarity," a tougher standard than mere preponderance of evidence. "Applying these standards, we consider that the proof presented to show actual malice lacks the convincing clarity which the constitutional standard demands," wrote Brennan.[33] Considered together, the actual malice standard of liability and the convincing clarity standard of proof provided a formidable obstacle that public officials would have to overcome to win a libel suit against a media defendant.

The Court wanted to make it clear that our constitutional system simply would not tolerate prosecution, whether in the form of criminal prosecution or civil libel suits, for seditious libel. In a democratic society one must be free to examine and criticize the public duties of officials charged with the responsibility of governing. Lest there be any doubt as to the continued validity of the Alien and Sedition Act of 1798, the Court laid to rest any notion that prosecutions for seditious libel were consistent with the First Amendment: "Although the Sedition Act was never tested in this Court, the attack on its validity has carried the day in the court of history."[34]

Some scholars, in analyzing *New York Times v. Sullivan*, correctly observed that the Court, although it had the opportunity, did not base its decision on the clear and present danger, redeeming social value, or balancing tests; instead, the Court looked to the central meaning of the First Amendment, and concluded that the meaning was identified in Madison's statement "that the censorial power is in the people over the Government, and not in the Government over the people."[35]

Professor Harry Kalven recognized the importance of the *New York Times* case in revealing the core of the First Amendment:

> The Court did not simply, in the face of an awkward history, definitively put to rest the status of the Sedition Act. More important, it found in the controversy over seditious libel the clue to "the central meaning of the First Amendment." The choice of language was unusually apt. The Amendment has a "central meaning"—a core of protection of speech without which democracy cannot function. . . . This is not the whole meaning of the Amendment. There are other freedoms protected by it. But at the center there is no doubt what speech is being protected and no doubt why it is being protected.[36]

Kalven was convinced that the decision was among the Court's most important: "My thesis is that the Court, compelled by the political realities of the case to decide it in favor of the *Times*, yet equally compelled to seek high ground in justifying its result, wrote an opinion that may prove to be the best and most important it has ever produced in the realm of freedom of speech."[37] He was able to reduce to syllogism the significance of the case:

> The central meaning of the Amendment is that seditious libel cannot be made the subject of government sanction. The Alabama rule on fair comment is

closely akin to making seditious libel an offense. The Alabama rule therefore violated the central meaning of the Amendment.[38]

Despite the broad language of the opinion, it was not certain what impact the opinion would have. Because the plaintiff was a public official, it was necessary for the Court to carve some rule that allowed the citizen-critic freedom to criticize the public conduct of its officials. But the Court went beyond simply deciding the case on the relatively narrow ground that the First Amendment had ended the law of seditious libel. The Court spoke in broad and eloquent terms about the importance of the freedom to exchange information in a self-governing society, and provided constitutional status to even false statements if they related to the conduct of public officials. Although not providing explicit language indicating what was to come, it must have understood that there would be individuals who may not hold official elected or appointed positions, but whose prominence or activities have a profound effect on public institutions and public policy decisions. In *New York Times*, the Court did not speak of public figures as it would a few years later,[39] but it surely knew that *New York Times* was but the first step in recalibrating a scale that was badly out of whack after 170 years of state autonomy in libel. The Court may not have known that balancing First Amendment and reputational interests would be all the more difficult because its initial contribution weighed in so heavily on the First Amendment side. By relying on the "central meaning of the First Amendment," rather than a test that did not involve to such a substantial degree fundamental constitutional questions, it subjected First Amendment interpretation to exposure, and therefore criticism, to which it was not accustomed. By dusting off phrases that had long enjoyed largely symbolic significance, the Court risked the possibility that the First Amendment's vitality could be injured by the very fact that it had been used to provide counterbalance to clearly unacceptable state practices. Such exposure brought risk that while in the short run First Amendment interests would enjoy substantial victory in reversing state abuse in libel, over time the scales could shift, thus not only bolstering reputational interests but diminishing First Amendment interests in the process.

Having begun the process of establishing national standards in libel and enhancing the constitutional status of communication of governing importance, the Court was able to contemplate its *New York Times* decision for only a short time. A few months after the *Times* case, the Court had to decide if the First Amendment had eliminated criminal libel and if it had not, under what circumstances could such speech be made a crime.

Interestingly, the Court in *New York Times* had discussed how Alabama's action in handling civil libel suits arising from criticism of official conduct was dangerously close to seditious libel:

What a State may not constitutionally bring about by means of a criminal statute is likewise beyond the reach of its civil law of libel. The fear of damage awards under a rule such as that invoked by the Alabama courts here may be markedly more inhibiting than the fear of prosecution under a criminal statute.[40]

James Garrison, the district attorney of New Orleans, was convicted under Louisiana's criminal defamation statute for issuing a press conference statement criticizing judges of the parish for a backlog of cases, saying they were inefficient and lazy, and took excessive vacations.[41] Garrison also charged that by refusing to authorize disbursements to cover the expenses of undercover investigations of vice in New Orleans, the judges had hampered his efforts to enforce the vice laws. He said:

> The judges have now made it eloquently clear where their sympathies lie in regard to aggressive vice investigations by refusing to authorize use of the DA's funds to pay for the cost of closing down the Canal Street clip joints. . . . This raises interesting questions about the racketeer influences on our eight vacation-minded judges.[42]

Garrison was convicted of violating the Louisiana Criminal Defamation Statute, which included punishment for even true statements if they were made with "actual malice." Yet this was not the "actual malice" defined by the Supreme Court in *New York Times*. The Louisiana law included punishment for true statements made with "actual malice" in the sense of ill-will as well as false statements if made with ill-will or without reasonable belief that they were true. The statute read in part: "Defamation is the malicious publication or expression in any manner . . . which tends to expose any person to hatred, contempt or ridicule, or to deprive him of the benefit of public confidence or social intercourse."[43]

The Court had to determine if the *New York Times* actual malice rule also limited state power to impose criminal sanctions for criticism of the official conduct of public officials. By a unanimous vote, the Court held that the *New York Times* standard did apply; when it comes to evaluating or criticizing public officials, criminal libel statutes are as constitutionally suspect as were civil libel laws. The original justification for criminal libel laws was that the victim of the libelous statement would resort to physical redress to avenge wounded feelings of honor, and criminal libel laws were necessary to prevent a breach of the peace. However, as discussed in chapter 2, there developed a preference for civil libel remedies, and the need to prosecute the purveyor of the alleged libel became unnecessary.

At the time of *Garrison*, about half the states included an important limitation on the idea that truth constituted a defense in a criminal libel case. For truth to be a defense, the statement had to be published "with good motives and for justifiable ends."[44] The Court had to consider how the *New York Times* rule would affect this historical limitation on truth as a defense:

> We must ask whether this history [of requiring a showing of good motives and justifiable ends] permits negating the truth defense, as the Louisiana statute does, on a showing of malice in the sense of ill-will. . . . Where criticism is of public officials and their conduct of public business, the interest in private reputation is overborne by the larger public interest, secured by the Constitution, in the dissemination of truth.[45]

The Court, quoting from a state case, held that such a qualification on truth does not clear constitutional barriers: " 'It has been said that it is lawful to publish truth from good motives, and for justifiable ends. But this rule is too narrow. If there is a lawful occasion—a legal right to make a publication—and the matter true, the end is justifiable, and that, in such case, must be sufficient.' "[46]

The Court then renewed the argument it had made just a few months earlier in *New York Times*: even false statements in this area are protected by the First Amendment unless they are knowing or reckless falsehoods. And the Court ruled that just as a public official would find civil remedy in a libel suit only if the official established that the statement was made with knowledge of its falsity or reckless disregard of whether it was false or not, the same constitutional guarantees apply in a criminal libel case. The Court did caution that although it would allow substantial latitude for the discusssion of public issues, there were limits:

> The use of calculated falsehood, however, would put a different cast on the constitutional question. Although honest utterance, even if inaccurate, may further the fruitful exercise of the right of free speech, it does not follow that the lie, knowingly and deliberately published about a public official, should enjoy a like immunity. . . . That speech is used as a tool for political ends does not automatically bring it under the protective mantle of the Constitution. For the use of the known lie as a tool is at once at odds with the premises of democratic government and with the orderly manner in which economic, social, or political change is to be effected. . . . Hence the knowingly false statement and the false statement made with reckless disregard of the truth, do not enjoy constitutional protection.[47]

The Supreme Court recognized in *Garrison* that a substantial number of important questions would arise in the wake of its *New York Times* ruling and its beginning efforts to establish national standards in libel. In *Garrison* it considered an issue that is still hotly debated today. The judges who instituted charges against *Garrison* asserted, and the Louisiana courts sustained the view, that *Garrison*'s statements constituted attacks upon the personal integrity and honesty of the judges rather than official conduct. The Supreme Court rejected the view that such statements could be considered purely private defamation; they concerned how the judges did their jobs. Yet, the Court recognized that these were difficult questions:

> Of course, any criticism of the manner in which a public official performs his duties will tend to affect his private, as well as his public, reputation. The *New York Times* rule is not rendered inapplicable merely because an official's private reputation, as well as his public reputation, is harmed. The public-official rule protects the paramount public interest in a free flow of information to the people concerning public officials, their servants. To this end, anything which might touch on an official's fitness for office is relevant. Few personal attributes are more germane to fitness for office than dishonesty, malfeasance, or improper motivation, even though these characteristics may also affect the official's private character.[48]

The Court concluded that any statute that allowed punishment for truthful statements made with actual malice is abrogated by the *New York Times* rule. The Louisiana statute was also unconstitutional as it applied to false statements against public officials. The Louisiana Supreme Court affirmed *Garrison*'s conviction solely on the ground that the evidence supported the trial court's finding of "ill-will, enmity, or a wanton desire to injure."[49] The trial judge had said that he could not imagine that *Garrison* could have had a reasonable belief or an honest belief that the judges were guilty of what he charged them with in his statements. But the U.S. Supreme Court said the reasonable belief standard is not enough when it comes to protecting such important constitutional interests. "The test which we laid down in *New York Times* is not keyed to ordinary care; defeasance of the privilege is conditioned, not on mere negligence, but on reckless disregard for the truth."[50]

The Court's holding that the First Amendment protects defamatory statements made about the conduct of officials even though such statements can also injure their private reputations provided the media with substantial latitude when discussing public officials, yet it provides little guidance when it comes to "private" individuals who play a prominent or important role in influencing public affairs. As will be seen in the ensuing discussion of libel suits brought by private individuals against media defendants, the Court's rulings have perhaps had unintended results. Today media organizations may be on safer ground if they publish or broadcast statements about the private lives of public officials and public figures than if the statements concern the public activities of private persons. Nevertheless, in *Garrison*, the Supreme Court held that the constitutional protection is not forfeited simply because the statements may affect the private reputations of public officials.

Although Justice Douglas, in a concurring opinion in which Justice Black joined, applauded the decision of the Court, he deplored what he called the "gloss which the Court has put on" freedom of speech, declaring it "makes that guarantee almost unrecognizable."[51] Douglas harshly criticized the development of the actual malice standard in both *New York Times* and *Garrison* as being contrary to the principles of the First Amendment:

The presence of "actual malice" is made critical in seditious libel, as well as in civil actions involving charges against public officials, when in truth there is nothing in the Constitution about it, any more than there is about "clear and present danger."

While the First Amendment remains the same, the gloss which the Court has written on it in this field of the discussion of public issues robs it of much vitality.

Why does "the freedom of speech" that the Court is willing to protect turn out to be so pale and tame?

It is because . . . the Bill of Rights is constantly watered down through judicial "balancing" of what the Constitution says and what judges think is needed for a well-ordered society.[52]

Balancing of First Amendment and other societal interests is balancing regardless of which side of the scales is receiving the greatest weight at a particular time. Once First Amendment interests are put on a plane that requires an ad hoc balancing by judges on a case-by-case basis, there is always the danger that the First Amendment will lose its preferred status and will be thrust into the balancing process on equal footing with what may be less compelling societal interests. Douglas and Black vociferously argued that such balancing was not only inexact, unnecessary, and dangerous, but ignored the lessons of history, a history that included the jailing and fining of those who dared to criticize the government, suppression of publications, and the exercise of self-censorship. To Douglas and Black, it was constitutionally repulsive for the Supreme Court to adopt rules that would allow individuals, under certain circumstances, to be punished in a criminal or civil trial for criticizing their servants in government. Black and Douglas probably recognized that some negative consequences would follow the granting of such immunity to the press, but believed it was better for a self-governing society to suffer excesses by the press than to tolerate the punishing of individuals who criticize the conduct of public officials.

The Supreme Court in *New York Times* and *Garrison* may not have fully satisfied Black and Douglas, and other critics who thought the Court was establishing standards that in the short run looked promising for First Amendment interests but would later prove to be most troublesome, yet it nevertheless forged the beginning of a new era in First Amendment history. And it was called upon within a short time to identify again the circumstances under which a journalist could be sued for libel and the classes of individuals who have to meet the *New York Times* actual malice standard.

Unlike *New York Times* and *Garrison*, *Rosenblatt v. Baer* divided the Supreme Court over a number of key issues.[53] Decided in early 1966, it foreshadowed the frustration the Court would experience as it attempted to answer many difficult questions arising out of its previous decisions.

Frank Baer, a former supervisor of a county recreation area in New Hampshire, had successfully sued Alfred Rosenblatt, a newspaper columnist. Baer was employed by and directly responsible to the Belknap County commissioners, three elected officials in charge of the county government. A controversy had developed over the way Baer and the commissioners operated the recreation area, and in 1959 the New Hampshire legislature had transferred control of the area to a special commission. To give the new commission a fresh start, Baer had been dismissed.

Rosenblatt was a regular contributor to the *Laconia Evening Citizen*, and had been an outspoken proponent of transferring control of the recreation area to the new commission. In January 1960, during the first ski season under the new management and some six months after Baer had been dismissed, Rosenblatt wrote a column very disparaging of past management practices. It read, in part:

> This year, a year without snow till very late . . . the difference in cash income [is] simply fantastic, almost unbelievable. . . . When consider[ing] that last year was [an] excellent snow year . . . one can only ponder the following question: What happened to all the money last year? and every other year? What magic has Dana Beane [chairman of the new commission] and the rest of the commission, and Mr. Warner [new supervisor] wrought to make such a tremendous difference in net cash results?[54]

Baer sued, saying that the column suggested that he had mismanaged public monies and that it injured his reputation. He was awarded $31,500 in damages.[55] After the jury verdict but before the New Hampshire Supreme Court affirmed it, the U.S. Supreme Court issued its opinion in *New York Times v. Sullivan*.

Justice William Brennan, writing the majority opinion in *Rosenblatt*, expressed some of the same concerns raised in *New York Times*. As with L.B. Sullivan, one of the Montgomery, Alabama, commissioners, Brennan expressed doubt as to whether the newspaper column could be interpreted as referring to the respondent. The only persons mentioned by name in the column were the officials of the new regime; Baer was not mentioned by name. Brennan said that persons reading the column may have thought it was simply complimentary of the current management. Baer had asserted at his trial that the jury could award him damages if it found "that the column had cast suspicion indiscriminately on the small number of persons who composed the former management group, whether or not it found that the imputation of misconduct was specifically made of and concerning him."[56] Under New Hampshire law Baer was entitled to make such an argument.

Brennan rejected Baer's argument, asking "whether that theory of recovery is precluded by our holding in *New York Times* that, in the absence of sufficient evidence that the attack focused on the plaintiff, an otherwise impersonal attack on governmental operations cannot be utilized to establish a libel of those administering the operations."[57] Brennan then voiced a suspicion like the suspicion the Court had had in *New York Times*: the statements at issue could have been interpreted as referring to someone other than the plaintiff—in this case to Commissioner Sullivan. The Court required that there be evidence showing that the attack was read as specifically directed at the plaintiff, which in *New York Times*, it did not. Brennan had said at the outset that the newspaper column in *Rosenblatt* on its face contained no clearly actionable statement.[58]

The Court wanted to make it clear that if there is not a specific reference, then allowing recovery for such statements is too close to punishment for libeling the government: "A theory that the column cast indiscriminate suspicion on the members of the group responsible for the conduct of this governmental operation is tantamount to a demand for recovery based on libel of government, and therefore is constitutionally insufficient."[59]

The Court knew that addressing a more complex issue was unavoidable. Baer was clearly an appointed government employee, but was he a "public official," as was the elected commissioner, Sullivan? Brennan sought to limit any confusion over whether the Supreme Court or the states would make this decision:

> Turning, then, to the question whether respondent was a "public official" within *New York Times*, we reject at the outset his suggestion that it should be answered by reference to state-law standards. States have developed definitions of "public official" for local administrative purposes, not the purposes of national constitutional protection. . . . Our decision in *New York Times*, moreover, draws its force from the constitutional protections afforded free expression. The standards that set the scope of its principles cannot therefore be such that "the constitutional limits of free expression in the Nation would vary with state lines."[60]

In *New York Times*, the Court specifically stated that it was not determining how far down into the ranks of government employees the "public official" designation would extend. In *Rosenblatt* Brennan emphasized the strong interest in debate on public issues and the strong interest in debate on those who are in "a position significantly to influence the resolution of those issues."[61] Criticism of government is, to Brennan, at "the very center of the constitutionally protected area of free discussion." He then attempted for the first time to provide some guidance as to who is to be considered a "public official": "It is clear, therefore, that the 'public official' designation applies at the very least to those among the hierarchy of government employees who have, or appear to the public to have, substantial responsibility for or control over the conduct of governmental affairs."[62]

The Court thus held that even an appointed official must meet the same *New York Times* actual malice standard that must be met by an elected official. Brennan conceded that the Court decision should not be interpreted as ignoring the importance of defamation laws, saying that society has a substantial interest in preventing and redressing attacks upon reputation. But when those interests clash in cases involving criticism of public officials, the Constitution limits the protections afforded by the defamation laws and the official must prove that the statement was published or broadcast with actual malice. Because the trial was held before the Court handed down its decision in *New York Times*, it decided to remand the case so that Baer would have the opportunity to demonstrate that the statements were made with actual malice.

Brennan also remarked that it is for the trial judge in the first instance to determine whether the respondent is a "public official." In a footnote, he suggested that a jury should not be trusted with such a decision: "Such a course will both lessen the possibility that a jury will use the cloak of a general verdict to punish unpopular ideas or speakers, and assure an appellate court the record and findings required for review of constitutional decisions."[63]

The Court seemed to recognize, even at this relatively early stage of nationalizing libel laws, that determining who is a "public official" and who is not was going to be not only immensely important but exceedingly difficult. It probably did not know in 1966 that by the late 1970s limiting the types of individuals who could be considered "public officials" or "public figures" would prove to be one of the Court's favorite vehicles by which it added to the reputational side of a scale it believed had come to overwhelmingly and unfairly favor media organizations. In the early cases the Court was taking one step at a time, deciding on a case-by-case basis what standard of liability would be appropriate for what type of plaintiff. Yet, in requiring cherished First Amendment interests to rest on a ledge whose width was determined by the status of the plaintiff and not the intrinsic rights suggested in the amendment, the Court chose a road that was to lead to substantial confusion and less protection for both First Amendment and reputational interests.

Justice William Douglas, as he had in *New York Times* and *Garrison*, concurred, stating that it would be very difficult for the Court to determine how far into the lower ranks of public employees the "public official" designation should be used, and he raised new questions that were later to lead to the "public figure" designation and would demonstrate the inadequacy of the Court's efforts to provide guidance in libel:

> If free discussion of public issues is the guide, I see no way to draw lines that exclude the night watchman, the file clerk, the typist, or, for that matter, anyone on the public payroll. And how about those who contract to carry out governmental missions? Some of them are as much in the public domain as any so-called officeholder.... And the industrialists who raise the price of a basic

> commodity? Are not steel and aluminum in the public domain? And the labor leader who combines trade unionism with bribery and racketeering?[64]

He added:

> If the term "public official" were a constitutional term, we would be stuck with it and have to give it content. But the term is our own; and so long as we are fashioning a rule of free discussion of public issues, I cannot relate it only to those who, by the Court's standard, are deemed to hold public office.[65]

Douglas then reiterated his view that the First and Fourteenth Amendments have displaced state libel laws and that if the Court is providing protection for the discussion of important public issues, "why is it . . . not applicable to speech at the lower levels of science, the humanities, the professions, agriculture, and the like?"[66] Finally, he said that if the protections in the Bill of Rights as applied to the states through the Fourteenth Amendment are no different from those that apply to the federal government, then both Congress and the states cannot constitutionally pass libel laws: "Then the question is whether a public *issue*, not a public official, is involved."[67]

Justice Potter Stewart, in a concurring opinion in *Rosenblatt*, said he had agreed with the Court's decision in *Garrison* but cautioned that such rulings had not robbed private individuals of their ability to vindicate damaged reputations:

> The First and Fourteenth Amendments have not stripped private citizens of all means of redress for injuries inflicted upon them by careless liars. The destruction that defamatory falsehood can bring, is, to be sure, often beyond the capacity of the law to redeem. Yet, imperfect though it is, an action for damages is the only hope for vindication or redress the law gives to a man whose reputation has been falsely dishonored.[68]

Justice John Marshall Harlan, breaking a string of unanimous Supreme Court decisions in libel, objected to part of the majority opinion. In his dissent he agreed that the reference in the advertisement in *New York Times* to "police" was so general that it could not be interpreted as "of and concerning" the plaintiff. The Court stated at the time that the liberty of expression embodied in the Fourteenth Amendment forbade a state from permitting "an otherwise impersonal attack on governmental operations" to be used as the basis of "a libel of an official responsible for those operations."[69] But in *Rosenblatt* the group may be small enough that people could reasonably think the defamatory statement referred to the plaintiff. Suggesting that traditional tort law permitted Baer to bring an action, it being sufficient that Baer was a member of small group on which suspicion was cast, Harlan distinguished *Rosenblatt* from *New York Times*:

It seems manifest that in instructing the jury as to a "small group," the trial judge was not allowing the plaintiff to transform impersonal governmental criticism into an individual cause of action, but was simply referring to this traditional tort doctrine that more than one person can be libeled by the same statement. I cannot understand why a statement which a jury is permitted to read as meaning "A is a thief" should become absolutely privileged if it is read as meaning "A, B, C, and D are thieves."[70]

Justice Abe Fortas, dissenting, objected to the Court's taking the case because the trial had occurred before the *New York Times* decision was handed down.[71] Although Fortas's dissent was brief and based on technical grounds, it foreshadowed decisions in which the Court would be bitterly divided over a number of fundamental issues in libel.

Two years after deciding *Rosenblatt*, the Supreme Court had to define further what it meant by "actual malice" and how much latitude the Constitution gives individuals when they discuss the conduct of public officials. *St. Amant v. Thompson*[72] involved a televised political speech, thus raising some interesting issues related to the broadcasting of allegedly libelous statements. However, the Court was mostly concerned with further defining "actual malice" and only indirectly interested in how its libel decisions related to the electronic media.

St. Amant v. Thompson was a rather confusing case, the details of which are less important than what the Supreme Court said about the standard of liability that should be applied in cases involving public officials and what constitutes "reckless disregard" as first discussed in *New York Times v. Sullivan*. In 1962, Phil St. Amant, a candidate for the United States Senate in Louisiana, made a television speech in which he read a series of questions that he had put to J.D. Albin, a member of a Teamsters Union local, and Albin's answers to those questions. At one point, he referred to a Herman Thompson, a deputy sheriff in East Baton Rouge Parish, while discussing the nefarious activities of the local union president, which allegedly included the passing of money to Thompson:

> Now, we knew that this safe was gonna be moved that night, but imagine our predicament, knowing of Ed's [local union president] connections with the Sheriff's office through Herman Thompson, who made recent visits to the Hall to see Ed. We also knew of money that had passed hands between Ed and Herman Thompson . . . from Ed to Herman.[73]

Thompson sued for defamation, alleging that the statement suggested he was guilty of gross misconduct. He was awarded $5,000 in damages by the trial judge. The trial was concluded before the Supreme Court handed down its *New York Times v. Sullivan* decision, but the trial judge, upon reviewing the present case with the rules laid down in *New York Times*, let the judgment stand. The Louisiana Court of Appeal reversed on the grounds that Thompson had failed to prove that St. Amant had acted with actual malice. The Louisiana Supreme Court reversed, saying that Thompson had proved that St. Amant recklessly disregarded whether the statements about Thompson were true or false.[74]

There was no dispute about whether Thompson was a public official. In considering the test developed by the Court in *Rosenblatt v. Baer*, the Louisiana Supreme Court concluded that a deputy sheriff has "substantial responsibility for or control over the conduct of public affairs . . . at least where law enforcement and police functions are concerned."[75] The key issue, therefore, was whether the statements were made in such a way as to satisfy the *New York Times* actual malice test.

The Supreme Court noted that the Louisiana Supreme Court ruled that St. Amant had broadcast false information about Thompson recklessly, though not knowingly. St. Amant had no personal knowledge of Thompson's activities, relying instead on the union official's affidavit; he had failed to verify the information with those in the union office who might have known the facts; and he mistakenly believed that he had no responsibility for the broadcast because he was merely quoting the words of the union official.

To the Supreme Court, these considerations fell short of proving that St. Amant showed reckless disregard for the accuracy of his statements:

> "Reckless disregard," it is true, cannot be fully encompassed in one infallible definition. Inevitably its outer limits will be marked out through case-by-case adjudication, as is true with so many legal standards for judging concrete cases, whether the standard is provided by the Constitution, statutes, or case law. . . . Reckless conduct is not measured by whether a reasonably prudent man would have published, or would have investigated before publishing. There must be sufficient evidence to permit the conclusion that the defendant in fact entertained serious doubts as to the truth of his publication. Publishing with such doubts shows reckless disregard for truth or falsity and demonstrates actual malice.[76]

Justice White admitted that such a standard in a sense encouraged journalists to be less careful by not investigating a subject as thoroughly and then claiming that they did not know that the statement was false. In addition, White realized that the plaintiff's ability to collect damages hinged to a substantial degree on the defendant's testimony that he published the statement in good faith and was unaware of its probable falsity. White conceded such a strict standard would allow recovery of damages in fewer cases than those in which proof was based on a *reasonable man* standard or a *prudent publisher* standard. But he acknowledged that in cases dealing with comments about official conduct, *New York Times*, *Garrison*, and *Rosenblatt* had made it clear that the nation has a substantial stake in allowing the public's business to be freely discussed and the standard of ordinary care was not sufficient when it involved such fundamental constitutional principles.

So public officials who bring libel suits against media defendants may realize there is some hope of winning, White outlined what they would have to do to prove actual malice:

> The defendant in a defamation action brought by a public official cannot, however, automatically insure a favorable verdict by testifying that he published with a belief that the statements were true. The finder of fact must determine whether the publication was indeed made in good faith. Professions of good faith will be unlikely to prove persuasive, for example, where a story is fabricated by the defendant, is the product of his imagination, or is based wholly on an unverified anonymous telephone call. Nor will they be likely to prevail when the publisher's allegations are so inherently improbable that only a reckless man would have put them in circulation.[77]

White's statement that a "failure to investigate does not itself establish bad faith"[78] would appear in other forms in future libel cases and did grant the media substantial latitude in which they could make errors and still be protected from libel suits. But as juries began to demonstrate impatience with sloppy journalism, appellate courts eventually became more critical of journalistic practices that departed from what they considered to be responsible behavior and grew increasingly critical of the failure of journalists to pursue leads that may have refuted the defamatory statements they published or broadcast.

While Black and Douglas concurred by referring to the reasons they stated in *New York Times v. Sullivan* and *Garrison v. Louisiana*, Fortas wrote one of the first and most biting dissents in any libel case considered by the Supreme Court. Acknowledging that Thompson was a public official, he argued that the affidavit broadcast by St. Amant contained a "seriously libelous" statement:

> Petitioner's casual, careless, callous use of the libel cannot be rationalized as resulting from the heat of a campaign. Under *New York Times*, this libel was broadcast by petitioner with "actual malice"—with reckless disregard of whether it was false or not. . . . The First Amendment is not so fragile that it requires us to immunize this kind of reckless, destructive invasion of the life, even of public officials, heedless of their interests and sensitivities. The First Amendment is not a shelter for the character assassinator, whether his action is heedless and reckless or deliberate. The First Amendment does not require that we license shotgun attacks on public officials in virtually unlimited open season. The occupation of public officeholder does not forfeit one's membership in the human race.[79]

Fortas declared that St. Amant had a duty to check the accuracy of his statement. If he had made a good-faith effort to check the facts, Fortas would grant him protection even if the statement was false. But because no such check was made, he would sustain the judgment of the Louisiana Supreme Court.

Considered together, *New York Times*, *Garrison*, *Rosenblatt*, and *St. Amant v. Thompson* probably seemed like a dream come true for journalists. They had received from the highest court in the land not only a substantial amount of breathing space when writing about public officials, but protection from libel suits if they could convince a jury or an appellate court that they did not know something was false.

These early Supreme Court efforts to establish national standards in libel can be examined chronologically, but because they encompass a number of general areas related to the developing national standards, it is appropriate to consider them by subject. Although it may seem disjointed to return to a period before *New York Times*, a 1959 case raised important issues about the immunity afforded public officials to make allegedly libelous statements. This and other cases are discussed before a more chronological examination of the development of the actual malice standard continues.

Libel *by* Public Officials

The cases discussed above concerned criticism of public officials and how much protecton the First Amendment affords such discussion. In 1959, the Supreme Court in *Barr v. Matteo*[80] held that public officials enjoyed a substantial degree of immunity when *making* allegedly libelous statements. When petitioner William Barr was acting director of the Office of Rent Stabilization, he issued a press release on February 5, 1953 criticizing a plan developed by a number of his subordinates that would allow them to circumvent congressional efforts to reduce the number of federal agencies and employees. Barr announced that when he assumed the position of acting director, his first act would be to suspend the subordinates. He also ordered that a press release be issued, which was to become the subject of the libel suit and which read in part:

> William G. Barr, Acting Director of Rent Stabilization, today served notice of suspension on the two officials of the agency who in June 1950 were responsible for the plan which allowed 53 of the agency's 2,681 employees to take their accumulated annual leave in cash. . . . The employees are John J. Madigan, Deputy Director for Administration, and Linda Matteo, Director of Personnel. . . . When I did learn that certain employees were receiving cash annual leave settlements and being returned to agency employment on a temporary basis, I specifically notified the employees . . . that if they applied for such cash settlements I would demand their resignations.[81]

The respondents sued Barr, charging that the press release, along with news accounts of negative reaction in the U.S. Senate to publicity about the plan, injured their reputations and that Barr had made the statements with malice. The jury, rejecting the argument that the press release was protected by either a qualified or absolute privilege, found for the respondents.[82] A badly divided Supreme Court reversed the judgment.

Writing the majority opinion, Justice John Harlan emphasized the importance of allowing public officials to be immune from libel suits when the statements concerned their official duties. Members of Congress enjoy absolute immunity with respect to any speech made, vote cast, or action taken in session.[83] Judges also enjoy immunity from actions taken by them in the exercise of their judicial functions. The Supreme Court has extended such immunity to executive officers as well, such as the postmaster general.[84]

Harlan summarized the need for such a privilege:

> It has been thought important that officials of government should be free to exercise their duties unembarrassed by the fear of damage suits in respect of acts done in the course of those duties—suits which would consume time and energies which would otherwise be devoted to governmental service and the threat of which might appreciably inhibit the fearless, vigorous, and effective administration of policies of government.[85]

The Court said that it would be difficult to determine how far down executive ranks such a privilege should apply. "The complexities and magnitude of governmental activity have become so great that there must of necessity be a delegation and redelegation of authority as to many functions, and we cannot say that these functions become less important simply because they are exercised by officers of lower rank in the executive hierarchy."[86] Considering the importance of such a privilege, the majority held that the Barr's plea of absolute privilege must be sustained, although Harlan admitted that it was a difficult decision:

> The question is a close one, but we cannot say that it was not an appropriate exercise of the discretion with which an executive officer of petitioner's rank is necessarily clothed to publish the press release here at issue in the circumstances disclosed by this record. . . . It would be an unduly restrictive view of the scope of the duties of a policy-making executive official to hold that a public statement of agency policy in respect to matters of wide public interest and concern is not action in the line of duty.[87]

Justice Black's concurring opinion emphasized the need for the public to be informed about the activities of its administrative agencies and the way public employees do their jobs. But Chief Justice Earl Warren, with whom Justice Douglas joined, sharply criticized the majority view, saying that the opinion provides very little guidance and creates many problems:

On the one hand the principal opinion sets up a vague standard under which no government employee can tell with any certainty whether he will receive absolute immunity for his acts. On the other hand, it has not given even the slightest consideration to the interest of the individual who is defamed. It is a complete annihilation of his interest.[88]

Warren then traced the development of legislative and executive privilege and argued that society also had a substantial interest in a free and open discussion of government and its officials without being subjected to unfair and absolutely privileged retorts by the public official.[89]

Brennan, who was later to write so eloquently in expanding the role of the First Amendment in protecting discussion about public issues, also dissented, declaring that the Court's decision unnecessarily deprived citizens of all redress of malicious defamation made by public officials. Brennan was concerned about the scope of the majority opinion, particularly that it could include the obscure employee who has been given the authority to hire and fire and who maliciously defames a person discharged. Brennan also questioned whether the public interest is necessarily served by allowing executive officers such a privilege. He suggested that if there should be such a privilege, it should be developed in statutes passed by Congress, not in the Supreme Court.[90]

In a brief dissent, Justice Stewart stated that the issuance of the press release was not "action in the line of duty" and did not serve any agency function. By publicizing the action of dismissing the employees, the petitioner, in Stewart's view, was "seeking only to defend his own individual reputation."[91]

In 1973 the Supreme Court again had to decide whether statements made by officials were within the boundaries of privileged communication. *Doe v. McMillan*[92] primarily concerned the scope of congressional immunity under the speech or debate clause of the United States Constitution, and was less directly related to libel. The House of Representatives Committee on the District of Columbia released a report in late 1970 concerning the public school system that included materials related to the disciplinary problems of certain students who were named. The report said that the materials were included to give a "realistic view" of a troubled school and the lack of administrative efforts to correct problems there.[93]

The petitioners, using pseudonyms, brought suit against the chairman and members of the House committee; the clerk, staff director, and counsel of the committee; a consultant and an investigator for the committee; the superintendent of documents and the public printer; the president and members of the D.C. Board of Education; the superintendent of public schools; the principal and one of the teachers at the school in question; and the United States of America.[94] They said that the report violated their children's right to privacy and "would cause grave damage to the children's mental and physical health and to their reputations, good names, and future careers."[95]

The district court, with a divided United States Court of Appeals affirming, dismissed the action on the ground that the conduct complained of was absolutely privileged. The lower courts cited *Barr v. Matteo* in upholding the official immunity doctrine. The Supreme Court reversed the decision and remanded the case to the lower courts; in its view the immunities of the speech or debate clause and of the doctrine of official immunity had been applied too broadly.[96] The Court held that the members of the congressional committee, members of their staff, the consultant, and the investigator were absolutely immune under the speech or debate clause, but that the others did not enjoy such immunity. Although technically not a libel case, it provided the Court with an opportunity to elaborate further on principles first enunciated in *Barr v. Mateo*, although in *Doe*, members of the Court had many different reasons for the decision they reached.[97]

Actual Malice Evolves

In *Barr v. Matteo* and *Doe v. McMillan*, the Supreme Court made it clear that public officials must be allowed to make statements in their official capacity without having to endlessly venture to court to defend defamation suits. Yet the Court also recognized that it would give public officials an unfair advantage if they could make libelous statements with absolute immunity, while citizen-critics did not enjoy at least some equivalent immunity. The Court had implied in a number of opinions that discussion and criticism on both sides are necessary for there to be free debate on public issues. In 1965 in a short *per curiam* opinion, the Court reinforced the principle that citizens must given substantial latitude in which they can discuss and criticize public officials, and it continued the evolution of the actual malice standard.

In *Henry v. Collins*,[98] the Court reversed the judgment of the Mississippi Supreme Court that had awarded damages to a county attorney and chief of police. After Aaron E. Henry was arrested on a charge of disturbing the peace, he issued a statement to the effect that his arrest was the result of a "diabolical plot" in which the respondents were implicated.[99] At the request of the respondents, and with the approval of the trial judge, the following statement was read to the jury: "The court instructs the jury for the plaintiff that malice does not necessarily mean hatred or ill will, but that malice may consist merely of culpable recklessness or a willful and wanton disregard of the rights and interests of the person defamed."[100]

The jury was also instructed, at the request of the respondents, that

if you believe from the evidence that defendant published a false statement charging that his arrest . . . was the result of a diabolical plot . . ., you may infer malice, as defined in these instructions, from the falsity and libelous nature of the statement, although malice as a legal presumption does not arise from the fact that the statement in question is false and libelous. It is for you to determine as a fact, if you have first determined from the evidence that defendant published the statement in question and that it is false, whether or not the statement in question was actually made with malice.[101]

The Supreme Court was concerned that the jury might well have understood the instructions "to allow recovery on a showing of intent to inflict harm, rather than intent to inflict harm through falsehood." The Court repeated its holding in *New York Times* that a public official, to recover damages for a defamatory falsehood relating to the official's conduct, must prove that the statement was made with knowledge that it was false or with reckless disregard of whether it was false or not. Justices Black, Douglas, and Goldberg added that they concurred in the result, not merely for error in the instructions read to the jury, but "on the ground that it would violate the First and Fourteenth Amendments to subject petitioner to any libel judgment solely because of his publication of criticisms against respondents' performance of their public duties."[102]

Although the Court did not elaborate, it did indicate that the federal rule of privilege granted to officials making statements within their official capacities would also be extended to the citizen who criticized the activities of public servants. The criticism of both now enjoyed constitutional status.

The actual malice standard with its requirement of reckless disregard did pose a number of problems, some of which suggest that the standard did not provide very clear guidelines. Some state courts, for example, seemed either terribly confused by the requirement or chose instead to ignore the dictates of the Supreme Court. That seemed to be the case in a 1967 decision, *Beckley Newspapers v. Hanks*.[103]

Beckley was another short *per curiam* opinion in which the Court expressed impatience with the inablility of state courts to understand its rulings in *New York Times* and *Garrison*. C. Harold Hanks, the elected clerk of the criminal and circuit courts of Raleigh County, West Virginia, sued the petitioner's newspaper, the *Beckley Post-Herald* after it published three editorials during Hanks's reelection campaign criticizing his official conduct. The jury awarded Hanks $5,000 in damages. The State Supreme Court declined to review the case.

The U.S. Supreme Court seemed irritated that it had to deal with the case. The trial was held after the opinions in *New York Times v. Sullivan, Garrison v. Louisiana, Henry v. Collins,* and *Rosenblatt v. Baer* had been issued, and the Court said:

Despite the fact that it was recognized at trial that the principles of *New York Times* were applicable, the case went to the jury on instructions which were clearly impermissible. The jury was instructed in part that it could find for the respondent if it were shown that petitioner had published the editorials "with bad or corrupt motive," or "from personal spite, ill will or a desire to injure plaintiff."[104]

The petitioner had failed, in the Court's view, to challenge what it called the erroneous interpretation of *New York Times* at the trial; therefore, the Supreme Court was technically unable to review the instructions directly. However, the Court sidestepped the issue by holding that because it was clear the jury verdict was rendered upon instructions that "misstated the law and since petitioner has properly challenged the sufficiency of the evidence," the Court undertook an independent examination of the record as a whole.

Hanks contended that the newspaper had failed to investigate properly before publishing the charges, and that omission entitled the jury to find that "the offending charges" were published with reckless disregard of whether they were true or not. Following is some of the testimony of the president and general manager of the newspaper:

Q.   But you can't tell this jury that any specific investigation was made before this man was attacked in any of these articles, can you?

A.   We watch the activities of the public servant. You don't have to make an investigation. His whole life is out front of everybody.

And then referring to the substance of the editorials, petitioners said, "It was our opinion that that was as near the facts and truth as we could get."[105]

The Supreme Court rejected the respondent's contention. It said that nothing in the record indicated "the high degee of awareness of . . . probable falsity demanded by *New York Times*," and added that "it cannot be said on this record that any failure of petitioner to make a prior investigation constituted proof sufficient to present a jury question whether the statements were published with reckless disregard of whether they were false or not."[106]

Justice Fortas took no part in the case; Justices Black and Douglas dissented, citing reasons stated in *New York Times* and *Garrison*. By holding that failure to investigate does not in itself constitute reckless disregard, the Supreme Court made the actual malice standard a powerful weapon in the hands of media organizations when fighting libel suits. Although the Court did not specifically address the issue until later, implicit in its early rulings is the notion that journalism is not a developed profession in the sense that there are approved codes of standards or behavior, and that the degree of commitment to investigation cannot be standardized and depends on individual circumstances. Although the Court in a very important 1967 case recognized departure from standards of responsible journalism when it saw such depar-ture,[107] it seemed to say that those determinations need to be made on a case-by-case basis, with the benefit of the doubt going to the First Amendment and those charged with the responsibility of disseminating news. Yet the Court may have recognized the dangers involved in a system of standards that prac-tically rewarded the failure to investigate, with media organizations able to claim that they did not know in advance that what they were publishing or broadcasting was false. A more thorough investigation might reveal the ac-curacy of the statements and it may be to the advantage of the media organi-zation, determined to publish defamatory statements about public officials, not to check the accuracy of the facts.

The media organization, however, is not simply concerned about bolstering its defenses when sued for libel. One of the most precious possessions of a newspaper or broadcasting station is its reputation. During the early years of Supreme Court libel rulings it may have been able to publish defamatory statements and been spared, on appeal, having to pay monetary damages. Yet such cases attract substantial publicity and curiosity, and competing newspa-pers or other media outlets may follow them closely, thus a serious loss of credibility may result for the news organization being sued. So, even though the Court may have provided very substantial constitutional protection during its initial rulings, it did not give newspapers or broadcasting stations unre-strained license to destroy the reputations of public officials. Public officials may disagree with this statement, particularly in regard to the Court's initial rulings, but journalistic credibility—despite a history of American journalism that includes examples to the contrary—remains an important goal of any media organization. In addition, public officials, as the Supreme Court recog-nized in later cases, have at least some access to other media outlets to rebut criticisms made in a given newspaper or broadcast program.

A few years after *Beckley Newspapers v. Hanks*, the Court realized that its efforts to explain the actual malice test were only partially successful. Cases continued to arrive that required the Court's scrutiny, for juries had awarded damages in cases where media organizations had not received the First Amendment protection to which they were entitled by previous court rulings. Granted, the evolutionary process of developing actual malice would certainly include cases where juries, whether misguided by poorly informed judges or stirred by passions of the moment to vent their anger against a media organi-zation, would continue to find for plaintiffs in libel cases that, if they con-formed to the previous rulings of the Supreme Court, should have been de-cided the other way.

Some members of the Supreme Court were beginning to show signs of im-patience as they again tried to explain in *Greenbelt Publishing Association v. Bresler*[108] what the actual malice standard required. Decided by a unanimous

Court in 1970, *Greenbelt* involved a privilege enjoyed for years by media organizations to report accurately and fairly what takes place at official meetings of legislative bodies.

Charles S. Bresler, a prominent real estate developer in Greenbelt, Maryland, won $17,500 from the *Greenbelt News Review* after it published derogatory remarks made about him in two city council meetings. Bresler owned land that the city wanted for construction of a new high school. He also was negotiating with the city for a zoning change in other land that he owned. The council members realized that if they could not reach some agreement with him, it would mean extensive litigation over compensation for the school site. The negotiations evoked substantial controversy in the community, and the council meetings were reported in the *Greenbelt News Review*. Bresler's negotiating position was described as "blackmail" in several articles; the word appeared several times, both with and without quotation marks, and was used once as a subheading.[109] Bresler was awarded $5,000 in compensatory damages and $12,500 in punitive damages.

Bresler's lawyer conceded that his client was a "public figure" and thus had to meet the same *New York Times* actual malice standard, as would a public official. First introduced in *Curtis Publishing Company v. Butts*[110] in 1967, the concept of the public figure will be discussed in detail in chapter 4. For present purposes, what matters are the elaboration and clarification of the actual malice test that must be met by both public officials and public figures.[111] In the view of the Court, the trial judge's instructions to the jury permitted a finding of liability under an "impermissible constitutional standard, whichever status Bresler might be considered to occupy."

The trial judge repeatedly instructed the jurors that Bresler could recover if the articles had been published with malice or with a reckless disregard of whether they were true or false. The judge then defined malice as including "'spite, hostility or deliberate intention to harm.' Moreover, he instructed the jury that 'malice' could be found from the 'language' of the publication itself. Thus the jury was permitted to find liability merely on the basis of a combination of falsehood and general hostility."[112]

With some impatience, the Court declared, "This was error of constitutional magnitude, as our decisions have made clear." The Court then repeated the definition of malice it had first enunciated in *New York Times v. Sullivan*: a public official may collect damages only if the official establishes that the statement was false and that it was made with knowledge of its falsity or in reckless disregard of whether it was false or true. The Court quoted its decisions in *Rosenblatt*, *Garrison*, and *Beckley Newspapers* in reminding lower courts what was required to meet the actual malice standard.

The Court could have reversed the judgment in *Greenbelt* on that ground alone, but instead chose to address another issue of much importance. It noted that this case involved newspaper reports of public meetings of the citizens of a community concerned with matters of local government interest and importance. The Court emphasized the importance of allowing freedom of discussion: "Because the threat or actual imposition of pecuniary liability for alleged defamation may impair the unfettered exercise of these First Amendment freedoms, the Constitution imposes stringent limitations upon the permissible scope of such liability."[113]

The newspaper articles were accurate and truthful reports of what was said at the council meetings. Thus, the Court held that Bresler could not claim that the petitioners were guilty of any "departure from the standards of investigation and reporting ordinarily adhered to by responsible publishers,"[114] much less the knowing of falsehood or a reckless disregard of whether the statements were true or false. But Bresler claimed that because the newspaper knew he had not committed the crime of blackmail, it could be held liable for the knowing use of falsehood. The Supreme Court rejected such a view, and said use of the word "blackmail" in these circumstances was not slander when spoken, and not libel when reported in the *Greenbelt News Review*.[115]

The Court recognized that the issue caused heated debate at the council meetings, yet as long as the newspaper acurately and fairly reported what was said, it was performing what the Court called "its wholly legitimate function." If the reports had been inaccurate or distorted in such a way as to use the word *blackmail* out of context, it would be a different case. In the articles Bresler's proposal was accurately described, along with the statement that some people at the meetings had referred to the proposal as blackmail, and others had indicated they thought Bresler's position was unreasonable.[116]

The Court dismissed the notion that such reporting constituted knowing falsehood:

> It is simply impossible to believe that a reader who reached the word "blackmail" in either article would not have understood exactly what was meant: it was Bresler's public and wholly legal negotiating proposals that were being criticized. No reader could have thought that either the speakers at the meetings or the newspaper articles reporting their words were charging Bresler with a criminal offense.[117]

To permit infliction of financial liability for publishing the two articles, the Court concluded, "would subvert the most fundamental meaning of a free press, protected by the First and Fourteenth Amendments."[118]

By the time *Greenbelt* was decided in 1970, the Supreme Court and lower courts had experimented with providing a workable definition of actual malice for six years. It was clear by 1979 that not all the questions had been answered, and by then a different Court was concerned that actual malice had evolved in such a way that it presented an almost insurmountable barrier to recovery for damage to reputation.

Herbert v. Lando,[119] decided by a divided Supreme Court in 1979, was but one step in a case that took over ten years just to get to the trial stage. It is one of the most important libel suits against a television network ever considered by United States courts, but for present purposes it is the Supreme Court's pronouncements on the actual malice standard that are of interest.

Anthony Herbert, a retired Army officer who had spent an extended period of time in Vietnam, received widespread media attention in 1969-70 when he accused his superior officers of covering up reports of atrocities and other war crimes.[120] In 1973 CBS broadcast a report in its critically acclaimed "60 Minutes" program entitled "The Selling of Colonel Herbert," which cast doubt on his allegations. The report was produced and edited by Barry Lando, and narrated by Mike Wallace. Lando later published an article on the subject in *Atlantic Monthly* magazine. Herbert sued Lando, Wallace, CBS, and *Atlantic Monthly* for defamation, asking $45 million in damages. He claimed that the program and article "falsely and maliciously portrayed him as a liar and a person who had made war-crimes charges to explain his relief from command."[121]

Herbert conceded that he was a "public figure" and thus had to prove that respondents had published or broadcast a defamatory falsehood with "actual malice"—that is, with knowledge that it was false or with reckless disregard of whether it was false or not. During the pretrial discovery process, Herbert's attorneys asked Lando a series of questions that he refused to answer on the grounds that the "First Amendment protected against inquiry into the state of mind of those who edit, produce, or publish, and into the editorial process."[122] The questions were directed at Lando's state of mind when he was putting the report together. The district court held that the defendant's state of mind was of "central importance" to the issue of malice in the case, but the court of appeals reversed, on the grounds that the First Amendment provided sufficient protection to the editorial processes to protect Lando from inquiry about his thoughts, opinions, and conclusions with respect to gathering material for the program and about his conversations with his editorial colleagues.[123] By a 6-3 vote, the Supreme Court overruled the appeals court, holding that Lando must answer the questions.

Justice Byron White, writing the majority opinion, traced the development of constitutional standards in libel, emphasizing that *New York Times* and subsequent cases made it essential to proving liability that the plaintiff focus on the "conduct and state of mind" of the defendant. For a public official or public figure to win a libel suit, either has to prove that the publisher of the alleged libel must have known or have had reason to suspect that the statements were false. White believed that the thoughts and editorial processes of the alleged defamer must be open to examination.

White spent much of his opinion recounting the numerous cases in which inquiry into the state of mind of the defendant had been fully explored. In fact,

White said such "state-of-mind evidence... is deeply rooted in the common-law rule, predating the First Amendment, that a showing of malice on the part of the defendant permitted plaintiffs to recover punitive or enhanced damages."[124] Furthermore, long before *New York Times* was decided, certain qualified privileges had developed to protect a publisher from liability for libel unless the publication was made with malice:

> Malice was defined in numerous ways, but in general depended upon a showing that the defendant had acted with improper motive. This showing in turn hinged upon the intent or purpose with which the publication was made, the belief of the defendant in the truth of his statement, or upon the ill will which the defendant might have borne toward the plaintiff.[125]

White expressed irritation that the court of appeals had apparently misunderstood the history and importance of free inquiry into the state of mind of libel defendants, and rejected the notion that a privilege existed that allowed journalists to refuse to answer such questions:

> In sum, contrary to the views of the Court of Appeals, according an absolute privilege to the editorial process of a media defendant in a libel case is not required, authorized, or presaged by our prior cases, and would substantially enhance the burden of proving actual malice, contrary to the expectations of *New York Times*, *Butts*, and similar cases.[126]

White rejected the contention of the defendants that the First Amendment provided an immunity from such questions, and expressed confusion over the scope of the defendants' claim:

> Although we are told that respondent Lando was willing to testify as to what he "knew" and what he had "learned" from his interviews, as opposed to what he "believed," it is not at all clear why the suggested editorial privilege would not cover knowledge as well as belief about the veracity of published reports. . . . Respondents would also immunize from inquiry the internal communications occuring during the editorial process and thus place beyond reach what the defendant participants learned or knew as the result of such collegiate conversations or exchanges. . . . We thus have little doubt that Herbert and defamation plaintiffs have important interests at stake in opposing the creation of the asserted privilege.[127]

White concluded by emphasizing the importance of the discovery process and acknowledging that the Court had expressed concern in the past over undue and uncontrolled discovery that can prolong the pretrial stages of a case. But he said that is a problem not peculiar to libel and slander. He also said that judges have ample powers to prevent abuse of the discovery process.

None of the dissenters objected to allowing inquiry into the mental processes of defendants, but several justices disagreed with the majority opinion in other respects. Justice Powell, in concurring with the judgment of the Court, wanted to add the point that a trial judge "has a duty to consider First Amendment interests as well as the private interests of the plaintiff."[128] Powell criticized the widespread abuse of the discovery process which he said was the prime cause of delay and expense in civil litigation. He urged trial judges to exercise their discretion in restricting the discovery process "in the interest of justice or to protect the parties from undue burden or expense."[129] He added: "I join the Court's opinion on my understanding that in heeding these admonitions, the district court must ensure that the values protected by the First Amendment, though entitled to no constitutional privilege in a case of this kind, are weighed carefully in striking a proper balance."[130]

Justice Brennan, the author of the Court's opinion in *New York Times v. Sullivan*, dissented in part, saying that he agreed that no "editorial privilege" insulates factual matters that may be sought during discovery and that such a privilege should not shield respondents' "mental processes." But he added:

> I would hold, however, that the First Amendment required predecisional communication among editors to be protected by an editorial privilege, but that this privilege must yield if a public-figure plaintiff is able to demonstrate to the prima facie satisfaction of a trial judge, that the publication in question constitutes defamatory falsehood.[131]

Justice Potter Stewart filed a strong dissent, expressing great frustration with the actual malice standard:

> I have come to greatly regret the use . . . of the phrase "actual malice." For the fact of the matter is that "malice" as used in the *New York Times* opinion simply does not mean malice as that word is commonly understood. In common understanding, malice means ill will or hostility, and the most relevant question in determing whether a person's action was motivated by actual malice is to ask "why." As part of the constitutional standard enunciated in the *New York Times* case, however, "actual malice" has nothing to do with hostility or ill will, and the question "why" is totally irrelevant.[132]

And Stewart lamented the amount of time the case had already taken:

> By the time the case went to the Court of Appeals, the deposition of the respondent Lando alone had lasted intermittently for over a year and had filled 2,903 pages of transcript, with an additional 240 exhibits. The plaintiff had, in Chief Judge Kaufman's words, "already discovered what Lando knew, saw, said and wrote during his investigation." That, it seems to me, was already more than sufficient.[133]

Finally, Justice Thurgood Marshall argued in a long dissent that some constraints on pretrial discovery are essential to ensure the "uninhibited [and] robust debate on public issues which *Sullivan* contemplated":

The possibility of such abuse is enhanced in libel litigation, for many self-perceived victims of defamation are animated by something more than a rational calculus of their chances of recovery. . . . Plaintiffs' pretrial maneuvers may be fashioned more with an eye to deterrence or retaliation than to unearthing germane material.[134]

And in phrases that might well reflect the thinking of many journalists who had defended a libel suit, he added: "Faced with the prospect of escalating attorney's fees, diversion of time from journalistic endeavors, and exposure of potentially sensitive information, editors may well make publication judgments that reflect less the risk of liability than the expense of vindication."[135]

Herbert v. Lando is a libel case that was fought for the better part of ten years. It demonstrates not only how complicated such an inquiry can be but also how long and expensive the process of litigating such a case can be for all parties concerned.[136]

When the Supreme Court sent the case back to the trial level with instructions that Lando must answer the questions about his state of mind, some media organizations unleashed a storm of protest. Allen Neuharth, then president of the American Newspaper Publishers Association, denounced *Herbert v. Lando* as a threat to First Amendment freedoms, describing the Court as "the imperial judiciary . . . that is bending the First Amendment at every turn" and creating an "atmosphere of intimidation."[137] William Leonard, then president of CBS News, was quoted as saying the decision denied "constitutional protection to the journalist's most precious possession—his mind, his thoughts, and his editorial judgment."[138] Sanford indicated that other members of the press, such as Clayton Kirkpatrick, editor of the *Chicago Tribune*, considered *Herbert v. Lando* to be of minor legal significance.[139]

The widespread reaction to *Herbert v. Lando* prompted Justice William Brennan to respond in a speech that he delivered on October 17, 1979. Expressing concern that the press might have been not only overreacting to some Court decisions, but missing their significance, Brennan said:

In recent years the press has taken vigorous exception to decisions of the Court circumscribing the protections the First Amendment extends to the press. . . . I have dissented from many of these opinions as hampering, if not shackling the press' performance of its crucial role in helping maintain our open society. . . . I am concerned, however, that in the heat of the controversy the press may be misapprehending the fundamental issues at stake, and may consequently fail in its important task of illuminating these issues for the Court and the public.[140]

Brennan asserted that in some cases the "vehemence of the press' reaction has been out of all proportion to the injury suffered." Referring to *Herbert*, Brennan chided the press for its reaction to the case:

I can say with some degree of confidence that the decision deserved a more considered response on the part of the press than it received. The injury done the press was simply not of the magnitude to justify the resulting firestorm of acrimonious criticism. . . . Being asked about one's state of mind can be a demeaning and unpleasant experience. Nevertheless, the inquiry into a defendant's state of mind, into his intent, is one of the most common procedures in the law. . . . And, in the area of libel, it would scarcely be fair to say that a plaintiff can only recover if he establishes intentional falsehood and at the same time to say that he cannot inquire into a defendant's intentions.[141]

Brennan made note of the part of his dissent that would have held that there should be a "qualified" privilege for "predecisional communications" among editors, saying that such communication could be curtailed if they may later be used as evidence in libel suits:

Since a democracy requires an informed and accurate press, and since predecisional editorial communications contribute to an informed and accurate editorial judgments, I would have held that such communications should receive a qualified privilege. I say a *qualified* privilege because even the executive privilege bestowed upon the President of the United States . . . is . . . a qualified privilege.[142]

By the time of *Herbert v. Lando*, in 1979, the Supreme Court had written many words about the actual malice standard in libel cases, yet more often than not it merely reiterated the components of the test first enunciated in *New York Times v. Sullivan*. A few years after that historic decision of 1964, the Court expanded the applicability of the actual malice test to public figures, but in doing so, it had to face squarely an issue that would trouble the Court and the press for many years to come: Who is a public official or public figure and who is a private person? And what standards of liability must a private person meet? After discussing those issues in many decisions over a period of fifteen years, the Court has yet to provide clear answers.

Notes

1. 376 U.S. 254 (1964).
2. Ibid. at 256.
3. Among those signing the advertisement were Harry Belafonte, Marlon Brando, Diahann Carroll, Nat "King" Cole, Ossie Davis, Sammy Davis, Jr., Nat Hentoff, Langston Hughes, Mahalia Jackson, Eartha Kitt, Hope Lange, Sidney Poitier, Jackie Robinson, Eleanor Roosevelt, Maureen Stapleton, and Shelley Winters.
4. 376 U.S. at 257.
5. Sullivan had actually filed suit against The *New York Times*, and four other media defendants. Other state officials had filed lawsuits against the *Times*,

seeking $5.6 million, and five such suits against CBS seeking $1.7 million. Ibid. at 295.

6. Ibid. at 257.
7. Ibid. at 257-58.
8. Ibid. at 258.
9. Ibid. at 259.
10. Ibid.
11. The *Times* did write Sullivan a letter stating, among other things, that "we . . . are somewhat puzzled as to how you think the statements in any way reflect on you," and "you might, if you desire, let us know in what respect you claim that the statements in the advertisement reflect on you." Ibid. at 261. Sullivan filed the suit without answering the letter. Interestingly, though, the *Times* did subsequently publish a retraction upon the demand of Governor John Patterson of Alabama, who said that the publication charged him with "grave misconduct and . . . improper actions and omissions as Governor of Alabama and Ex-Officio Chairman of the State Board of Education of Alabama." Ibid. at 261. When asked to explain why there had been a retraction for the governor but not for Sullivan, the secretary of the *Times* testified: "We did that because we didn't want anything that was published by *The Times* to be a reflection on the State of Alabama and the Governor was, as far as we could see, the embodiment of the State of Alabama and the proper representative of the State and, furthermore, we had by that time learned more of the actual facts which the ad purported to recite and, finally, the ad did refer to the action of the State authorities and the Board of Education presumably of which the Governor is the ex-officio chairman . . . ." Ibid. at 261-62.
12. 273 Ala. 656; 144 So. 2d 25.
13. See discussion of libel *per se* and *per quod* in chapter 2.
14. 376 U.S. at 262.
15. Ibid. at 263.
16. 273 Ala. at 676; 144 So. 2d at 40.
17. 376 U.S. at 265.
18. 316 U.S. 52 (1942).
19. 376 U.S. at 265.
20. Ibid. at 266.
21. Ibid.
22. Ibid. at 270-71.
23. Ibid. at 271-72.
24. Ibid. at 279.
25. Ibid. at 279-80.
26. *Curtis Publishing Company v. Butts* and *Associated Press v. Walker*, 388 U.S. 130 (1967), and other cases that developed the public figure status of plaintiffs will be discussed in the next chapter.
27. Brennan all but suggested that it would not be appropriate for Alabama authorities to try the case again. The Court said, "Since respondent may seek a new trial, we deem that considerations of effective judicial administration require us to review the evidence in the present record to determine whether it could constitutionally support a judgment for respondent." 376 U.S. at 284-85. Brennan then summarized the Court's main points, indicating that a new trial would not change the result.
28. Ibid. at 292.
29. Ibid. at 293.

30. Ibid.
31. Ibid. at 294-95.
32. Ibid. at 297. Justice Goldberg in a concurring opinion that Justice Douglas joined, would have gone beyond the Court's holding:

> In my view, the First and Fourteenth Amendments to the Constitution afford to the citizen and to the press an absolute, unconditional privilege to criticize official conduct despite the harm which may flow from excesses and abuses. . . . The right should not depend upon a probing by the jury of the motivation of the citizen or press. The theory of our Constitution is that every citizen may speak his mind and every newspaper express its view on matters of public concern and may not be barred from speaking or publishing because those in control of government think that what is said or written is unwise, unfair, false, or malicious. Ibid. at 298-99.

Goldberg would, however, apply different standards to "private" defamation:

> This is not to say that the Constitution protects defamatory statements directed against the private conduct of a public official or private citizen. . . . Purely private defamation has little to do with the political ends of a self-governing society. The imposition of liability for private defamation does not abridge the freedom of public speech or any other freedom protected by the First Amendment. Ibid. at 301-02.

But in a footnote Goldberg discussed an issue that would later cause the Supreme Court many problems: "In most cases, as in the case at bar, there will be little difficulty in distinguishing defamatory speech relating to private conduct from that relating to official conduct. I recognize, of course, that there will be a gray area." Ibid. at 302 n. 4.
33. Ibid. at 285-86.
34. The act expired by its terms in 1801. Ibid. at 276. Kalven believed that the Court was being unusually candid about its reliance on history in establishing legal doctrine. He quoted Brennan as writing in *New York Times* that "the attack on upon its [the Sedition Act of 1798] validity has . . . carried the day in the court of history." To Kalven, this was "heady doctrine": "The Court has never before been quite so candid about its use of history. A major issue in constitutional doctrine thus beckons." Harry Kalven, Jr., "The *New York Times* Case: A Note on "the Central Meaning of the First Amendment," *The Supreme Court Review* 191 (1964): 193.
35. Ibid., pp. 213-18.
36. Ibid., p. 208.
37. Ibid., pp. 193-94.
38. Ibid., p. 209.
39. *Curtis Publishing Co. v. Butts*, 388 U.S. 130 (1967).
40. 376 U.S. at 277, referring to *Farmers Union v. WDAY*, 360 U.S. 525 (1959) at 535.
41. *Garrison v. Louisiana*, 379 U.S. 64 at 66.
42. Ibid.
43. La. Rev. Stat., 1950, Tit. 14.
44. 379 U.S. at 70.
45. Ibid. at 71-73.
46. Ibid. at 73, quoting a New Hampshire court in *State v. Burnham*, 9 N.H. 34 at 42-43 (1837).
47. Ibid. at 75.

48. Ibid. at 77.
49. Ibid. at 78.
50. Ibid. at 79.
51. Ibid. at 80.
52. Ibid. at 81-82.
53. 383 U.S. 75 (1966).
54. Ibid. at 78-79.
55. Clifton O. Lawhorne, *The Supreme Court and Libel* (Carbondale: Southern Illinois University Press, 1981), p. 41.
56. 383 U.S. at 79-80.
57. Ibid. at 80.
58. Ibid. at 79.
59. Ibid. at 83.
60. Ibid. at 84, quoting *Pennekamp v. Florida*, 328 U.S. 331 (1946) at 335.
61. Ibid. at 85.
62. Ibid.
63. Ibid. at 88 n. 15.
64. Ibid. at 89.
65. Ibid. at 90.
66. Ibid.
67. Ibid.; emphasis in original.
68. Ibid. at 93.
69. Ibid. at 97.
70. Ibid. at 100.
71. Ibid.
72. 390 U.S. 727 (1968).
73. Ibid. at 728-29.
74. Ibid. at 729.
75. Ibid. at 730 n. 2.
76. Ibid. at 730-31.
77. Ibid. at 732.
78. Ibid. at 733.
79. Ibid. at 734.
80. 360 U.S. 564 (1959).
81. Ibid. at 567-68 n. 5.
82. The case went to the Supreme Court twice. Barr appealed the first time, raising only the issue of absolute privilege. The judgment of the trial court was affirmed by the court of appeals, which held that "in explaining his decision [to suspend respondents] to the general public [petitioner] . . . went entirely outside his line of duty" and thus the absolute privilege, assumed otherwise to be available, did not attach. Ibid. at 568. The Supreme Court granted certiorari, vacated the court of appeals judgment, and remanded the case "with directions to pass upon petitioner's claim of a qualified privilege." On remand the court of appeals held that the press release was protected by a qualified privilege, but that there was evidence from which a jury could reasonably conclude that petitioner had acted maliciously, or had spoken with lack of reasonable grounds for believing his statement was true, and that either conclusion would defeat the qualified privilege. The court of appeals remanded the case to the district court for retrial, at which point Barr sought, and the Supreme Court again granted, certiorari "to determine whether in the circumstances of this case petitioner's claim of absolute

privilege should have stood as a bar to maintenance of the suit despite the allegations of malice made in the complaint." Ibid. at 568-69.

83. U.S. Constitution, Article I, Section 6. In *Hutchinson v. Proxmire*, 443 U.S. 111 (1979), to be discussed in chapter 5, the Supreme Court rejected the claim of U.S. Senator William Proxmire that criticism of the way public research money was spent, made outside the Senate floor, was protected by the speech or debate clause.

84. *Spalding v. Vilas*, 161 U.S. 483 (1896).

85. 360 U.S. at 571.

86. Ibid. at 573.

87. Ibid. at 574-75.

88. Ibid. at 578.

89. Ibid. at 584.

90. Ibid. at 591.

91. Ibid. at 592. In a companion case to *Barr*, *Howard v. Lyons*, 360 U.S 593 (1959), the Court ruled that statements made by a military officer were absolutely privileged.

92. 412 U.S. 306 (1973).

93. Ibid. at 308-09.

94. Ibid. at 309.

95. Ibid.

96. Ibid. at 324.

97. Justice White was joined in the majority opinion in *Doe* by Justices Douglas, Brennan, Marshall and Powell. Douglas wrote a concurring opinion which Brennan and Marshall joined. Chief Justice Burger filed an opinion concurring in part and dissenting in part. Justice Harry Blackmun filed an opinion concurring in part and dissenting in part that was joined by Burger. Justice William Rehnquist wrote an opinion concurring in part and dissenting in part, which Burger and Blackmun joined, and in one part of which Justice Stewart joined.

98. 380 U.S. 356 (1965).

99. Ibid. at 356.

100. Ibid. at 357.

101. Ibid.

102. Ibid. at 358.

103. 389 U.S. 81 (1967).

104. Ibid. at 82.

105. Ibid. at 84.

106. Ibid. at 84-85.

107. *Curtis Publishing Company v. Butts*, 388 U.S. 130 (1967).

108. 398 U.S. 6 (1970).

109. Ibid. at 6-7.

110. 388 U.S. 130 (1967).

111. Bresler was also a member of the Maryland House of Delegates from a neighboring district at the time the articles were published. The Court did not think it necessary to specify whether Bresler was a "public figure" or a "public official": "Whether as a state legislator representing another county, or for some other reason, Bresler was a 'public official' within the meaning of the *New York Times* rule is a question we need not determine." 398 U.S. at 9.

112. Ibid. at 10.

113. Ibid. at 12.

114. Ibid. In *Curtis Publishing Company v. Butts,* to be considered in the next chapter, the Court discusses in some detail the concept of "responsible journalism."
115. Ibid. at 13.
116. Ibid. at 14.
117. Ibid.
118. Ibid.
119. 441 U.S. 153 (1979).
120. Ibid. at 155-56.
121. Ibid. at 156.
122. Ibid. at 157.
123. Ibid. at 157-58.
124. Ibid. at 161-62.
125. Ibid. at 163-64.
126. Ibid. at 169.
127. Ibid. at 170-71.
128. Ibid. at 178.
129. Ibid. at 180.
130. Ibid.
131. Ibid. at 181. Brennan's detailed dissent in *Herbert v. Lando* will be examined in more detail in a later chapter.
132. Ibid. at 199.
133. Ibid. at 202.
134. Ibid. at 205.
135. Ibid.
136. More than a decade after Herbert filed his lawsuit against CBS, the case had still not come to trial.
137. Bruce W. Sanford, "No Quarter from This Court," *Columbia Journalism Review* (September/October, 1979): 60.
138. Ibid.
139. Ibid. Sanford quoted Charles W. Baily, editor of the *Minneapolis Tribune* and chairman of the Freedom of Information Committee of the American Society of Newspaper Editors, as saying, "The Allen Neuharths overreacted . . . but it was really a reaction to the Court's general hostility to the press." Sanford, "No Quarter from This Court," p. 60.
140. William J. Brennan, Jr., "Press and the Court: Is the Strain Necessary?" *Editor and Publisher,* 27 October 1979, p. 10.
141. Ibid., p. 33.
142. Ibid., p. 34.

4

"Public Figures" and the "Public Interest": The Search for Standards Continues

The ink used to write the landmark decision in *New York Times v. Sullivan* was barely dry when the United States Court of Appeals for the Second Circuit discussed its significance in a libel case involving Dr. Linus Pauling, a biochemist from California who had won a Nobel Prize. Pauling had sued the *New York Daily News*, which in an editorial had all but accused Pauling and Norman Cousins, the editor of the *Saturday Review*, of being disloyal to the United States.[1] Pauling lost at the trial court level and the appeals court affirmed in *Pauling v. News Syndicate*, decided July 7, 1964.[2]

The case was decided for the most part on the complicated issue of whether the judge issued the appropriate instructions to the jury, but the judges of the court of appeals demonstrated remarkable prescience as they referred to *New York Times v. Sullivan* in discussing the status of Pauling. Although not specifically calling him a public figure, they clearly had such a concept in mind:

> We realize that the sole point actually determined by that decision [*New York Times v. Sullivan*] was that the First Amendment requires a state to recognize a "privilege for criticism of official conduct" . . . extending to misstatements of fact, this being regarded as in some way the reciprocal of the privilege of federal officials against liability for defamatory statements "within the outer perimeter" of their duties. . . . Although the public official is the strongest case for the constitutional compulsion of such a privilege, it is questionable whether in principle the decision can be so limited.

Recognizing that *New York Times* granted protection to discuss "public officials," the judges of the court of appeals suggested that the privilege probably needs to be extended:

> A candidate for public office would seem an inevitable candidate for extension; if a newspaper cannot constitutionally be held for defamation when it states

111

without malice, but cannot prove, that an incumbent seeking re-election has accepted a bribe, it seems hard to justify holding it liable for further stating that the bribe was offered by his opponent. Once that extension was made, the participant in public debate on an issue of grave public concern would be next in line.[3]

This may be the first time that any court foreshadowed the coming of the public figure to constitutional litigation in a post-*New York Times* decision. The court of appeals not only suggested the existence of a public figure without calling it that, but made mention of the fact that Pauling had become a willing participant in public debate, an issue the Supreme Court considered in detail a decade later:

> A Fourth Defense asserted [by the newspaper] that plaintiff, having achieved a good professional reputation in education and scientific research, "became an outspoken advocate of causes, policies, organizations and individuals sympathetic to communism, and he sought wide-spread publicity for such advocacy," thereby creating "for himself a reputation that could not and did not suffer any damage by reason of the editorial complained of."[4]

Not yet ready to designate certain plaintiffs in libel suits as public figures, the Court gave further hints two years later that it was heading toward extending constitutional protection to discuss the activities of such individuals. As mentioned before, the Court indicated in *Rosenblatt v. Baer* that it had "no occasion to determine how far down into the lower ranks of government employees of the 'public official' designation would extend . . . or otherwise to specify categories of persons who would or would not be included."[5] But the Court foreshadowed decisions to come when it suggested that the constitutional status of the plaintiff may be related to the nature of the issue involved:

> We expressed [in *New York Times*] "a profound national commitment to the principle that debate on public issues should be uninhibited, robust and wide-open *and* that such debate may include vehement, caustic, and sometimes unpleasantly sharp attacks on government and public officials." There is, first, a strong interest in debate on public issues, and, second, a strong interest in debate about those persons who are in a position significantly to influence the resolution of those issues.[6]

The Court seemed to be strongly suggesting that individuals who are not public officials, but are in a position to influence the activities of government and the resolution of public issues, may need to meet the same strict constitutional standard that protects media organizations when discussing bona fide public officials. It also indicated that the type of issue involved would be relevant, that the public is entitled to hear discussion about and criticism of those individuals who are associated with the resolution of issues of public importance no matter what their status.

It was not until a year later, in 1967, that the Court created the public figure status for plaintiffs in libel cases against the media and required that such individuals meet the same *New York Times* test of actual malice. But it was clear in *Pauling v. News Syndicate* and *Rosenblatt v. Baer* that if the Court was to provide substantial protection to discussion about public issues and private persons who may be involved in them, it would have to decide how far and to whom such protection would extend.

Five months before the Court's creation of the public figure status in *Curtis Publishing Company v. Butts*,[7] the Court applied the actual malice test in a privacy case involving a family that sued *Life* magazine after it published an article about a play on Broadway based roughly on the experiences of James Hill and his family.[8] They had been held hostage by escaped convicts in their home near Philadelphia. The play differed from the actual experiences of the Hill family in a number of significant ways. Hill sued for invasion of privacy under New York law and was awarded $30,000 in damages.[9]

Although a privacy and not a libel case, it provided the Supreme Court with an opportunity, which it seized, to extend directly the public-official actual malice standard adopted in *New York Times* by applying it to plaintiffs involved in matters of public interest: "We hold that the constitutional protections of speech and press preclude the application of the New York statute to redress false reports of matters of public interest in the absence of proof that the defendant published the report with knowledge of its falsity or in reckless disregard of the truth."[10]

Anxious to extend protection to discussion of public issues as well as the activities and fitness of public officials, the Court said that both private citizens and public officials must understand that occasional exposure to public view is part of living in a society like ours:

> The guarantees for speech and press are not the preserve of political expression or comment upon public affairs, essential as those are to healthy government. One need only pick up any newspaper or magazine to comprehend the vast range of published matter which exposes persons to public view, both private citizens and public officials. Exposure of self to others in varying degrees is a concomitant of life in a civilized community. The risk of this exposure is an essential incident of life in a society which places a primary value on freedom of speech and of press.[11]

The Hills were clearly private citizens who involuntarily became the subjects of public interest, yet the Court felt that there should be widespread discussion of issues of public interest and that the actual malice standard should protect such discussion. It must be noted that in privacy cases, the truthfulness of the statements is not necessarily a key issue. Privacy can be invaded even if the statements subsequently published or broadcast are truthful. Rules governing the privilege of defendants in privacy cases have developed very differently from those in defamation cases.[12] Yet it was clear that having adopted the actual malice test in *New York Times*, the Court was beginning the process of deciding to whom and in what types of controversies the rule would apply. It was now ready to designate by name a category of individuals who would share the same constitutional status of public officials and thus the task of overcoming substantial obstacles if they were to be successful in a libel suit against a media defendant.

Public Figures

Including "public figures" in the category of individuals who must meet the *New York Times* actual malice standard was but one aspect of two immensely complicated Supreme Court decisions handed down on June 12, 1967. Combining *Curtis Publishing Company v. Butts*[13] with *Associated Press v. Walker*, the Court sustained a large libel judgment against a media organization and warned journalists that there would be limits beyond which they could not go in defending libel suits. Even as the Court enlarged the scope of First Amendment protection on one level, it showed substantial impatience with what it considered to be irresponsible reporting.

Justice Harlan, writing the majority opinion, stated at the outset that there had been substantial confusion among state courts as to which individuals should meet the actual malice test before collecting damages in a libel suit. He wrote that combining the two cases into one opinion would provide the Court with the opportunity to discuss further the relationship of the First Amnendment to libel laws.

Wally Butts, the athletic director of the University of Georgia, was accused in an article in the Curtis Publishing Company's *Saturday Evening Post* of conspiring to "fix" a football game between the University of Georgia and the University of Alabama played in 1962. Georgia is a state university, but Butts was actually employed by a private corporation, the Georgia Athletic Association, rather than by the state itself. Butts had been head coach of the football team at Georgia and was "a well-known and respected figure in the coaching ranks."[14] At the time the article appeared, he was negotiating for a position with a professional football team.

"The Story of a College Football Fix" ran on March 23, 1963 and was prefaced by a note from the editors:

> Not since the Chicago White Sox threw the 1919 World Series has there been a sports story as shocking as this one. This is the story of one fixed game of college football. Before the University of Georgia played the University of Alabama . . . Wally Butts . . . gave [to its coach] . . . Georgia's plays, defensive patterns, all the significant secrets Georgia's football team possessed.[15]

The article said that Atlanta insurance salesman George Burnett had overheard a phone conversation between Butts and Alabama coach Paul Bryant when his phone became hooked by accident into a long distance circuit carrying the conversation. This is how the conversation was reported in the *Post*:

> "Hello, Bear," Butts said. "Hello, Wally. Do you have anything for me?" As Burnett listened, Butts began to give Bryant detailed information about the plays and formations Georgia would use in its opening game eight days later . . . Butts mentioned both players and plays by name. Occasionally Bryant asked Butts about specific offensive or defensive maneuvers, and Butts either answered in detail or said, "I don't know about that. I'll have to find out."[16]

The article went on to relate that Alabama won decisively over Georgia, 35-0, the most lopsided score between the two teams since 1923. Georgia's quarterback was quoted as having said, "They just seemed to know every play we were going to run."[17] The article added that the "Georgia players, their moves analyzed and forecast like those of rats in a maze, took a frightful physical beating."

Quoting Georgia's coach, the article added this final note: "'I never had a chance, did I?'" Coach Johnny Griffith said bitterly to a friend the other day. 'I never had a *chance*.' When a fixer works against you, that's the way he likes it."[18]

The article concluded, "The chances are that Wally Butts will never help any football team again. . . . The investigation by Southern Conference officials is continuing; motion pictures of other games are being scrutinized; where it will end no one so far can say. But careers will be ruined, that is sure."[19]

Butts brought a diversity libel suit in federal court in Georgia seeking $5 million in compensatory and $5 million in punitive damages. The jury returned a verdict for $60,000 in compensatory damages and $3 million in punitive damages. The trial judge reduced the total to $460,000.[20] The complaint was filed and the trial completed before the Court handed down its decision in *New York Times v. Sullivan*, thus the Court had to consider whether the standards applied by the judge and the decision reached by the jury conformed with its dictates in that case.

There was much disagreement at the trial over the accuracy of the article. Georgia law required a finding of "malice" for a plaintiff in a libel cases to collect punitive damages. The judge instructed the jury that "malice" was defined in part as "the notion of ill will, spite, hatred and an intent to injure one. Malice also denotes a wanton or reckless indifference or culpable negligence with regard to the rights of others."[21]

The evidence showed that Burnett had indeed overheard a conversation between Butts and Bryant, but the content of that conversation was disputed. Butts contended that the conversation had been "general football talk" and nothing that he said to Bryant would have been of any particular value to an opposing football coach. Justice Harlan noted that expert witnesses supported Butts by analyzing Burnett's notes about the conversation and films of the game itself. The *Post*'s version of the game and of the players' remarks about the game was "severely contradicted."[22]

The trial judge rejected the publishing company's motion for a new trial on the grounds that *New York Times* was inapplicable because Butts was not a public official. He also said that "there was ample evidence from which a jury could have concluded that there was reckless disregard by defendant of whether the article was false or not."[23] The Court of Appeals for the Fifth Circuit affirmed the judgment by a 2-1 vote, writing that "what the Post did was done with reckless disregard of whether the article was false or not."[24]

The Supreme Court, in a 5-4 vote, affirmed the decision and allowed Butts to keep his $460,000, although the majority had varying reasons for its decision. Justice Harlan, in a lengthy discussion of First Amendment history and previous libel decisions, held that the public interest in the circulation of the materials involved in *Butts* and *Walker* (to be discussed shortly), and the publisher's interest in circulating them, is not less than that involved in *New York Times*:

> Both Butts and Walker commanded a substantial amount of independent public interest at the time of the publications; both, in our opinion, would have been labeled "public figures" under ordinary tort rules. . . . Butts may have attained that status by position alone and Walker by his purposeful activity . . . but both commanded sufficient continuing public interest and had sufficient access to the means of counterargument to be able to "to expose through discussion the falsehood and fallacies" of the defamatory statements.[25]

To Harlan and the three justices who joined his opinion, the First Amendment required that states, when considering the appropriate standards for libel suits, not be left on their own to decide the burden that certain plaintiffs must meet in libel actions, and that *New York Times* did not provide the final word on how far First Amendment protection is extended to media defendants in libel cases. Yet Harlan would not go so far as to extend the exact actual malice standard of *New York Times* to "public figures":

> We consider and would hold that a "public figure" who is not a public official may also recover damages for a defamatory falsehood whose substance makes substantial danger to reputation apparent, on a showing of highly unreasonable conduct constituting an extreme departure from the standards of investigation and reporting ordinarily adhered to by responsible publishers.[26]

In a footnote, Harlan said the jury must have decided that the investigation undertaken by the *Saturday Evening Post* was "grossly inadequate." He referred to the argument of Butts's lawyer, who, although not contending that the *Post* held preexisting animosity toward Butts, asserted that it had failed to exercise a minimum of care: "That is not fair journalism . . . that is not true, careful reporting."[27]

Considering the serious deficiencies in investigatory procedure, wrote Harlan, and the severe harm inflicted on Butts, "we would not feel justified in ordering a retrial of the compensatory damage issue, either on the theory that this aspect of the case was submitted to the jury only under the issue of 'truth,' or on the very slim possibility that the jury finding regarding punitive damages might have been based on Curtis' attitude toward Butts rather than on Curtis' conduct."[28] What Harlan seemed to be saying is that even though the case was not submitted to the jury under instructions based on the *New York Times* decision, it satisfied the requirements set out in that case.

Harlan then criticized the methods by which the *Post* reported the story, asserting that such a departure from responsible reporting could be used to forge a new constitutional standard:

> The evidence showed that the Butts story was in no sense "hot news" and the editors of the magazine recognized the need for a thorough investigation of the serious charges. Elementary precautions were, nevertheless, ignored. *The Saturday Evening Post* knew that Burnett had been placed on probation in connection with bad check charges, but proceeded to publish the story on the basis of his affidavit without substantial independent support. Burnett's notes were not even viewed by any of the magazine's personnel prior to publication. . . . No attempt was made to screen the films of the game to see if Burnett's information was accurate, and no attempt was made to find out whether Alabama had adjusted its plans after the alleged divulgence of information. . . . *The Saturday Evening Post* was anxious to change its image by instituting a policy of "sophisticated muckraking," and the pressure to produce a successful expos´ might have induced a stretching of standards. In short, the evidence is ample to support a finding of highly unreasonable conduct constituting an extreme departure from the standards of investigation and reporting ordinarily adhered to by responsible publishers.[29]

Curtis Publishing Company had argued that whether or not it was required to compensate Butts for any injury it may have caused him, it could not be subjected to an assessment of punitive damages limited only by the "enlightened conscience" of the community.[30] The magazine had argued that unlimited punitive damages constitute an effective prior restraint by giving the jury the power to destroy a publisher's business. In this regard, Harlan held, publishers are not different from anyone else:

> We cannot accept this reasoning. Publishers like Curtis engage in a wide variety of activities which may lead to tort suits where punitive damages are a possibility. To exempt a publisher, because of the nature of his calling, from an imposition generally exacted from other members of the community, would be to ex-

tend a protection not required by the constitutional guarantee. . . . We think the constitutional guarantee is adequately served by judicial control over excessive jury verdicts . . . and by the general rule that a verdict based on jury prejudice cannot be sustained even when punitive damages are warranted.[31]

Harlan acknowledged that punitive damages also serve to deter others from committing the same abuses:

Where a publisher's departure from standards of press responsibility is severe enough to strip from him the constitutional protection our decision acknowledges, we think it entirely proper for the State to act not only for the protection of the individual injured but to safeguard all those similarly situated against like abuse.[32]

Chief Justice Earl Warren, providing the fifth and deciding vote that allowed Butts to keep the money awarded by the jury, disagreed with the reasoning of the Harlan group, declaring that it departed from the standard enunciated in *New York Times* only three years before. Warren, arguing that the distinction between governmental and private sectors was increasingly blurred, seemed to agree that public figures should meet the same actual malice standard as do public officials, claiming their "views and actions with respect to public issues and events are often of as much concern to the citizen as the attitudes and behavior of 'public officials' with respect to the same issues and events." Yet, Warren argued, the majority in *Butts*, in departing from the *New York Times* standard, had created new problems:

Mr. Justice Harlan's opinion departs from the standard of *New York Times* and substitutes in cases involving "public figures" a standard that is based on "highly unreasonable conduct" and is phrased in terms of "extreme departure from the standards of investigation and reporting ordinarily adhered to by responsible publishers." I cannot believe that a standard which is based on such an unusual and uncertain formulation could either guide a jury of laymen or afford the protection for speech and debate that is fundamental to our society and guaranteed by the First Amendment.[33]

Warren criticized the Court's efforts to develop one set of standards for public officials and one for public figures, maintaining that such a distinction has no basis in law, logic, or First Amendment policy. He suggested that power has become dispersed in our society in such a way that media organizations need to be able to cover the activities of a wide range of organizations:

In many situations, policy determinations which traditionally were channeled through formal political institutions are now originated and implemented through a complex array of boards, committees, commissions, corporations, and associations, some only loosely connnected with the Government. This blending of positions and power has also occurred in the case of individuals so that many who do not hold public office at the moment are nevertheless intimately involved in the resolution of important public questions or, by reason of their fame, shape events in areas of concern to society at large.[34]

Warren claimed that the *New York Times* actual malice test is a "manageable standard, readily stated and understood," and that because it allows recovering for reckless disregard and not just in cases of knowing falsehood, it is not overly restrictive. Even though the judge in *Butts* did not have the advantage of *New York Times* in instructing the jury, Warren believed that the judge "recognized the essential principle [of *New York Times*] and conformed with it to a substantial degree."[35] In addition, after *New York Times* was brought to the judge's attention in a posttrial motion, he held that the jury verdict should not be disturbed because "there was ample evidence from which a jury could have concluded that there was reckless disregard by the [petitioner] of whether the article was false or not."[36] To Warren, the *Saturday Evening Post* had clearly demonstrated reckless disregard and he concluded by saying, "Freedom of the press under the First Amendment does not include absolute license to destroy lives or careers."[37]

Justice Black, with whom Justice Douglas joined, dissented in *Butts*, writing that the struggle of the Court majority to develop appropriate standards only proved the point he had been making in a number of previous cases. "These cases illustrate, I think, the accuracy of my prior predictions that the *New York Times* constitutional rule concerning libel is wholly inadequate to save the press from being destroyed by libel judgments"[38] Black and Douglas were critical not only of the decision reached by the Court majority, but of the Court's abuse of its self-imposed limits. The Court is not supposed to second-guess juries but to leave to them the finding of facts. The Court is confined, by a self-imposed limitation that has evolved over many years, to considering whether the non-fact-finding aspects of the case meet with constitutional requirements. Black saw the Court's conclusions in *Butts* and *Walker* as conflictive and as a departure from the normal standard of leaving fact-finding to juries:

> Here the Court reverses the case of *Associated Press v. Walker*, but affirms the judgment of *Curtis Publishing Company v. Butts*. The main reason for this quite contradictory action, so far as I can determine, is that the Court looks at the facts in both cases as though it were a jury and reaches the conclusion that the *Saturday Evening Post*, in writing about Butts, was so abusive that its article is more of a libel at the constitutional level than is the one by the Associated Press. That seems a strange way to erect a constitutional standard for libel cases. If this precedent is followed, it means that we must in all libel cases hereafter weigh the facts and hold that all papers and magazines guilty of gross writing or reporting are constitutionally liable, while they are not if the quality of the reporting is approved by a majority of us. In the final analysis, what we do in these circum-

stances is to review the factual questions in cases decided by juries—a review which is a flat violation of the Seventh Amendment.[39]

The Supreme Court seemed to have little choice in the matter. When reviewing the constitutionality of libel laws, the Court must consider actual cases; those cases involve individuals who are trying to meet the standards of liability established by the Supreme Court. The actual malice standard is not just difficult for juries to apply, it is difficult for them to understand. As a number of cases discussed in the previous chapter indicated, in post-*New York Times* cases, both judges and juries had a difficult time either understanding the actual malice test or accepting the authority of the Supreme Court to define it. A review of such a case necessarily requires some examination of how they jury applied the test. Because First Amendment interests of paramount importance are involved, the Supreme Court is entitled to, and in fact probably obligated to, subject the jury decision to more exacting judicial scrutiny. While the jury system is clearly important and valuable, deference to lay jurors struggling to apply crucial First Amendment standards is neither constitutionally required nor administratively convenient when it comes to libel cases. If the Supreme Court is going to establish immensely complicated and often vague standards, it must be willing to help lower courts when they apply them. Inasmuch as defamation cases decided by juries are won overwhelmingly by plaintiffs, appellate courts cannot sit idly by as First Amendment rights are abused on the grounds that self-restraint or judicial deference prevents them from acting.[40]

Associated Press v. Walker contrasts with *Curtis Publishing Company v. Butts*, decided the same day and combined with it, in a number of respects. As tensions mounted at the University of Mississippi, where a black student was being enrolled for the first time, Edwin Walker, a retired major general in the U.S. Army who actively opposed integration, apparently became involved in a riot that erupted on the campus on the night of September 30, 1962. The dispatch of the Associated Press reporter at the scene said that Walker had taken command of the violent crowd and had personally led a charge against federal marshals who were there to enforce the court-ordered integration. The dispatch also described Walker as encouraging rioters to use violence. The reporter, who was only twenty-one, was able to pass as a college student:

> This allowed me to follow the crowd—a few students and many outsiders—as they charged federal marshals surrounding the century old Lyceum Building. It also brought me into direct contact with former Maj. Gen. Edwin A. Walker. . . .
>
> One unidentified man queried Walker as he approached the group. "General, will you lead us to the steps?"
>
> I observed Walker as he loosened his tie and shirt and nodded "Yes" without

speaking. He then conferred with a group of about 15 persons who appeared to be the riot leaders.

The crowd took full advantage of the near-by construction sticks and broken soft drink bottles.

Walker assumed command of the crowd, which I estimated at 1,000. [41]

Walker was a civilian at the time of the publication. In Harlan's majority opinion in the case, he made note of Walker's long and honorable career in the army and that he had, in fact, been in command of federal troops during the school segregation confrontation in Little Rock, Arkansas, in 1957. Since his retirement, he had become active in political affairs and was prominent as a conservative who opposed forced integration. [42]

As a result of the AP dispatch, Walker filed a series of libel suits against newspapers that had carried the story, asking a total of more than $33 million. [43] The Court reviewed a case from Texas courts. Although there was some disagreement about the events of that evening, Walker admitted that he was there but stated that he "had counseled restraint and peaceful protest," and that he exercised no control over the crowd. He denied taking part in any charge against the federal marshals. There was not very much evidence relating to the preparation of the AP report, but it was clear that the reporter was actually at the scene and some discrepancies about whether Walker had spoken to the group before or after approaching the marshals did not seem to concern the Court majority. [44] The Court noted that there was no evidence of personal prejudice or incompetency on the part of the reporter or the Associated Press.

The jury in the Texas case awarded $500,000 in compensatory damages and $300,000 in punitive damages. The trial judge disallowed the punitive damages because there was "no evidence to support the jury's answers that there was actual malice." There were some minor discrepancies between the oral and written versions of the incident as relayed by the reporter on the scene to the AP bureau in Atlanta. As reported by the Supreme Court, the trial judge concluded:

> The failure further to investigate the minor discrepancy between the oral and written versions of the incident could not "be construed as that *entire want of care* which would amount to a *conscious indifference* to the rights of the plaintiff. Negligence, it may have been; malice, it was not. Moreover, the mere fact that AP permitted a young reporter to cover the story of the riot is not evidence of malice." [45]

And then, apparently failing to comprehend the significance of *New York Times*, the judge, as summarized by the Supreme Court, rejected the applicability of that case to the one at hand:

The trial judge also noted that this lack of "malice" would require a verdict for the Associated Press if *New York Times* were applicable. But he rejected its applicability since there were "no compelling reasons of public policy requiring additional defenses to suits for libel. Truth alone should be an adequate defense."[46]

The Court unanimously agreed that the $500,000 libel judgment had to be reversed, but was sharply divided over the reasons for doing so. Harlan wrote that in contrast with the article in the *Butts* case, the AP dispatch in *Walker* was "news which required immediate dissemination." The AP had received the information from a reporter at the scene of an on-going story and he "gave every indication of being trustworthy and competent."[47] Harlan added, "Considering the necessity of rapid dissemination, nothing in this series of events gives the slightest hint of a severe departure from accepted publishing standards."[48]

Chief Justice Warren agreed with the results of both cases, yet disagreed with Harlan's reasons for reaching them, arguing that both decisions departed from the standards of *New York Times*. In *Walker*, the trial judge expressly ruled that no showing of malice in any sense had been made, and he reversed the award of punitive damages for that reason. "Under any reasoning," wrote Warren, "General Walker was a public man in whose public conduct society and the press had a legitimate and substantial interest."[49] As discussed before, Warren concurred in the majority opinion in *Butts* because he believed the actions of the *Saturday Evening Post* constituted the kind of reckless disregard discussed in *New York Times* and *Garrison*. He was most dissatisfied with Harlan's "departure from responsible journalism" standard.

The individual opinions in the two cases could be discussed at great length, but the most important doctrine to emerge from them was the Court's ruling that public figures as well as public officials must meet the actual malice test. Thus, the Court had begun the process of deciding which classes of plaintiffs must meet the actual malice test that provided substantial protection to media organizations. It was only a matter of time before the Court, as it had hinted a number of times before, considered extending such protection to the discussion of public issues as well as public figures.

Between *New York Times* in 1964 and *Butts* and *Walker* in 1967, the Supreme Court had made it clear that it was willing to review aggressively the decisions by juries and the efforts of lower courts to interpret the new constitutional standards in libel cases. Although the Court sometimes expressed much impatience with lower court efforts to apply the new standards, it recognized that states still needed a certain amount of discretion in deciding such cases. The Court was heading toward the high-water mark of constitutional protection for media organizations when covering news events and defending libel suits, but that road was not always smooth. The Court was willing to leave undisturbed a verdict that exemplified the vagueness of some of the standards and the trouble the lower courts had in applying them.

On July 18, 1969 the United States Court of Appeals for the Second Circuit affirmed the decision of a federal district court to award former presidential candidate and United States Senator Barry Goldwater one dollar in compensatory damages and $75,000 in punitive damages against Ralph Ginzburg and *Fact Magazine*.[50] In the fall of 1964, Ginzburg, the publisher, president, and sole stockholder of *Fact Magazine*, published a special issue, "The Unconscious of a Conservative: A Special Issue on the Mind of Barry Goldwater." In two articles about Goldwater, Ginzburg strongly suggested that Goldwater was mentally unbalanced and unfit to be president. One of the articles was supposedly based on the replies of psychiatrists to questionnaires sent to them by Ginzburg. Among other questions, the survey asked the psychiatrists if they believed "Barry Goldwater is psychologically fit to serve as President of the United States?"[51] The court of appeals noted that the survey was conceived and planned by Ginzburg and his managing editor, neither of whom had training or prior experience in the techniques of polling and who had not consulted or gotten advice from any experts in the field.

There were numerous problems with the survey, not the least of which was that the psychiatrists had never personally interviewed or examined Goldwater. Throughout his testimony, Ginzburg repeatedly stated that he had no explanation for many of the statements made in the article and all but said that much of the information was false.[52] Ginzburg admitted that all statements favorable to Goldwater had been deleted and that sections of the article had been edited in such a way as to change the original meaning of the statements.

The appeals court recognized the importance of open discussion about the fitness and qualifications of presidential candidates, but it considered the *Fact Magazine* articles to be within the category of "calculated falsehood" discussed in *New York Times* that does not contribute to the exchange of ideas and discussion of important public issues. The court thought Ginzburg's actions clearly malicious:

> The district judge did not rely on a few isolated instances of derogatory statements which could be charitably thought of as being nonactionable negligent or good faith misstatements of fact, but rather upon the totality of appellants' conduct, as evidenced by the proffered materials, from which a jury might reasonably find a predetermined and preconceived plan to malign the Senator's character.[53]

Unlike *Associated Press v. Walker*, the articles about Goldwater were not "hot news," although it was clearly the intention of Ginzburg that the magazine be published before the presidential election of 1964. The court of appeals acknowledged the difference between a story like that about Goldwater and a breaking story like that in *Walker*:

> The [publishers] were very much aware of the possible resulting harm; the seriousness of the charge called for a thorough investigation but the evidence reveals only the careless utilization of slipshod and sketchy investigative techniques. . . . They persisted in their polling project despite warnings by reputable professional organizations that their techniques lacked validity. . . . This evidence, together with other facts brought out at trial established that the appellants not only knowingly published defamatory statements but also established with convincing clarity that the [publishers] were motivated by actual malice.[54]

The U.S. Supreme Court denied certiorari in 1970.[55] But Justice Black, who was joined by Justice Douglas, in an unusual dissent to the Court's decision not to hear a case, argued that the court of appeals and trial court decision in the *Goldwater* case denied to Ginzburg constitutional protection to which he was entitled:

> I firmly believe that the First Amendment guarantees to each person in this country the unconditional right to print what he pleases about public affairs. This case perhaps more than any I have seen in this area convinces me that the *New York Times* constitutional rule is wholly inadequate to assure the "uninhibited, robust, and wide-open" debate which the majority in that case thought it was guaranteeing.[56]

Black was especially concerned because the plaintiff in the libel suit had been seeking the office of president of the United States. Black strongly believed that the First Amendment granted complete immunity to those discussing persons seeking the highest office in the nation:

> In our times, the person who holds that high office has an almost unbounded power for good or evil. The public has an unqualified right to have the character and fitness of anyone who aspires to the Presidency held up for the closest scrutiny. Extravagant, reckless statements and even claims that may not be true seem to me an inevitable and perhaps essential part of the process by which the voting public informs itself of the qualities of a man who would be President.[57]

Black feared that the holding of the trial court and the court of appeals, and the Supreme Court's decision not to hear the case, would dampen political debate by persons who should feel totally free to discuss and criticize openly candidates for such high office. Black admitted that the jury was justified in determining that the publishers were guilty of actual malice in the preparation of the articles, but he believed that "the grave dangers of prohibiting or penalizing the publication of even the inaccurate and misleading information seem to me to more than outweigh any gain, personal or social, that might result from permitting libel awards such as the one before the Court today."[58]

Black found intolerable the reasoning of the jury as demonstrated by the monetary awards. Except for the one dollar awarded as compensatory damages, the monetary award was wholly punitive. To Black, the compensatory award of one dollar clearly established that Goldwater had suffered little if any actual harm as a result of the articles. For the jury, therefore, to punish Ginzburg and *Fact Magazine*, was clearly contrary to the First Amendment:

> It is bad enough when the First Amendment is violated to compensate a person who has actually suffered a provable injury as a result of libelous statements; it is incomprehensible that a person who has suffered no provable harm can recover libel damages imposed solely to punish defendants who have exercised their First Amendment rights.[59]

The Supreme Court does not normally give a reason for refusing the hear a case, and dissents to that decision, such as those of Justice Black in the *Goldwater* case, are relatively rare. It must be remembered that technically, the Supreme Court's denial of certiorari in no way means that the Court has approved the decision reached by the lower court; it simply means the Court has declined to review the case. It is likely that the Court approved of the decision of the court of appeals on the grounds that Ginzburg's behavior clearly constituted actual malice, a standard that the Court had now nurtured for six years. Yet, thinking about the breadth of the First Amendment had been influenced by such writers as Meiklejohn who believed that the freedom of speech and press provisions of the First Amendment provided special protection to "political" speech, or speech of "governing importance." Considering that Goldwater was the presidential nominee of one of the two major parties, debate about his fitness and qualifications would clearly come under a First Amendment umbrella especially protective of statements that add to public discussion of candidates for political office and that help us make intelligent decisions as citizens and voters. One could passionately argue that because of the scurrilous nature of the articles and the undisguised attempts of the authors to defame Goldwater, they abused the protection to which they would normally be entitled and therefore fell outside the ambit of constitutional protection. Yet, it must also be argued that as a presidential candidate and a U.S. senator, Goldwater enjoyed almost instant and virtually unlimited access to other channels of mass communication in which he could rebut the defamatory statements in the *Fact Magazine* articles. Few individuals enjoy better access to the news media than a nominee of one of the two major parties for president of the United States. Goldwater was clearly able not only to deflect but discredit totally the allegations made in the article. What had been true in Justice Louis Brandeis's dissent in *Whitney v. California*,[60] in 1927 was true in 1970: the answer to unpopular, distasteful, even false statements was not punishment but more debate, more discussion.[61] Goldwater could have fought back using channels of mass communication more powerful and influential than *Fact Magazine*. That he chose to pursue vindication of his reputation, to the extent it was actually damaged, in a libel suit suggests that even presidential candidates may find defamation suits and courts inviting when attempting to punish or silence those whose ideas or statements they find distasteful. The articles were hardly specimens of solid journalism, but they could have been fought and discredited in arenas other than those that have the potential to diminish vital First Amendment interests.

The Supreme Court chose not to review *Goldwater*, but it continued on a journey that would lead to its strongest endorsement of First Amendment protection in a libel case. And while the Court was at times struggling to apply the standards it had adopted in libel cases, it was still determined, for at least a few more years, to grant media organizations substantial latitude when they discuss the activities of public officials and public figures.

The Supreme Court's refusal to hear *Goldwater* did not indicate that it was having second thoughts about the public figure status of plaintiffs adopted in *Butts* and *Walker*. Just one month after the Court denied certiorari in *Goldwater*, the Court reaffirmed the public figure status of plaintiffs in *Greenbelt Cooperative Publishing Association v. Bresler*,[62] discussed in in the previous chapter. In overturning a jury award of $17,500 to a prominent real estate developer, Justice Potter Stewart held that "debate on public issues will not be uninhibited if the speaker must run the risk that it will be proved in court that he spoke out of hatred. . . . And the constitutional prohibition in this respect is no different whether the plaintiff be considered a 'public official' or a 'public figure.'"[63]

For some time the Supreme Court had recognized that individuals other than public officials would eventually face the substantial obstacle of proving that a media organization was malicious in publishing or broadcasting defamatory statements. A theme running through Court decisions addressing that issue was that, in addition to the status of the plaintiff, the nature of the controversy had some relevance to the standard of liability that would apply in a particular case. The Court suggested in a number of decisions that when discussing issues of public importance, media organizations would be entitled to broad constitutional protection. The issues of the status of the plaintiff and the nature of the controversy were related, but they raised some separate questions that would eventually create problems for the Court.

During this period, the Court continued to find ways to protect media organizations from libel suits brought by public figures, sometimes stretching precedents to fit the case at hand. On the eve of the Court's adoption of the public interest test, a decision that could be described as a dream come true for those concerned about the vitality of the First Amendment,[64] the Court considered three cases that would provide the path it needed to get from the public figure rule to the public interest test. These cases marked the end of an era in constitutional interpretation that granted substantial protection to media defendants to discuss a wide range of issues and individuals, and a beginning of the Court's decade-long effort to recalibrate the scales to provide more protection to reputation. If journalists want to point to a golden period of maximum First Amendment protection, it would be in the early months of 1971.

In *Monitor Patriot Company v. Roy*,[65] the first of three cases decided on February 24, 1971 the Court had to decide whether a newspaper could publish during a campaign a story about a candidate's criminal conduct even though that conduct had taken place twenty-six years before. Alphonse Roy was one of several individuals seeking the Democratic nomination for U.S. senator from New Hampshire. On September 10, 1960, three days before the primary, several newspapers in the state carried a syndicated column written by Drew Pearson that described some of the political "maneuvering" in the primary campaign, referred to the criminal records of several of the candidates, and characterized Roy as a "former small-time bootlegger."[66] After Roy lost the primary, he filed a libel suit against the Monitor Patriot Company, publisher of the *Concord Monitor*, in Concord, New Hampshire, and the North American Newspaper Alliance (NANA), the distributor of the column. The defendants offered truth as a defense, presenting evidence that Roy had in fact been a bootlegger during the Prohibition era, and they claimed that they had published the column in "good faith, without malice, with a reasonable belief in the probable truth of the charge, and on a lawful occasion."[67]

In instructing the jury, the trial judge said the actual malice rule of "knowledge of falsity or reckless disregard" would apply so long as the libel concerned "official conduct" as opposed to "private conduct." While holding that a candidate for public office would fall into the same constitutional category as one who already holds office, the judge questioned whether Roy's bootlegging activities of so many years before were relevant to his fitness to run in this election:

> As a candidate for the United States Senate, the plaintiff was within the public official concept, and a candidate must surrender to public scrutiny and discussion so much of his private character as affects his fitness for office. That is, anything which might touch on Alphonse Roy's fitness for the office of United States Senator would come within the concept of official conduct. If it would not touch upon or be relevant to his fitness for office for which he was a candidate but was rather a bringing forward of the plaintiff's long forgotten misconduct in which the public had no interest, then it would be a private matter in the private sector.[68]

The judge then told the jury that if it considered the defamatory statements to be within the "public sector," it must find for NANA and the newspaper because there was no evidence of actual malice. He explained that if the publication was in the private sector, the libel could be justified for two reasons: if the jury found the article was both true and published on a "lawful occasion"; and a conditional privilege, which he explained to mean that the publication was made "on a lawful occasion, in good faith, for a justifiable purpose, and with a belief founded on reasonable grounds of the truth of the matter published."[69] The judge's definition of "lawful occasion" sounded like it belonged to an era where proving the truthfulness of the statements was not enough and application of First Amendment protection was severely limited: "If the end to be attained by the publication is justifiable, that is, to give useful information to those who have a right and ought to know in order that they may act upon such information, the occasion is lawful."[70] The judge also placed the burden of showing a "lawful occasion" on the defendants. The jury awarded Roy $20,000, of which $10,000 was against the newspaper and $10,000 against NANA.[71]

In unanimously overturning the jury's award, the Supreme Court recognized that the jury in *Roy* got the case after its decisions in *New York Times* and *Garrison*, but before *Butts* and *Greenbelt*. The Court did not quibble with the judge's determination that as a candidate for the United States Senate, Roy was to be treated as a "public official." The Court noted that it would have been less confusing if the trial judge had used the term "public figure" in describing Roy, but it understood that the public figure characterization had not been clearly stated until *Butts* and *Walker*. As if to ignore the suggestions of Harlan that a different constitutional standard applied to public figures, the Court said, "It is abundantly clear that, whichever term is applied, publications concerning candidates must be accorded at least as much protection under the First and Fourteenth Amendments as those concerning occupants of public office."[72]

Because the jury returned verdicts against both the newspaper and NANA, it must have determined that the charge that Roy had been a bootlegger was in the private sector. The Court speculated that the jury also determined that the charge may have been true, but was "unjustified"—that is, that it had been published without a "lawful occasion."[73] Justice Stewart, writing for the Court, said that because such standards are "far less stringent than that of knowing falsehood or reckless disregard of the truth, the judgment must be reversed unless it can be shown that the *New York Times* rule is not applicable because of the nature of the libel in question."[74]

The First Amendment, in the Court's view, does not make such a fine distinction between public and private conduct. Referring to *Garrison*, the Court rejected the notion that criticisms of the judges' vacation and work habits constituted a personal attack on their integrity and honesty and not criticism of their official duties. The Court restated its commitment to protect discussion of the fitness and qualifications of those who seek political office:

The principal activity of a candidate in our political system, his "office," so to speak, consists in putting before the voters every conceivable aspect of his public and private life that he thinks may lead the electorate to gain a good impression of him. A candidate who, for example, seeks to further his cause through the prominent display of his wife and children can hardly argue that his qualities as a husband or father remain of "purely private" concern. And the candidate who vaunts his spotless record and sterling integrity cannot convincingly cry "Foul!" when an opponent or an industrious reporter attempts to demonstrate the contrary.[75]

The Court simply could not tolerate a standard of liability based on "relevance" instead of the maliciousness standard, which is a measure of liability based on the "care" taken by the publisher in preparing and printing the story. Such a "relevance" standard is, in the Court's view, "unlikely to be neutral with respect to the content of speech and holds a real danger of becoming an instrument for the suppression of those 'vehement, caustic, and sometimes unpleasantly sharp attacks,'" which must be protected.[76] And the Court concluded that even if Roy's misconduct happened years before, statements about it are still protected: "We therefore hold as a matter of constitutional law that a charge of criminal conduct, no matter how remote in time or place, can never be irrelevant to an official's or a candidate's fitness for office for purposes of application of the . . . rule of *New York Times v. Sullivan.*"[77]

The same day the Court handed down its decision in *Monitor Patriot v. Roy*, it also announced rulings in two other cases, *Time, Inc. v. Pape*[78] and *Ocala Star-Banner Company v. Damron.*[79] In *Pape*, the Court refused to allow a Chicago police officer to pursue a lawsuit against *Time* magazine after it discussed the results of a report issued by the U.S. Commission on Civil Rights dealing with police brutality.

The 307-page study, entitled *Justice*, included several specific examples of what the commission considered to be police brutality, naming Deputy Chief of Detectives Frank Pape as the person who had led thirteen police officers on a raid on a black couple's apartment that included mistreatment of the couple and their children:

> [It was alleged] that: Chicago police officers led by . . . Pape, broke through two doors of the Monroe apartment, woke the Monroe couple with flashlights, and forced them at gunpoint to leave their bed and stand naked in the center of the living room; that the officers roused the six Monroe children and herded them into the living room; that Detective Pape struck Mr. Monroe several times with his flashlight, calling him "nigger" and "black boy"; that another officer pushed Mrs. Monroe; that other officers hit and kicked several of the children and pushed them to the floor; that the police ransacked every room . . . that Mr. Monroe was then taken to the police station . . . [and] was interrogated about a murder.[80]

The report also said that Monroe had not been advised of his procedural rights, had not been brought before a magistrate, had not been permitted to call his family or an attorney, and eventually had been released without criminal charges having been filed against him. In *Monroe v. Pape*[81] the Supreme Court permitted Monroe to bring suit against several police officers for violation of the Federal Civil Rights Acts.

A week after the commission's report was issued, *Time* did a story that included accounts of the experiences of the Monroe family. In the words of the Supreme Court, "The *Time* article went on to quote at length from the summary of the Monroe complaint, without indicating in any way that the charges were those made by Monroe rather than independent findings of the Commission."[82]

After Pape filed a libel suit in federal court, *Time* moved to dismiss the suit on the grounds that the article was fair comment on a government report and therefore privileged under Illinois law. The district court granted the motion, but it was reversed by the U.S. Court of Appeals for the Seventh Circuit.[83] After the decision by the court of appeals, the Supreme Court handed down its decision in *New York Times*. In light of the holding in that case, the district judge again dismissed the lawsuit against *Time*, with the court of appeals again reversing that decision, holding that Pape was entitled to a chance to prove *Time* acted with actual malice.

Evidence was presented at trial, with Pape calling policemen who had participated in the Monroe raid. They all testified that nothing like the events described in the *Time* article had taken place, although it is worth noting that on January 24, 1963 a jury awarded Monroe $8,000 in the civil rights suit brought against Pape.[84] Pape did not appeal.

The author of the *Time* article testified that it was based entirely on the commission's report, and a *Time* researcher defended the article as true even though the word *alleged* was omitted in the article when describing Monroe's charges. At the close of evidence, the trial court judge granted *Time*'s motion for a directed verdict and Pape again appealed. As remarkable as it may seem, the court of appeals again reversed the district court, holding that it was for the jury to determine whether omission of the word *alleged* constituted "actual malice."

By an 8-1 vote, the Supreme Court reversed the court of appeals, holding that even though the account in *Time* had "significantly" altered the wording of the commission report,[85] it "can hardly be said that *Time* acted in reckless disregard of the truth."[86] In the discussing the way *Time* had handled the case, the Supreme Court noted that a "vast amount of what is published in the daily and periodical press purports to be descriptive of what somebody *said* rather than what anybody *did*."[87] Many news stories about government are based on "reports, speeches, press conferences and the like." The Court recognized that question of the "truth" of such indirect reports presents rather complicated problems.

It was difficult to tell from reading the commission's report if it was relaying information that it had independently confirmed or was merely passing on allegations. In one section the report said that what was to follow was "11 typical cases of police brutality," each of which "contribute[s] to an understanding of the problem," and was "substantial enough to justify discussion" in the study. But the reader was also told that these were "alleged facts," "allegations of misconduct," which had not been "determined conclusively" to be "correct."[88] Later sections of the report made it even more difficult to determine if it had made an independent investigation or was simply relying on Monroe's account.

In the Court's view, *Time*'s omission of the word *alleged* "amounted to the adoption of one of a number of possible rational interpretations of a document that bristled with ambiguities." While critical of *Time*'s reporting, the Court held that such an omission was "not enough to create a jury issue of 'malice' under *New York Times*."[89] But media organizations should not read the Court's opinion in *Pape* as an endorsement of such reporting practices, particularly in view of the Court's cautionary note concluding its opinion:

> Nothing in this opinion is to be understood as making the word "alleged" a superfluity in published reports of information damaging to reputation. Our decision today is based on the specific facts of this case, involving as they do a news report of a particular government publication. ... [But] neither lies nor false communications serve the ends of the First Amendment, and no one suggests their desirability or further proliferation. But to insure the ascertainment and publication of the truth about public affairs, it is essential that the First Amendment protect some erroneous publications as well as true ones.[90]

Justice Harlan dissented, warning that the Supreme Court's decision in *Pape* put the Court in the position of reviewing not just jury instructions or questions of law but factual disputes as well. He urged self-restraint if the Court did not want to find itself overwhelmed by such cases:

> While it is true, of course, that this Court is free to reexamine for itself the evidentiary bases upon which rest decisions that allegedly impair or punish the exercise of Fourteenth Amendment freedoms, this does not mean that we are of necessity always, or even usually, compelled to do so. Indeed, it is almost impossible to conceive how this Court might continue to function effectively were we to resolve afresh the underlying factual disputes in all cases containing constitutional issues.[91]

Harlan recognized that the Court was not intentionally inviting libel suits in which it could take over the fact-finding function of juries, but was concerned that "what is done today may open a door that will prove difficult to close."[92] He would have affirmed the judgment of the court of appeals.

The door remained open at least long enough to announce the decision in one more case on that day in February 1971. *Ocala Star-Banner v. Damron*[93] was a fairly complicated case involving an editor who questioned the accuracy of a reporter's story, and it gave the Supreme Court a chance to cite *Monitor Patriot*, announced the same day, in defending a newspaper's right to discuss a public official and a candidate for office even when it made a serious mistake in doing so.

The *Ocala Star-Banner*, a small newspaper in rural Florida, published a story to the effect that Leonard Damron, then the mayor of Crystal River and a candidate for county tax assessor, had been charged in a federal court with perjury. The only problem was that it was not Leonard Damron who had been charged with perjury, but his brother James. Apparently the reporter's story, which had been "substantially accurate," had been changed by a new editor who had run several stories about Leonard, but had never heard of James. Assuming that the reporter had made an error, the editor changed the name in the story, an act the newspaper called "a mental aberration."[94]

Despite the newspaper's printing of two retractions before the election, Leonard Damron lost the race for county tax assessor. He sued, asking for $50,000 in compensatory damages and $500,000 in punitive damages. The judge instructed the jury, which eventually awarded Damron compensatory damages of $22,000 but no punitive damages, that the *New York Times* standard did not apply because the article was not about Leonard Damron's political career. In denying the newspaper's motion for a new trial, the judge held that *New York Times* and later cases "relating to public officials or public figures in the official conduct of their office or position are not applicable to this cause of action which was founded upon a newspaper publication of the Defendants which was libelous per se and made no reference to the public offices held or sought by the Plaintiff."[95]

The Florida District Court of Appeal affirmed the judgment on the grounds that the plaintiff's official conduct was not the basis for the inaccuracies in the article and, "hence, it does not come within the protection afforded by the rule announced in the *New York Times* case. It follows therefore that the trial judge correctly held that it was unnecessary for the plaintiff to show malice."[96] The Florida Supreme Court refused to review the case.

The Supreme Court unanimously reversed the decision on the grounds that Damron was "without question" a public official within the meaning of the term in *New York Times*, and thus must meet the actual malice standard.[97] The judge had told the jury it should decide only the issue of damages, and Damron was permitted to recover without a finding that the newspaper either knew the article was false or recklessly disregarded whether it was false or not. In citing *Monitor Patriot v. Roy*, the Court reiterated that a charge of criminal conduct against an official or candidate, no matter how remote in time or place, is always "relevant to his fitness for office" for purposes of applying the *New York Times* rule. The Court concluded by holding that "under any test we can conceive, the charge that a local mayor and candidate for county elective post has been indicted for perjury in a civil rights suit is relevant to his fitness for office."[98]

In concurring in the Court's judgment, Justice White criticized the lack of care exercised by the newspaper, writing that the "First Amendment is not . . . construed . . . to award merit badges for intrepid but mistaken or careless reporting. Misinformation has no merit in itself; standing alone it is as antithetical to the purposes of the First Amendment as the calculated lie."[99] White admitted that forcing public officials and public figures to meet the strict "actual malice" standard will "result in extending constitutional protection to lies and falsehoods which, though neither knowing or reckless, do severe damage to personal reputation."[100]

Although clearly a victory for the First Amendment, the case may have tested the patience of the Court when dealing with errors made by journalists. The newspaper admitted during the trial that the story was "wholly false" as to the respondent, and explained the error as the result of a "mental aberration" of one of the editors. The Court majority did not discuss the issue in any detail and there was no suggestion that it would now allow evidence of such mental lapses to defeat libel suits. Nevertheless, the case demonstrated the lengths to which the Court would go during this period to excuse "innocent" errors on the part of journalists.

By 1971 media organizations could look to Supreme Court decisions in libel cases with increasing approval. In the few years since 1964 the Court, after being silent as to the appropriate standards in libel cases for many years, truly revolutionized libel laws and provided strict instructions to the states as to what procedures and standards they must follow when handling libel cases involving public officials and public figures. And the Court had proved, particularly from 1967 to 1971, that it was willing to enforce its standards by vigorously reviewing state and federal court libel decisions. By 1971 it was clear that any public official and individual who could be considered a public figure would have a very difficult time collecting damages against media defendants.

Although the Court had shown during this period some impatience with the sometimes sloppy practices of media organizations, and dissenters in some cases criticized the standards in the *New York Times*, *Butts*, and *Walker* decisions, or at least the way the standards were applied, a plurality of the Court was still determined to provide journalists with substantial First Amendment protection in discussing not only certain types of individuals, but certain issues as well. Yet, the decision in *Rosenbloom v. Metromedia* demonstrated that the Court was becoming increasingly divided over how the competing societal interests should be balanced, and it would not be long before the reputational side would receive a significant amount of the Court's favor.

The Public Interest Test:
A Badly Divided Court

Decided June 7, 1971, only a few months after the Court's trio of pro-First Amendment libel decisions in *Monitor Patriot*, *Pape*, and *Ocala Star-Banner* were announced, *Rosenbloom v. Metromedia*[101] badly splintered the Court and brought to a head many difficult issues that the Court knew it would have to consider if there was to be an appropriate balancing of these vital, yet often competing, societal interests.

As mentioned before, the Court had suggested for a number of years that the nature of the controversy, not just the status of the plaintiff, would be relevant in deciding the standard of liability in libel cases. The Court had interpreted the First Amendment as protecting and encouraging wide-open discussion of public issues and preventing interference with the exchange of information that the public needs if it is to make intelligent decisions as citizens and voters. Having committed itself to the proposition that the First Amendment protects discussion of certain ideas in which the public has an interest, the Court found itself in a difficult position as it tried to cope with the issues in *Rosenbloom*. The decision in the case signaled more than the deep divisions among members of the Court on libel; it marked the end of what some might have called the "golden age" of the First Amendment when journalists were given maximum latitude and protection to report news events and defend any libel suits brought by those who were unhappy with the way they had been portrayed in news stories. After *Rosenbloom*, with a change in not only membership of the Court but attitude toward the press, journalists found the Court's pronouncements on libel increasingly hostile to their interests and more accommodating and encouraging to those suing media organizations.

The case is especially interesting because it involved a radio station whose news department probably thought it was reporting an almost routine news story, but ended up causing a major constitutional storm. As part of a police crackdown on the sale and distribution of pornography, George Rosenbloom, whose occupation could be described as that of selling "nudist magazines," was arrested along with about twenty newsstand operators on charges of selling obscene materials. The police had not been looking for Rosenbloom, but as they were making an arrest at one of the newsstands, Rosenbloom showed up to deliver his magazines. A few days later the police searched Rosenbloom's home and a rented barn he used as a warehouse and seized the materials found at those locations.

When Rosenbloom, who had been released on bail, heard that his home and barn had been searched, he surrendered to police and was arrested for a second time. Captain Ferguson, who was part of the Philadelphia Police Department's Special Investigations Squad, called Metromedia's WIP Radio and another local radio station, a wire service, and a local newspaper to inform them of the raid on Rosenbloom's properties and his arrest.[102] WIP, which broadcast news reports every half hour to the Philadelphia metropolitan area, had this story on its 6:00 p.m. newscast on October 4, 1963:

City Cracks Down on Smut Merchants

The Special Investigations Squad raided the home of George Rosenbloom in the 1800 block of Vesta Street this afternoon. Police confiscasted 1,000 allegedly obscene books at Rosenbloom's home and arrested him on charges of possession of obscene literature. The ... Squad also raided a barn in the 20 Hundred block of Welsh Road near Bustleton Avenue and confiscated 3,000 obscene books. Captain Ferguson says he believes they have hit the supply of a main distributor of obscene material in Philadelphia.[103]

The report was broadcast again at 6:30 p.m. in "substantially the same form"; at 8:00 p.m. the third sentence was changed to read "reportedly obscene." News of Rosenbloom's arrest was broadcast five more times in the following twelve hours, but each time the seized books were described as "allegedly" or "reportedly" obscene. A week later Rosenbloom filed suit against several media organizations, not including WIP Radio, saying that the magazines that he distributed were not obscene and asking for an injunction restraining the police from further interfering with his business.[104] WIP broadcast ten reports over several days on Rosenbloom's lawsuit, although not mentioning him by name:

Federal District Judge Lord, will hear arguments today from two publishers and a distributor all seeking an injunction against Philadelphia Police Commissioner Howard Leary ... District Attorney James C. Crumlish ... a local television station and a newspaper ... ordering them to lay off the smut literature racket.

The girlie-book peddlers say the police crackdown and continued reference to their borderline literature as smut or filth is hurting their business.[105]

A few days later Rosenbloom, after being told by a friend that WIP had done a news report about him, had a brief conversation with a member of the news department over the radio station's lobby telephone. Rosenbloom contended that the magazines were not obscene, and the newsperson apparently told him that they had been informed by the district attorney that they were. Rosenbloom later testified that the conversation ended abruptly at that point.

In May of 1964, Rosenbloom was acquitted of criminal obscenity charges under instructions of the trial judge that the nudist magazines distributed by him were not legally obscene. He then filed a libel suit in federal court against WIP, claiming that WIP's unqualified characterization of the books seized as "obscene" in the first broadcast constituted libel *per se* and was proved to be false when Rosenbloom was acquitted of obscenity charges. He also claimed that the subsequent broadcasts defamed him and his associates by describing them as "smut distributors" and "girlie-book peddlers."

The jury returned a verdict for Rosenbloom and awarded him $25,000 in general damages and $725,000 in punitive damages. The district court reduced the punitive damages to $250,000.[106] WIP had argued at trial that its news department received the information from official sources, namely, Captain Ferguson, and because of the time pressure involved in putting frequent newscasts on the air, apparently did not seek additional verification.[107]

The United States Court of Appeals for the Third Circuit reversed the judgment, emphasizing that the broadcasts were about matters of public interest and that they involved "hot news" prepared under deadline pressure. The court of appeals concluded that "the fact that plaintiff was not a public figure cannot be accorded decisive importance if the recognized important guarantees of the First Amendment are to be adequately implemented."[108] For that reason, it held that the *New York Times* actual malice standard did apply to the case, and because Rosenbloom had failed to show reckless disregard, it ordered that a judgment be entered for Metromedia.[109]

Rosenbloom conceded that police efforts to enforce obscenity laws were matters of public interest. But he claimed that because he was not a public official or public figure but a private individual, he was obligated to meet the standards in force under Pennsylvania libel laws, namely, that Metromedia had failed to exercise reasonable care in preparing the reports.[110]

By a 5-3 vote the Supreme Court sustained the judgment of the court of appeals, but the justices offered many reasons for the decision. Five opinions were written, and there were as many justices dissenting, three, as there were signing the plurality opinion written by Justice William Brennan. The Court was badly divided over the issues in the case, but all of the eight justices participating did recommend that more protection of varying degree be given statements about private individuals than was available under many state libel laws and the old standard of "strict liability."[111] The dissenters were unwilling, however, to require private individuals caught up in matters of public interest to meet the actual malice test. Yet the dissenters, too, thought that the First Amendment side should be enhanced by arguing that the authority of the states to award damages should be tied to the standard of liability used in the case.

Brennan's lead opinion, which was joined by Chief Justice Warren Burger and Justice Harry Blackmun, reasoned that the Constitution "places in private hands vast areas of economic and social power that vitally affect the nature and quality of life in the Nation."[112] Freedom of speech and press are not limited to political expression but embrace "all issues about which information is needed or appropriate to enable the members of society to cope with the exigencies of their period." Brennan quoted the concurring opinion of Chief Justice Warren in *Curtis Publishing Company*, which stated that the distinctions between the governmental and private sectors are blurred and that individuals who do not hold public office are "nevertheless intimately involved in the resolution of important public questions."[113] Brennan held that the public is primarily interested in the event, and not the participant's status:

> If a matter is a subject of public or general interest, it cannot suddenly become less so merely because a private individual is involved, or because in some sense the individual did not "voluntarily" choose to become involved. The public's primary interest is in the event; the public focus is on the conduct of the participant and the content, effect, and significance of the conduct, not the partipant's prior anonymity or notoriety.[114]

Brennan cited as an example the *Walker* case by saying that the public's interest in that issue, namely, the integration of a university and the violence that was taking place at the time, would not have been any less if "the speaker had been an anonymous student and not a well-known retired Army general."[115] To Brennan, the *Walker* case showed how impracticable it is to tie the standard of liability to the status of the plaintiff, for in *Walker* the general's fame stemmed from events completely unrelated to the incidents at the University of Mississippi. Brennan argued that "it seems particularly unsatisfactory to determine the extent of First Amendment protection on the basis of factors completely unrelated to the newsworthy events being reported."[116] As the author of the Court's famous *New York Times* decision, Brennan's reaffirming the commitment announced in that case had special significance in *Rosenbloom*: "We honor the commitment to robust debate on public issues, which is embodied in the First Amendment, by extending constitutional protection to all discussion and communication involving matters of public or general concern, without regard to whether the persons involved are famous or anonymous."[117]

Brennan recognized the reluctance of those, including Justice White as expressed in his concurring opinion, who would not extend such blanket protection to issues of public or general concern. White believed it was unnecessary in the *Rosenbloom* case to make such broad changes. *Rosenbloom* involved the official actions of police and the public's interest in such actions by public officials is especially keen. As will be seen, White concurred on the grounds that a police arrest of a person for distributing allegedly obscene literature did constitute an issue of public interest. Brennan understood White's hesitancy to extend such protection to any issue considered of public importance, but rejected such a narrow interpretation, writing that "we think the time has come forthrightly to announce that the determinant whether the First Amendment applied to state libel actions is whether the utterance involved concerns an issue of public or general concern, albeit leaving the delineation of the reach of that term to future cases."[118] Brennan quickly added that there will be issues and activities that are not within the area of public or general interest, but that the Court was intentionally leaving that question for future decisions.

Rosenbloom had argued that as a private person he did not thrust himself into the public controversy, and that he did not have access to media organizations to counter the defamatory statements and vindicate his reputation. Brennan rejected such arguments, holding that the *New York Times* standard is designed to encourage discussion of public issues and that public officials have just as much interest in protecting their reputations as do private persons.

Brennan also turned aside Rosenbloom's argument that as a private person he was much less able to protect himself. Brennan held that although some very prominent people may have such excellent access to media organizations that they can counter attacks upon their character, for most people the argument is not relevant. It is very rare, said Brennan, for the denial to "overtake the original charge"; denials, retractions, and corrections are not "hot" news and do not receive the prominence of the original story. In some cases, the public official holds a minor position, and in some, like *Rosenblatt v. Baer*, the public official who was the subject of a defamatory story had already left the official position, thus lessening the chances that the media would be interested in his efforts to rebut the defamation. To Brennan the suggestion that there is a class of "public figures" involved in matters of public concern that is better able than private individuals to respond through the media "seems too insubstantial a reed on which to rest a constitutional distinction."[119] Without indicating just how complicated a suggestion it was, Brennan added that if the states were concerned that private citizens would not be able to respond adequately to publicity involving them, "the solution lies in the direction of ensuring their ability to respond, rather than in stifling public discussion of matters of public concern."[120]

Brennan, writing in 1971, had no way of knowing that just a few years later, in *Gertz v. Welch*,[121] one of the most important libel cases ever decided by the Supreme Court, the majority would grant constitutional status to the argument that private individuals need special protection because they do not enjoy access to media attention to rebut defamatory statements. The majority in *Gertz* would also reject another of Brennan's arguments. In *Rosenbloom* he claimed that it was a "legal fiction" to assume that certain public figures had "voluntarily exposed their entire lives to public inspection, while private individuals have kept theirs carefully shrouded from public view." And Brennan seemed to know what would happen if the Court followed that road:

Such a distinction could easily produce the paradoxical result of dampening discussion of issues of public or general concern because they happen to involve private citizens while extending constitutional encouragement to discussion of aspects of the lives of "public figures" that are not in the area of public or general concern.[122]

The Court did not heed his warning and in subsequent libel cases, traveled down the very path that Brennan had warned would lead to the morass in which the Court finds itself today.

Justice White, whose concurring opinion was mentioned before, surveyed the attitudes of his brethren and concluded that five of his colleagues would support the following rules:

For public officers and public figures to recover for damage to their reputations for libelous falsehoods, they must prove either knowing or reckless disregard of the truth. All other plaintiffs must prove at least negligent falsehood, but if the publication about them was in an area of legitimate public interest, then they too must prove deliberate or reckless error. In all actions for libel or slander, actual damages must be proved, and awards of punitive damages will be strictly limited.[123]

White was unable to join Brennan's opinion because, in his view, it displaced more state libel law than was necessary for the decision in the *Rosenbloom* case. The dissenters, Justices Harlan, Marshall, and Stewart, found Brennan's opinion unacceptable on several fronts. For various reasons they held that the public issue standard provided insufficient protection to either the press or the individual whose reputation had been harmed. Justice Marshall, who was joined in part of his opinion by Harlan and in total by Stewart, argued that lower courts, and ultimately the Supreme Court, would have to determine if events are of legitimate public interest. But he doubted that courts could or should make those decisions. Under Brennan's rule, "Courts are not simply to take a poll to determine whether a substantial portion of the population is interested or concerned in a subject, courts will be required to somehow pass on the legitimacy of interest in a public event or subject; what information is relevant to self-government."[124] Marshall thought that the danger in such a doctrine seemed "apparent."

Marshall was also concerned that because all human events are arguably within the area of "public or general concern," society's interest in protecting private individuals from being thrust into the public eye was also threatened. He anticipated that the Court would be involved in a constant and continuing supervision of defamation litigation throughout the country if it were required to "weigh the nuances of each particular circumstance on its scale of values regarding the relative importance of society's interest in protecting individuals from defamation against the importance of a free press."[125]

Marshall was also alarmed at the potential for huge damage awards, and the ability of juries to punish those whose ideas are unorthodox or unpopular. In his view, the self-censorship that results from the award of punitive damages requires an accommodation between freedom of the press and the ability of individuals to be compensated for damage to their reputation:

> I believe that the appropriate resolution of the clash of societal values here is to restrict damages to actual losses. Of course, damages can be awarded for more than direct pecuniary loss but they must be related to some proved harm. If awards are so limited in cases involving private individuals—persons first brought to public attention by the defamation that is the subject of the law-suit—it will be unnecessary to . . . engage in ad hoc balancing of the competing interests involved. States would be essentially free to continue the evolution of the common law of defamation and to articulate whatever fault standard best suits the State's need.[126]

Marshall did add that the old standard of "strict liability," imposing liability without fault, is inconsistent with the concepts of freedom of the press. He would have remanded the case to determine if Rosenbloom could show any actual loss.

The issue of damages did not concern Justice Harlan to the same degree. If the standard of care required is appropriately adjusted to take account of the "special countervailing interests in an open exchange of ideas," the fact that compensation for the harm that publishers have caused may involve substantial sums of money cannot "plausibly be said to raise serious First Amendment problems."[127] Even though he recognized that the awarding of punitive damages could induce self-censorship, Harlan would allow punitive damages if the "amount awarded bears a reasonable and purposeful relationship to the actual harm done."[128]

Harlan also argued that private individuals should be treated differently from public officials and public figures. "I would not construe the federal constitution to require that the States adhere to a standard other than that of reasonable care where the plaintiff is an ordinary citizen."[129] Harlan would not overrule *New York Times* or *Curtis Publishing Company*, but he felt that neither case was applicable in *Rosenbloom*. Disagreeing with Brennan's plurality opinion, Harlan wrote that private persons did need special protection: "For me, it does seem quite clear that the public person has a greater likelihood of securing access to channels of communication sufficient to rebut falsehoods concerning him than do private individuals in this country who do not toil in the public spotlight."[130]

Harlan's concern for private individuals was not idle talk. In *Gertz* the Court majority expressed many of the same sentiments in trying to recalibrate a scale that, in the Court's view, had come to unfairly favor First Amendment interests. Harlan was no longer on the Court when those decisions were made, but his views were certainly influential.

The public interest test had been adopted, but its impact would be short-lived. It had been the result of seven years of Supreme Court efforts to define the appropriate standards that would balance First Amendment and reputational interests. It alarmed some members of the Court because in their view, the test granted too little protection to private persons seeking to recover for damage to their reputation, and others were concerned that because almost any issue could be considered a matter of public interest, the test could not be generally applied as a balance between the interests in protecting individuals from defamation and the interests in protecting freedom of the press. If all issues are a matter of public interest, then the test becomes useless as a constitutional standard.

Nevertheless, *Rosenbloom* marked the end of a seven-year period when the Supreme Court went from virtual silence on these important issues to an active role that resulted in progressively pro-First Amendment decisions. But the Court had become alarmed over the amount of protection granted to media defendants in libel suits, and it had a chance a few years later to provide additional protection to individuals attempting to recover damages in libel suits by giving constitutional status to one more category of plaintiffs in libel cases, the private person. Although the Court left substantial discretion to the states to determine the standard of liability in cases involving private persons, and issued opinions that primarily favored reputational interests, there were some bright spots about which journalists could feel positive. But in leaving so much discretion to the states, the Supreme Court subjected precious First Amendment rights to interpretation by fifty state court systems, some of which seemed unable to understand or seemed impatient with the First Amendment claims of journalists when defending libel suits.

Notes

1. The allegedly libelous statements appeared in an editorial in the *New York Daily News* on 2 September 1961. It read in part:

    > For years, a couple of semi-prominent American loudmouths have been agitating against nuclear weapons and weapon tests—the best defense the West has against Soviet Russia and Chinese Red Manpower.

    > The pair are Linus Pauling, a California biochemist who once won a Nobel Prize, and Norman Cousins, editor of something called the *Saturday Review*.

    > Cousins and Pauling now profess to be horrified by Khrushchev's announcement of Soviet resumption of nuclear weapon tests.

> But all that Pauling has done about it is to record a plea to his friend in the Kremlin to reconsider.
>
> . . . It's nice to have these two on the American side for once, however belatedly and lukewarmly. 335 F. 2d (1964) at 661-62 n. 1.

2. Ibid. at 659.
3. Ibid. at 671.
4. Ibid. at 662.
5. 383 U.S. 75 (1966) at 85, quoting *New York Times v. Sullivan*, 376 U.S. 254 (1964) at 283 n. 23.
6. Ibid.; emphasis in *Rosenblatt*.
7. 388 U.S. 130 (1967).
8. 385 U.S. 374 (1967).
9. Ibid. at 379.
10. Ibid. at 387-88.
11. Ibid. at 388.
12. Harry Kalven, Jr., "The Reasonable Man and the First Amendment: Hill, Butts, and Walker," *Supreme Court Review* (1967): 280.
13. 388 U.S. 130 (1967).
14. Ibid. at 136.
15. Ibid.
16. *Saturday Evening Post*, 23 March 1963, p. 80.
17. Ibid.
18. Ibid., p. 82; emphasis in original.
19. Ibid.
20. 388 U.S. at 137-38.
21. Ibid. at 138.
22. Ibid. at 137.
23. Ibid. at 139.
24. 351 F. 2d at 719, in 388 U.S. at 139.
25. 388 U.S. at 154-55.
26. Ibid. at 155.
27. Ibid. at 156 n. 20.
28. Ibid. at 157.
29. Ibid. at 157-58.
30. Ibid. at 159.
31. Ibid. at 159-60.
32. Ibid. at 161.
33. Ibid. at 163.
34. Ibid. at 163-64.
35. Ibid. at 167.
36. Ibid. Warren also noted that the same law firm that had represented the *New York Times* when it fought the lawsuit filed by L.B. Sullivan and others in the state courts was also involved in the *Curtis Publishing Company* case. The trial in *Butts* had taken place before the Court's decision in *New York Times* was handed down, although it had already announced that it would review the *New York Times* case. Warren believed that counsel for Curtis Publishing Company was certainly familiar with the *New York Times* case and that failure to raise the issue of the "actual malice" test was not sufficient grounds for forcing Butts to go through another trial:

> Lead counsel in the cases conferred periodically, and one of the members of the Alabama law firm [that represented the *New York Times*]... sat at the counsel table throughout this trial. The same Alabama law firm was retained to represent petitioner [Curtis Publishing Company] in a lawsuit filed by Coach Paul Bryant, who was also libeled by the magazine article here in question. First Amendment defenses were raised both at the trial of the *New York Times* case and by the pleadings in the Bryant lawsuit, which was settled for a substantial amount of money. But counsel did not raise such defenses here. Given the importance of the case to petitioner and the interplay between overlapping counsel aligned on the same sides of related lawsuits, I can only conclude that tactical or public relations considerations explain the failure here to defend on First Amendment grounds. 388 U.S. at 168.

37. Ibid. at 170.
38. Ibid. at 171.
39. Ibid. Justices Brennan and White dissented in *Curtis Publishing Company* largely on procedural grounds. They agreed that the evidence in the case "unmistakably would support a judgment for Butts under the *New York Times* standard," but would remand the case for a new trial "since the charge to the jury did not comport with that standard." Specifically, Brennan and White were concerned that the instructions to the jury allowed the awarding of compensatory damages on a "finding of mere falsehood." And the judge also had told the jury that punitive damages could be awarded on a finding of actual malice, which he defined to encompass "the notion of ill-will, spite, hatred and an intent to injure one," and also to include "a wanton or reckless indifference or culpable negligence with regard to the rights of others." Ibid. at 172-73. Those instructions were significantly different from the actual malice test that the Supreme Court had adopted, and Brennan and White would have ordered another trial to make certain that the jury believed the *New York Times* standard was satisfied.
40. As will be seen in a later chapter, a recent study done by the Libel Defense Resource Center indicated that as many as eight or nine out of ten libel cases decided by juries are won by plaintiffs.
41. Clifton O. Lawhorne, *The Supreme Court and Libel* (Carbondale: Southern Illinois University Press, 1981), pp. 50-51.
42. Ibid., p. 50.
43. Ibid., p. 51.
44. 388 U.S. at 141.
45. Ibid. at 142; emphasis in original.
46. Ibid. at 142.
47. Ibid. at 158.
48. Ibid. at 159.
49. Ibid. at 165.
50. 414 F. 2d 324 (1969); 261 F. Supp. 784 (S.D.N.Y.) 1966.
51. 414 F. 2d at 329. According to the story, the questionnaire had been sent to 12,356 psychiatrists and 2,417 of them responded. Of the those, 571 said they did not know enough about Senator Goldwater to answer the question; 657 answered yes, that they thought Senator Goldwater was psychologically fit to serve as president; and 1,189 answered no, in the belief that he was not. The court also noted that 1,749 out of the 2,417 responses were unsigned. Ibid. at 334.

52. Ibid. at 331-35.
53. Ibid. at 337.
54. Ibid. at 339-40.
55. 396 U.S. 1049 (1970).
56. Ibid. at 1050-51.
57. Ibid. at 1051-52.
58. Ibid. at 1052.
59. Ibid. at 105-53.
60. 274 U.S. 357 (1927).
61. In a concurring opinion joined by Justice Holmes, Brandeis wrote:
    > Those who won our independence by revolution were not cowards.
    > They did not fear political change. They did not exalt order at the cost
    > of liberty. To courageous, self-reliant men, with confidence in the
    > power of free and fearless reasoning applied through the processes of
    > popular government, no danger flowing from speech can be deemed
    > clear and present, unless the incidence of the evil apprehended is so
    > imminent that it may befall before there is opportunity for full discus-
    > sion. If there be time to expose through discussion the falsehood and
    > fallacies, to avert the evil by the processes of education, the remedy to
    > be applied is more speech, not enforced silence. Ibid. at 377.
62. 398 U.S. 6 (1970).
63. Ibid. at 10-11. The Court, recognizing that Bresler was also a member of the
    state legislature, focused on Bresler as a "public figure" and did not consider the
    issue of his being a state legislator to be relevant:
    > Whether as a state legislator representing another county, or for some
    > other reason, Bresler was a "public official" within the meaning of the
    > *New York Times* rule is a question we need not determine. . . . For the
    > instructions to the jury in this case permitted a finding of liability under
    > an impermissible constitutional standard, whichever status Bresler
    > might be considered to occupy. Ibid. at 9.
64. *Rosenbloom v. Metromedia*, 403 U.S. 29 (1971).
65. 401 U.S. 265 (1971).
66. Ibid. at 266.
67. Ibid. at 268.
68. Ibid. at 269.
69. Ibid. at 269-70.
70. Ibid. at 269 n. 2.
71. Ibid. at 270.
72. Ibid. at 271.
73. Ibid. at 272.
74. Ibid.
75. Ibid. at 274.
76. Ibid. at 277; the phrase is from *New York Times v. Sullivan*, 376 U.S. at 270.
77. 401 U.S. at 277.
78. Ibid. at 279.
79. Ibid. at 295.
80. Ibid. at 280-81.
81. 365 U.S. 167 (1961).
82. 401 U.S. at 282.
83. 318 F. 2d 652. The district court and the court of appeals were in agreement that
    Pape was a "public official" by virtue of his position as deputy chief of detec-

tives of the Chicago Police Department, and that the "charges contained in the Monroe complaint, the Justice report, and the Time story concerned his 'official conduct.'" The two courts differed only in their application of the rule of *New York Times v. Sullivan.* 401 U.S. at 284.

84. 401 U.S. at 283.
85. Ibid. at 285.
86. Ibid. at 292.
87. Ibid. at 285; emphasis in original.
88. Ibid. at 287-88.
89. Ibid. at 290.
90. Ibid. at 292; quoting *St. Amant v. Thompson,* 390 U.S. 727 (1968) at 732.
91. Ibid. at 294.
92. Ibid.
93. Ibid. at 295.
94. Ibid. at 297.
95. Ibid. at 298.
96. Ibid. at 299.
97. Ibid.
98. Ibid at 301.
99. Ibid.
100. Ibid.
101. 403 U.S. 29 (1971).
102. Ibid. at 33.
103. Ibid.
104. Ibid. at 34.
105. Ibid. at 34-35.
106. Ibid. at 40.
107. Ibid. at 37.
108. 415 F. 2d at 896; 403 U.S. at 40.
109. 403 U.S. at 40.
110. Ibid. at 40-41.
111. Justice Douglas took no part in the case.
112. 403 U.S. at 41.
113. Ibid. at 42; quoting *Curtis Publishing Company v. Butts,* 388 U.S. at 163-64.
114. 403 U.S. at 43.
115. Ibid., n. 11.
116. Ibid.
117. Ibid. at 43-44.
118. Ibid. at 44-45.
119. Ibid. at 46-47.
120. Ibid. at 47.
121. 418 U.S. 323 (1974).
122. 403 U.S. at 48.
123. Ibid. at 59.
124. Ibid. at 79.
125. Ibid. at 81.
126. Ibid. at 86.
127. Ibid. at 67.
128. Ibid. at 75.
129. Ibid. at 69.
130. Ibid. at 70.

5

Recalibrating the Scales:
The Private Person

In a system of government that both appreciates and fears the awesome power granted to the judiciary, judges have felt substantial pressure to avoid constant tampering with the Constitution. Courts often attempt to decide questions of law on other than purely constitutional grounds.[1] Such self-restraint or deference to other branches of government is particularly difficult for courts in cases involving individuals who are suing media organizations for libel. The issues raised in such cases invariably involve compelling First Amendment interests that the courts have a responsibility to consider. When disputes involve the information process by which we govern ourselves, judges cannot watch from the sidelines and assume the political process will provide an appropriate balancing of the various interests.[2]

At the same time it is important that constitutional interpretation have some structure and uniformity. Constant reinterpretation of vital constitutional provisions can diminish the psychological legitimacy that the courts need to gain acceptance of and compliance with their decisions. The principle of following precedents has provided much of that stability. Yet in libel such stability seems to be missing. The Supreme Court apparently decided that the Constitution meant one thing in the period 1964 to 1971, but something very different after 1974. A change in membership of the Court partially explains its changing attitude in libel cases, but does not free the justices from the responsibility of providing guidance to those in society who are responsible for informing the public and who desperately need to know what the rules are.[3] When courts interpret the First Amendment, they must avoid ad hoc tampering that sometimes appears to be less related to principles that have developed over a period of time than to the undisguised personal opinions of the justices.

Clearly, the libel decisions from 1974 to the present reflect more than a change in the membership of the Supreme Court. The justices had become increasingly alarmed that the first seven years of activity in libel had provided so much protection to media defendants in libel suits that individuals had been all but stripped of means by which they could be compensated for damage to their reputations. The public interest test in *Rosenbloom v. Metromedia*[4] seemed to require that all but a few individuals would have to meet the strict standard of actual malice if they were to win a libel suit. The plurality in *Rosenbloom* provided an expansive definition of which issues would be considered a matter of public interest and which individuals caught up in such issues would have to meet the *New York Times* test.

But the Court's recent libel decisions reflect more than just an effort to recalibrate a scale it considered to be out of whack; they demonstrate substantial hostility to the role of journalists in our society and contain phrases that make little effort to disguise the impatience with which the Court views the First Amendment assertions of the news media.

Three years after *Rosenbloom*, the Supreme Court handed down what could be considered, after *New York Times v. Sullivan*, its most important libel decision, a case that is second to none in complexity. *Gertz v. Welch*,[5] decided on June 25, 1974 by a closely divided Court, changed the libel laws of all fifty states and ushered in an era in which journalists could legitimately claim that they do not know in advance what kind of mistakes would subject them to potentially huge libel judgments. Yet *Gertz* also provided those concerned about the First Amendment with a number of provisions about which they could feel positive, although subsequent application of those provisions has dampened their spirits.

After Chicago policeman Richard Nuccio shot and killed seventeen-year-old Ronald Nelson, Elmer Gertz, a prominent attorney, was retained by the family of the youth to bring a civil suit against the policeman. Nuccio had been convicted of second degree murder in the case.[6] Robert Welch was the publisher of *American Opinion*, a monthly magazine of the John Birch Society. For some time the magazine had been concerned about what it considered to be a nationwide effort to discredit law enforcement agencies and "create in their stead a national police force capable of supporting a Communist dictatorship."[7]

In March 1969, the magazine published an article about the case under the title "FRAME-UP: Richard Nuccio And The War On Police." The article stated that testimony against Nuccio at his criminal trial was false and that his prosecution was part of the Communist campaign against the police.[8] Gertz, in a capacity as a lawyer representing the Nelson family, had attended the coroner's inquest into the boy's death and had initiated the civil suit for damages, but had played no part in the criminal proceeding against Nuccio.

The article in *American Opinion* portrayed Gertz as an "architect of the 'frame-up,'" stating that he had been an official in the "Marxist League for

Industrial Democracy, originally known as the Intercollegiate Socialist Society, which has advocated the violent seizure of our government."[9] The article labeled Gertz as a "Leninist" and a "Communist-fronter." It also said that Gertz had been an officer of the National Lawyers Guild, described as a Communist organization that "probably did more than any other outfit to plan the Communist attack on the Chicago police during the 1968 Democratic Convention."[10]

The Supreme Court noted that the statements in the article contained serious inaccuracies. The implication in the article that Gertz had a criminal record was false. He had been a member and officer of the National Lawyers Guild some fifteen years earlier, the Court noted, but there was no evidence that Gertz or the organization had taken any part in planning the 1968 demonstrations in Chicago. There was also no basis, the Court said, for the charge that Gertz was a "Leninist" or a "Communist-fronter," and he had never been a member of the "Marxist League for Industrial Democracy" or the "Intercollegiate Socialist Society."[11]

Gertz filed a libel suit in the United States District Court for the Northern District of Illinois. He asserted that the falsehoods published by Welch injured his reputation as a lawyer and citizen. Welch filed a pretrial motion for summary judgment, arguing that Gertz was a public official or a public figure and that the article concerned an issue of public importance. For those reasons Welch claimed that the *New York Times* actual malice standard was applicable to the case and that Gertz had failed to show that the article had been published with reckless disregard.

The trial court judge denied Welch's motion for summary judgment, but he did not dispute his claim that the *New York Times* standard was applicable; he concluded, instead, that Gertz was entitled to the opportunity to demonstrate that the article had been published with actual malice. However, during the course of the trial it became clear that the judge "had not accepted all of the respondent's asserted grounds for applying the *New York Times* rule to the case," ruling in effect that Gertz was neither a public official nor a public figure.[12] He noted that if Gertz were, the court would be required to grant a directed verdict for Welch apparently on the grounds that there was insufficient proof of actual malice; rather, the judge held that some statements in the article constituted libel per se under Illinois law, and thus he submitted the case to the jury "under instructions that withdrew from its consideration all issues save the measure of damages." The jury award $50,000 to Gertz.[13]

The judge was not finished with making more complicated an already complicated case. Upon further reflection, he decided that the *New York Times* standard should apply even though Gertz was neither a public official or a public figure. He accepted Welch's argument that the *New York Times* privilege "protected discussion of any public issue without regard to the status of the person defamed therein.''[14] The trial judge, reversing the verdict for Gertz, entered a judgment for Welch.[15] Without stating so specifically, the judge seemed to be anticipating the Supreme Court's decision in *Rosenbloom v. Metromedia*.

By the time the United States Court of Appeals for the Seventh Circuit heard the case, the Supreme Court had issued its decision in *Rosenbloom*. Although the court of appeals expressed some doubt about the trial judge's determination that Gertz was not a public figure, it nevertheless sustained his judgment on the grounds that the article concerned a matter of public interest and *Rosenbloom* required application of the *New York Times* standard to ''any publication or broadcast about an issue of significant public interest, without regard to the position, fame, or anonymity of the person defamed,'' and it concluded that the statements in the article concerned such an issue.[16] In expressing doubt about the trial judge's determination that Gertz was not a public figure, the court of appeals noted his prominence:

> [Gertz's] considerable stature as a lawyer, author, lecturer, and participant in matters of public import undermine[s] the validity of the assumption that he is not a ''public figure'' as that term has been used by the progeny of *New York Times*. Nevertheless, for purposes of decision we make that assumption and test the availability of the claim of privilege by the subject matter of the article.[17]

The court of appeals determined that Gertz had failed to prove by clear and convincing evidence that the article had been published with actual malice. There was no evidence that those who prepared the article knew of the falsity of the accusations.[18] The Supreme Court, acknowledging that the evidence in the case did not reveal that Welch had acted with a ''high degree of awareness of . . . probable falsity,'' recognized that if Gertz had been held to be a public figure, he would have lost the case.

The controversial 5-4 decision of the Supreme Court reversed the court of appeals. In the majority opinion written by Justice Lewis Powell, and joined by Justices Stewart, Marshall, Blackmun, and Rehnquist, the Court reversed many of the gains made by media organizations in libel cases in the years since *New York Times v. Sullivan* and altered the libel laws of all fifty states.

Powell saw the key issue to be whether an individual who is neither a public official nor a public figure must meet the strict actual malice standard of *New York Times*. In other words, was the public interest test announced by a plurality three years earlier in *Rosenbloom* applicable? Was the Court correct in *Rosenbloom* by holding that a private individual who was caught up in a matter of public interest must meet the same standard of liability as would a public official or public figure?

Powell began his opinion by describing the difficulty his brethren had had in *Rosenbloom* in agreeing on a rationale for the decision. He noted that the eight justices who participated in *Rosenbloom* announced their views in five opinions, none of which commanded more than three votes. In Powell's view, the "several statements not only reveal disagreement about the appropriate result in that case, they also reflect divergent traditions of thought about the general problem of reconciling the law of defamation with the First Amendment."[19]

After tracing the development of the public official and public figure categories of plaintiffs, and the constitutional standards developed in *New York Times v. Sullivan* and subsequent cases, Powell turned to Justice Brennan's lead opinion in *Rosenbloom*. In that case, Brennan had held that the *New York Times* protection extended to defamatory falsehoods relating to private persons if the statements concerned matters of general or public interest. He had criticized efforts to distinguish between public officials and public figures on the one hand and private individuals on the other. To Brennan, what was important was society's interest in learning about certain issues, and if the matter is a subject of public or general interest, it "cannot suddenly become less so merely because a private individual is involved, or because in some sense the individual did not 'voluntarily' choose to become involved."[20] Thus, a private individual involved in such matters of public interest would have to meet the *New York Times* actual malice standard to win a libel suit against a media organization.

Recognizing the importance of granting sufficient constitutional protection to the news media, Powell still asserted that avoiding self-censorship by the press is "not the only societal value" at issue. He argued that there is a legitimate state interest in compensating individuals for the harm inflicted on them by defamatory falsehood. To Powell, the *New York Times* standard provides an appropriate level of protection in defamation cases involving a public person:

> Those who, by reason of the notoriety of their achievements or the vigor and success with which they seek the public's attention, are properly classed as public figures and those who hold government office may recover for injury to reputation only on clear and convincing proof that the defamatory falsehood was made with knowledge of its falsity or with reckless disregard for the truth. This standard administers an extremely powerful antidote to the inducement to media self-censorship of the common-law rule of strict liability for libel and slander. And it exacts a correspondingly high price from the victims of defamatory falsehood. Plainly many deserving plaintiffs, including some intentionally subjected to injury, will be unable to surmount the barrier of the *New York Times* test.[21]

Although granting such protection to the news media abridges the "state law right" to compensation for wrongful hurt, Powell held that the Court was correct in extending the *New York Times* protection to publications and broadcasts of defamatory falsehood concerning public officials and public figures. But Powell believed that the *New York Times* rule is an accommodation between reputational and First Amendment interests in the "context of libel actions" brought by *public persons*; he and four of his brethren held that a different rule is required when the defamation involves private individuals.

Despite the warnings of Justice Brennan in *Rosenbloom*, the Court in *Gertz* calmly stated that it had no trouble distinguishing among defamation plaintiffs. A victim of defamation's "first remedy" is to use "available opportunities to contradict the lie or correct the error" and thus minimize the harm done to the victim's reputation. Despite some reservations, Powell asserted that public officials and public figures "usually enjoy significantly greater access to the channels of effective communication and hence have a more realistic opportunity to counteract false statements than private individuals normally enjoy."[22] Thus, he seemed to suggest that there is a class of individuals who have regular access to channels of mass communication by which they could rebut defamatory statements made about their reputations, although he also understood that the rebuttal or correction rarely gets the attention enjoyed by the original statement.[23] Private persons, on the other hand, do not enjoy such access and are therefore "more vulnerable to injury, and the state interest in protecting them is correspondingly greater."

Powell attempted to demonstrate that a distinction between public and private persons can be made based on the actions taken by the person defamed. As the Court had stated directly or indirectly since *New York Times*, someone who seeks public office must be willing to have personal fitness and qualifications closely examined by news organizations. The office seeker understands the risks of public scrutiny, which can include discussion of not only one's public life, but some aspects of one's private life as well. Public figures must also suffer such scrutiny, but the Supreme Court in *Gertz* viewed such individuals in a somewhat different light. In an effort to limit the types of individuals who would be considered public figures, and thus make it easier for them to bring a libel suit against a media organization successfully, the Court attempted to define a public figure as someone who has actively sought notoriety:

> Hypothetically, it may be possible for someone to become a public figure through no purposeful action of his own, but the instances of truly involuntary public figures must be exceedingly rare. For the most part those who attain this status have assumed roles of especial prominence in the affairs of society. Some occupy positions of such persuasive power and influence that they are deemed public figures for all purposes. More commonly, those classed as public figures have thrust themselves to the forefront of particular public controversies in order to influence the resolution of the issues involved. In either event, they invite attention and comment.[24]

The Court had been looking for some method by which it could recalibrate a scale that it felt had come to overwhelmingly favor First Amendment interests. Having committed itself to the public-figure/private-person test, it apparently chose to strike a fairer balance by restricting the categories of individuals who would be considered public figures. Yet it will be argued that no matter what efforts are made to precisely define public figures with the goal of providing clear guidelines to persons who gather and disseminate news, the public-figure/private-person standard fails to consider appropriately both First Amendment and reputational interests, and it has, in fact, created a morass from which the Court is having a very difficult time extricating itself.

Private individuals, the Court argued in *Gertz*, are "not only more vulnerable to injury than public officials and public figures; they are also more deserving of recovery." A private person has not sought public office and has not assumed an "influential role in ordering society." Because a private person has not voluntarily surrendered a part of personal privacy by seeking public office or thrusting himself or herself into a public controversy, the person has a "more compelling call on the courts for redress of injury inflicted by defamatory falsehood."[25]

If private persons are entitled to greater protection, the states, in the Court's view, should "retain substantial latitude in their efforts to enforce a legal remedy for defamatory falsehood injurious to the reputation of a private individual."[26] The states should not be hampered by an extension of the *New York Times* actual malice test, as was suggested by the plurality in *Rosenbloom*. Such an extension would force the states to determine on an ad hoc basis which statements address issues of "general or public interest" and which do not. The right of recovery for private individuals should not hinge on court efforts to make such distinctions:

> We doubt the wisdom of committing this task to the conscience of judges. Nor does the Constitution require us to draw so thin a line between the drastic alternatives of the *New York Times* privilege and the common law of strict liability for defamatory error. The "public or general interest" test for determining the applicability of the *New York Times* standard to private defamation actions inadequately serves both of the competing values at stake. On the one hand, a private individual whose reputation is injured by defamatory falsehood that does concern an issue of public or general interest has no recourse unless he can meet the rigorous requirements of *New York Times*. . . . On the other hand, a publisher or broadcaster of a defamatory error which a court deems unrelated to an issue of public or general interest may be held liable in damages even if it took every reasonable precaution to ensure the accuracy of its assertions. And liability may far exceed compensation for any actual injury to the plaintiff, for the jury may be permitted to presume damages without proof of loss and even to award punitive damages.[27]

To allow the awarding of damages in cases where news organizations have taken every reasonable step to ensure accuracy, and also in cases where juries are allowed to "presume" damages without any showing of actual harm, would, in the view of the Court, put intolerable burdens on the media. Thus, in what could be considered a rather drastic change in the libel laws of the fifty states, the Court offered to the press several new standards that it could consider to be accommodating to its interests. Among the most important of those was the formal end to the old standard of strict liability:

> We hold that, so long as they do not impose liability without fault, the States may define for themselves the appropriate standard of liability for a publisher or broadcaster of defamatory falsehood injurious to a private individual. This approach provides a more equitable boundary between the competing concerns involved here. It recognizes the strength of the legitimate state interest in compensating private individuals for wrongful injury to reputation, yet shields the press and broadcast media from the rigors of strict liability for defamation.[28]

The Court argued that the states are entitled to substantial latitude in determining the standard of liability in cases involving private individuals. And if they choose, they may impose liability on the publisher or broadcaster of defamatory falsehood on a "less demanding showing than that required by *New York Times*." Such a determination is based on the Court's recognition of the "strong and legitimate state interest in compensating private individuals for injury to reputation."[29] But Powell and his brethren were not willing to grant the states unlimited discretion. In a key phrase, the Court offered the news media the chance to be less vulnerable to the theoretically unlimited ability of juries to award punitive damages: "This countervailing state interest extends no further than compensation for actual injury. . . . We hold that the States may not permit recovery of presumed or punitive damages, at least when liability is not based on a showing of falsity or reckless disregard for the truth."[30]

Thus, as of *Gertz*, even a private individual suing for libel would have to meet the *New York Times* actual malice standard if he or she expected to collect punitive damages, and juries in libel suits could no longer "presume" damages; there would have to be at least some evidence of actual harm. Under traditional rules relating to actions for libel, which many states had observed, the existence of injury is presumed from the fact of publication. Juries were able to award huge sums of money without any proof that there had actually been harm to a person's reputation. That is why Powell called the common law of defamation an "oddity of tort law." The Court believed there were significant dangers in allowing juries freedom to award damages in such cases:

The largely uncontrolled discretion of juries to award damages where there is no loss necessarily compounds the potential of any system of liability for defamatory falsehood to inhibit the vigorous exercise of First Amendment freedoms. Additionally, the doctrine of presumed damages invites juries to punish unpopular opinion rather than to compensate individuals for injury sustained by the publication of a false fact. . . . States have no substantial interest in securing for plaintiffs . . . gratuitous awards of money damages far in excess of any actual injury.[31]

Having found it necessary to limit private plaintiffs to compensation for actual injury if they cannot prove knowledge of falsity or reckless disregard for the truth, the Court declined to define "actual injury," suggesting that trial courts have "wide experience in framing appropriate jury instructions in tort actions." But Powell did indicate that actual injury was not limited to compensation for monetary loss:

Suffice it to say that actual injury is not limited to out-of-pocket loss. Indeed, the more customary types of actual harm inflicted by defamatory falsehood include impairment of reputation and standing in the community, personal humiliation, and mental anguish and suffering. Of course, juries must be limited by appropriate instructions, and all awards must be supported by competent evidence concerning the injury, although there need be no evidence which assigns an actual dollar value to the injury.[32]

Powell expressed concern over the willingness of juries to award punitive damages in "wholly unpredictable amounts" bearing no relation to the actual harm caused. And he was especially concerned about the power of juries to punish unpopular views expressed by media organizations.

In ending one of the most important opinions written in any libel case, Powell returned briefly to the issue of whether Elmer Gertz could be considered a public figure. He understood that Gertz had long been active in community and professional affairs, had served as an officer of local civic groups and of various professional organizations, and was consequently well known in some circles, but believed "he had achieved no general fame or notoriety in the community." Powell noted that none of the prospective jurors called at the trial had ever heard of Gertz prior to the litigation, and that in the context of the trial he was a not a public figure:

He plainly did not thrust himself into the vortex of this public issue, nor did he engage the public's attention in an attempt to influence its outcome. . . . We therefore conclude that the *New York Times* standard is inapplicable in this case and the trial court erred in entering judgment for respondent. Because the jury was allowed to impose liability without fault and was permitted to presume damages without proof of injury, a new trial is necessary.[33]

Justice Harry Blackmun provided the fifth and decisive vote, despite expressing reservations about the logic of Powell's reasoning. He recognized that in *Gertz* the Court departed from the reasoning in *Rosenbloom*, decided only three years before, but he was willing to join the *Gertz* majority on the grounds that the removal of presumed and punitive damages in the absence of *New York Times* actual malice "eliminates significant and powerful motives for self-censorship" that are otherwise present in "traditional libel action." By doing so, the Court, in Blackmun's words, "leaves what should prove to be sufficient and adequate breathing space for a vigorous press. What the Court has done, I believe, will have little, if any, practical effect on the functioning of responsible journalism."[34]

Blackmun was also concerned that the Court had become so divided over appropriate standards in libel cases, it was time to form a clear majority of opinion. "The Court was sadly fractioned in *Rosenbloom*. A result of that kind inevitably leads to uncertainty."[35]

As might be expected, Justice William Brennan filed a vigorous dissent in which he repeated his statements in *Rosenbloom* to the effect that a matter of public interest does not become less so merely because a private individual is involved.[36] He also repeated his view that "risk of exposure" is an "essential incident of life in a society which places a primary value on freedom of speech and of press." Brennan was especially concerned that the new standards announced in *Gertz* would lead states to adopt a "reasonable-care standard" in cases where private individuals are involved in matters of public interest, and that would lead to self-censorship:

> Plainly a jury's latitude to impose liability for want of due care poses a far greater threat of suppressing unpopular views than does a possible recovery of presumed or punitive damages. Moreover, the Court's broad-ranging examples of "actual injury" ... inevitably allow a jury bent on punishing expression of unpopular views a formidable weapon for doing so.[37]

Brennan rejected Powell's argument that courts are unable to determine what is an issue of public importance. Brennan recognized in *Rosenbloom* that the "task would not always be easy," but he believed that courts making such a determination would be "performing one of their traditional functions."

Justice White bitterly dissented in a thirty-five page opinion that was both analytical and thoughtful, but showed his now predictable impatience with the First Amendment claims of news organizations. He sharply criticized what he considered to be the Court's efforts in *Gertz* to usurp the responsibility of states to determine the rights of an "ordinary citizen" to recover damages for false publication injurious to the person's reputation. The majority, in White's view, went far beyond the exceptions to state autonomy over libel laws enunciated in some cases since *New York Times*:

The Court, in a few printed pages, has federalized major aspects of libel law by declaring unconstitutional in important respects the prevailing defamation law in all or most of the 50 states. That result is accomplished by requiring the plaintiff in each and every defamation action to prove not only the defendant's culpability beyond his act of publishing defamatory material but also actual damage to reputation resulting from the publication.[38]

With some sarcasm, White criticized the Court for making such drastic changes:

I assume these sweeping changes will be popular with the press, but this is not the road to salvation for a court of law. As I see it, there are wholly insufficient grounds for scuttling the libel laws of the States in such wholesale fashion, to say nothing of deprecating the reputation interest of ordinary citizens and rendering them powerless to protect themselves.[39]

Because the *Gertz* majority required that even the private individual must demonstrate some type of "fault" to win a libel suit, it appeared that the burden of proof had clearly shifted to the plaintiff. Before *Gertz* state courts had been divided over whether a media defendant had the responsibility of proving that the statements at issue were true or that a plaintiff had to prove they were false. Because there must be evidence of some kind of fault, and presumably truthful statements would not satisfy that requirement, post-*Gertz* plaintiffs would now be required to prove that the statements were false and that they were published with at least some element of fault. To Justice White, such burdens on the plaintiff were intolerable and made recovery of damages unnecessarily difficult:

The Court evinces a deep-seated antipathy to "liability without fault." But this catch-phrase has no talismanic significance and is almost meaningless in this context where the Court appears to be addressing those libels and slanders that are defamatory on their face and where the publisher is no doubt aware from the nature of the material that it would be inherently damaging to reputation.[40]

To White, the Court's decision in *Gertz* unfairly favored the news media over the reputation of the individual, and they do not, in his view, need such special protection:

The press today is vigorous and robust. To me, it is quite incredible to suggest that threats of libel suits from private citizens are causing the press to refrain from publishing the truth. I know of no hard facts to support that proposition, and the Court furnishes none.

The communications industry has increasingly become concentrated in a few powerful hands operating very lucrative businesses reaching across the Nation and into almost every home. Neither the industry as a whole nor its individual components are easily intimidated, and we are fortunate that they are not. Requiring them to pay for the occasional damage they do to private reputation will play no substantial part in their future performance or existence.[41]

The new standard of permitting plaintiffs to win libel suits only if they demonstrate some type of fault would prove to be elusive. To Justice White and perhaps others, no one who publishes a false statement that is damaging to an individual's reputation is ever "faultless." That view has contributed to the difficulty of defining fault. Many states today require that private individuals offer evidence of "negligence" if they want at least to win compensatory damages. But the Court strongly suggested that the states can go beyond the negligence standard if they want to provide additional First Amendment protection to media organizations being sued by private individuals caught up in matters of public interest.

In *Gertz* the Supreme Court began the process of balancing a scale it believed had come to unfairly favor First Amendment interests at the expense of reputation. The vehicle it chose was to restrict the types of individuals who would be considered public figures. That Gertz was considered to be a private person may be partially due to the fact that the Supreme Court would be sympathetic to a lawyer who becomes involved in a public controversy by representing a client in a sensational case. The members of the Court may have seen themselves, in previous years, subjected to harsh criticism in the press for simply doing their jobs. More likely, the Court wanted to move away from the expansive First Amendment holding in *Rosenbloom* to a more restrictive standard that gave private individuals a greater chance to vindicate damaged reputations.

For those concerned about the First Amendment, *Gertz v. Welch* was not a victory for the news media, but it clearly could have been worse. By adopting the public figure test in *Gertz* rather than the public interest test in *Rosenbloom*, the Court had apparently moved toward the paradoxical result of underprotecting *and* overprotecting, in at least some respects, both First Amendment and reputational interests. Under such a formula, an individual could conceivably become a public figure in an issue that is not of public interest by voluntarily thrusting himself or herself into the controversy. At the same time, a person could remain a private figure even if involved in matters that are of the highest public interest. Even though Powell said such cases would be exceedingly rare, an "all-purpose" public figure would presumably have to prove actual malice for statements made about even the most private of such a figure's affairs. If the Court then attempted to establish a "privacy" exception in such cases, it would find itself in the very quagmire it rejected in *Rosenbloom*, that is, making a distinction between issues of public interest and those that are private. If the Court wants to leave undefined matters of public interest, then presumably it would not want to define more clearly matters of private interest either.[42]

Leaving public figures unable to protect certain aspects of their private lives from media scrutiny would force them to pursue privacy suits against news organizations. Unlike in libel, a plaintiff in a privacy case can pursue the litigation even if the statements were true, arguing instead that the very invasion of privacy, not the truthfulness of the statements, is the focus of the litigation.[43] But if the Court is committed to avoiding the problem of having trial and appellate judges determine which issues are public and which are private, it would not want to push defamation plaintiffs toward privacy suits where such determinations must necessarily be made.

The Supreme Court in *Gertz* invited states to establish their own standards that would apply to private persons in libel cases and except for the requirement that there be evidence of some degree of fault, left substantial discretion to the states to determine those standards. The states were even free to provide First Amendment protection beyond that required by the Court. Yet even while recognizing the importance of a federal system where states retain autonomy over some areas of the law, one is hard pressed to understand how the First Amendment's application could be contingent upon the status of the plaintiff. There may be an inherent conflict of interest when a state court knows both that if the plaintiff is determined to be a public figure, it must abide by standards set down by the Supreme Court, and that if the plaintiff is determined to be a private individual, it is able to apply familiar state laws and customs perhaps more to its liking. Without stretching the analogy too far, it may be similar to letting one team decide by which set of rules, *A* or *B*, the game will be played, knowing in advance that rules *A* were formulated by a distant court, and rules *B* were formulated by more sympathetic judges and legislators of the team's home state. Not only is there an incentive to designate a plaintiff in a libel case a private person so familiar state standards can be applied, but the Supreme Court, by narrowing the categories of individuals who can be considered public figures, has all but encouraged lower courts to take that step.

If those concerned about the First Amendment were surprised that the Court ruled that Gertz was a private citizen, they may have been more startled when two years later the Court determined that a prominent socialite, Mary Alice Firestone, was also not a public figure. In its 5-3 decision in *Time, Inc. v. Firestone*,[44] the Court, in an opinion written by Justice William Rehnquist, further narrowed the categories of individuals who could be considered public figures and put media organizations on notice that even innocent errors could be severely punished.

Mary Alice Firestone was granted a divorce from her husband Russell Firestone, the "scion of one of America's wealthier industrial families," in 1967. *Time* magazine had a "stringer," an individual who works for a media organization on a free-lance basis but not as a regular member of the staff, covering the divorce trial in Palm Beach County, Florida. Working with information supplied by the stringer, *Time*'s bureau chief in Miami, and wire-service reports, the magazine, at the conclusion of the long divorce trial, ran the following item in its "Milestones" section:

> Divorced. By Russell A. Firestone, Jr., 41, heir to the tire fortune: Mary Alice Sullivan Firestone, 32, his third wife; a onetime Palm Beach schoolteacher; on grounds of extreme cruelty and adultery; after six years of marriage, one son; in West Palm Beach, Fla. The 17-month intermittent trial produced enough testimony of extramarital adventures on both sides, said the judge, "to make Dr. Freud's hair curl."[45]

In language that would not win any awards for clarity, the trial judge's final judgment read in part:

> This cause came on for final hearing before the court upon the plaintiff wife's second amended complaint for separate maintenance [alimony unconnected with the causes of divorce], the defendant husband's answer and counterclaim for divorce on grounds of extreme cruelty and adultery, and the wife's answer thereto setting up certain affirmative defenses. . . .
>
> According to certain testimony in behalf of the defendant, extramarital escapades of the plaintiff were bizarre and of an amatory nature which would have made Dr. Freud's hair curl. Other testimony, in plaintiff's behalf, would indicate that defendant was guilty of bounding from one bedpartner to another with the erotic zest of a satyr. The court is inclined to discount much of this testimony as unreliable. Nevertheless, it is the conclusion and finding of the court that neither party is domesticated, within the meaning of that term as used by the Supreme Court of Florida.[46]

The judge then awarded Mrs. Firestone alimony of $3,000 a month to continue until her death or remarriage.[47] The issue of alimony was to become very important as the Supreme Court examined whether *Time* had exercised reasonable care in preparing the story.

It is possible that after listening for seventeen months to graphic descriptions of extramarital affairs and reading the judge's confusing final decree in the case, even the most well-meaning reporter could mistakenly assume that the divorce was granted on grounds of adultery. Mrs. Firestone, claiming the "Milestones" paragraph injured her reputation, demanded in writing a retraction from *Time*, alleging that a portion of the article was "false, malicious and defamatory." The retraction demand was a prerequisite for filing a libel action under Florida law, and if *Time* had complied, it would have limited Mrs. Firestone to compensatory damages. *Time* declined to issue the retraction, and Mrs. Firestone filed the libel suit in Florida Circuit Court. A jury awarded her $100,000 and both the state court of appeals and the state supreme court affirmed the judgment.[48]

In appealing to the Supreme Court, *Time* argued that Mrs. Firestone was a public figure and would therefore have to meet the *New York Times* standard of actual malice. It also argued that the report of the divorce constituted a "report of a judicial proceeding," which *Time* said "was a class of subject matter which . . . deserves the protection of the 'actual malice' standard even if the story is proved to be defamatorily false or inaccurate."[49] The Supreme Court rejected both arguments.

After reciting its definition of a public figure in *Gertz*, Justice Rehnquist, writing the majority opinion, held that Mrs. Firestone did not fall into that category:

> Respondent did not assume any role of especial prominence in the affairs of society, other than perhaps Palm Beach society, and she did not thrust herself to the forefront of any particular public controversy in order to influence the resolution of issues involved in it. Petitioner contends that because the Firestone divorce was characterized by the Florida Supreme Court as a "cause célèbre," it must have been a public controversy and respondent must be considered a public figure. But in doing so petitioner seeks to equate "public controversy" with all controversies of interest to the public.[50]

Rehnquist rejected the notion that "dissolution of a marriage" through judicial proceedings was the sort of "public controversy" referred to in *Gertz*. He acknowledged that the marital problems of extremely wealthy individuals may be of interest to "some portion of the reading public," but Mrs. Firestone had not freely chosen to make public the problems of her marriage. Under state law she had no choice but to go into a courtroom to pursue and defend a divorce action, and such an appearance is not voluntary. Rehnquist distinguished such action from that of General Walker in *Associated Press v. Walker*. Mrs. Firestone had assumed no "special prominence in the resolution of public questions."[51]

The Court also rejected the argument that the *New York Times* privilege extends to all reports of judicial proceedings. A year before *Firestone*, the Supreme Court in *Cox Broadcasting v. Cohn*[52] had held that states cannot impose civil liability based upon the publication of truthful information contained in official court records open to public inspection.[53] Rehnquist refused to extend such protection to what he considered to be "inaccurate and false statements," at least where actual malice has not been established. To the Court, that argument was asking too much:

> It may be that all reports of judicial proceedings contain some informational value implicating the First Amendment, but recognizing this is little different from labeling all judicial proceedings matters of "public of general interest," as that phrase was used by the plurality in *Rosenbloom*.[54]

In case there was any lingering confusion, Rehnquist reiterated that the public interest test in *Rosenbloom* had been put to rest in *Gertz*:

> Whatever their general validity, use of such subject-matter classifications to determine the extent of constitutional protection afforded defamatory falsehoods may too often result in an improper balance between the competing interests in this area. It was our recognition and rejection of this weakness in the *Rosenbloom* test which led us in *Gertz* to eschew a subject-matter test for one focusing upon the character of the defamation plaintiff.[55]

Rehnquist recognized that some reports of judicial proceedings would be protected, but to him and his brethren, "the details of many, if not most, courtroom battles would add almost nothing toward advancing . . . uninhibited debate on public issues." Most participants in some litigation will be like Mrs. Firestone, "drawn into a public forum largely against their will in order to obtain the only redress available to them or to defend themselves against actions brought by the State or by others."[56]

Time had argued, although unsuccessfully, that its report in the "Milestones" section was "factually correct." In its view, the article "faithfully reproduced the precise meaning of the divorce judgment."[57] The Florida courts rejected *Time*'s contention that the article was accurate and the Supreme Court believed the lower courts "properly could have found the . . . item to be false."

Although it is not appropriate to examine the reasons for the divorce in detail, they are worthy of some attention to illustrate why a reporter covering a long trial could be confused as to the grounds on which the divorce was granted. Perhaps forgetting that most reporters are not lawyers, the Court apparently expects the press to understand what a judge writes, no matter how ambiguous:

> For petitioner's report to have been accurate, the divorce granted Russell Firestone must have been based on a finding by the divorce court that his wife had committed extreme cruelty toward him *and* that she had been guilty of adultery. This is indisputably what petitioner reported in its "Milestones" item, but it equally indisputable that these were not the facts. Russell Firestone alleged in his counterclaim that respondent had been guilty of adultery, but the divorce court never made any such finding. Its judgment provided that Russell Firestone's "counterclaim for divorce be and the same is hereby granted," but did not specify that the basis for the judgment was either of the two grounds alleged in the counterclaim. The Supreme Court of Florida on appeal concluded that the ground actually relied upon by the divorce court was "lack of domestication of the parties," a ground not theretofore recognized by Florida. The Supreme Court nonetheless affirmed the judgment dissolving the bonds of matrimony because the record contained sufficient evidence to establish the ground of extreme cruelty.[58]

It seems nothing short of remarkable that the United States Supreme Court would expect a lay reporter to examine the judge's decree in the case and understand the grounds upon which the divorce was granted. The Court even admits that "lack of domestication" was not "theretofore recognized by Florida law." Considering the kinds of errors that the Court had excused in past libel cases, it was clear by *Firestone* that a Court determined to recalibrate the scales would allow punishment of what certainly could be described as innocent error. Those concerned about the First Amendment could be forgiven if they thought that cases like *Ocala Star-Banner v. Damron*, where a newspaper won a libel suit even when it, in a moment of "mental aberration," mistakenly accused the brother of a mayor of wrongdoing, were of another era.[59] In fact, the case had been decided only five years before. It was apparent by 1976 that the Supreme Court would make no effort to hide its impatience with journalists who make mistakes, even if those mistakes seemed minor when compared with errors forgiven in previous libel cases.

Rehnquist rejected any suggestion that the divorce decree was difficult to understand:

> Petitioner may well argue that the meaning of the court's decree was unclear, but this does not license it to choose from among several conceivable interpretations the one most damaging to the respondent. Having chosen to follow this tack, petitioner must be able to establish not merely that the item reported was a conceivable or plausible interpretation of the decree, but that the item was factually correct.[60]

Time stubbornly insisted that the article was true and represented a reasonable interpretation of the judge's decree. Assuming for a moment that those who prepared the news item genuinely believed they were publishing the truth, punishment for such error seems a galaxy away from the actual malice standard that would have to be met if Mrs. Firestone had been considered a public figure. It is arguable that the actual malice test does place an intolerable burden on even a public person because he or she has to prove either that the media organization *knew* its statement was false or recklessly disregarded whether it might have been false. But when a media organization honestly believed it was publishing the truth and had no reason to intentionally harm Mrs. Firestone's reputation, it seems strange that the decision as to which standard should apply in a libel case, one very protective of the First Amendment and one starkly unsympathetic to it, would rest on the thin line of whether Mrs. Firestone's activities qualified her for status as a public person.

Interestingly, although the Supreme Court would not reexamine the $100,000 award, it did send the case back for retrial to the Florida courts on the question of whether there was evidence of some fault on the part of *Time* that is required by *Gertz*. "No question of fault was submitted to the jury in the case,'' noted Rehnquist. Under Florida law, the only findings required for determination of liability were "whether the article was defamatory, whether it was true, and whether the defamation, if any, caused respondent harm."[61]

The Supreme Court had found itself in a bind. Rehnquist specifically noted that there is nothing in the Constitution that requires that a jury make the determination as to fault in a state civil case. Nor is there any "prohibition against such a finding being made in the first instance by an appellate, rather than a trial court." To Rehnquist, the "First and Fourteenth Amendments do not impose upon the States any limitations as to how, within their own judicial systems, factfinding tasks shall be allocated."[62] Stuck with the fault requirement from *Gertz*, the Court was unable to find that any Florida court had considered whether *Time* had actually been at fault. In fact, the Florida Supreme Court seemed to suggest that "a showing of fault was not required."[63]

The Florida Supreme Court, apparently choosing to ignore *Gertz*, chided *Time* for not knowing that under Florida law a wife found guilty of adultery could not get alimony. "Since petitioner had been awarded alimony, she had not been found guilty of adultery nor had the divorce been granted on the ground of adultery."[64] The Florida court held that if *Time* had checked the law, it would have known the divorce must have been granted on the grounds of extreme cruelty and not adultery, and Mrs. Firestone would have been saved the "humiliation of being accused of adultery in a nationwide magazine." To the Florida court, it was "a flagrant example of 'journalistic negligence.'"[65] Rehnquist was unwilling to accept this statement as proof that the Florida courts had examined the issue of fault. Thus, the Supreme Court vacated the judgment of the Florida Supreme Court and remanded the case for further proceedings consistent with its opinion.

Justice Powell, the author of the *Gertz* opinion, concurred in the judgment of the Court primarily because it was remanding the case, but he expressed some concern that *Time* had not been treated fairly by his brethren:

> My point in writing is to emphasize that, against the background of a notorious divorce case . . . and a decree that invited misunderstanding, there *was* substantial evidence supportive of *Time*'s defense that it was not guilty of actionable negligence. At the very least the jury or court assessing liability in this case should have weighed these factors and this evidence before reaching a judgment.[66]

Justice William Brennan, the author of the *New York Times v. Sullivan* decision and the plurality opinion in *Rosenbloom*, dissented on a number of grounds. He argued that *Gertz* had not specifically overruled *Rosenbloom* and that the public has a substantial interest in judicial proceedings. "At stake in the present case is the ability of the press to report to the citizenry the events transpiring in the Nation's judicial systems. There is simply no meaningful or constitutionally adequate way to report such events without reference to those persons and transactions that form the subject matter in the controversy."[67] He could have attacked Rehnquist's opinion in *Firestone* on a number of fronts, but largely confined himself to the issue that the media must have breathing space to report the activities of the judicial system:

> The First Amendment insulates from defamation liability a margin for error sufficient to ensure the avoidance of crippling press self-censorship in the field of reporting public judicial affairs. To be adequate, that margin must be both of sufficient breadth and predictable in its application. In my view, therefore, the actual-malice standard of *New York Times* must be met in order to justify the imposition of liability in these circumstances.[68]

While Brennan sharply criticized his brethren for their *Firestone* decision, which he felt "savages the cherished values encased in the First Amendment,"[69] Justice White, in dissent, was irritated that the case had been remanded to the Florida courts instead of being affirmed. He argued,

> To require proof of fault in this case—or in any other case predating *Gertz* and *Rosenbloom* in which a private figure is defamed—is to interfere with the State's otherwise legitimate policy of compensating defamation victims without furthering First Amendment goals *in any way at all.* . . . It appears to me that the Florida Supreme Court has made a sufficiently "conscious determination" of the fact of negligence.[70]

It was left to Justice Thurgood Marshall to argue in dissent that Mrs. Firestone was a public figure. He noted that she had been prominent in Palm Beach Society and that she appeared so often in the press that she subscribed to a press-clipping service.[71] And those who did the clipping were kept very busy:

> Mrs. Firestone brought suit for separate maintenance with reason to know of the likely public interest in the proceedings. . . . The 17-month trial and related events attracted national news coverage, and elicited no fewer than 43 articles in the Miami Herald and 45 articles in the Palm Beach Post and Palm Beach Times. Far from shunning the publicity, Mrs. Firestone held several press conferences in the course of the proceedings.[72]

To Marshall, those facts were enough to make Mrs. Firestone a public figure "for purposes of reports on the judicial proceedings she initiated." Recalling that in *Gertz* the Court sought to distinguish individuals who could command media attention to rebut the defamatory statements from those who could not, Marshall argued that Mrs. Firestone was able to get media coverage:

> Mrs. Firestone is hardly in a position to suggest that she lacked access to the media for purposes relating to her lawsuit. It may well be that she would have had greater difficulty countering alleged falsehoods in the national press than in

Miami and Palm Beach papers that covered the proceedings so thoroughly. But presumably the audience Mrs. Firestone would have been most interested in reaching could have been reached through the local media.[73]

Marshall claimed that in any case, *Gertz* did not require that a person be able to counter falsehoods fully through "self-help" in order to be considered a public figure. He also argued that Mrs. Firestone had willingly become an active member of what he called the "sporting set"—a social group with "especial prominence in the affairs of society" whose lives, in his words, "receive constant media attention":

> Having placed herself in a position in which her activities were of interest to a significant segment of the public, Mrs. Firestone chose to initiate a lawsuit . . . and most significantly, held several press conferences in the course of that lawsuit. If these actions for some reason fail to establish as a certainty that Mrs. Firestone "voluntarily exposed [herself] to increased risk of injury from defamatory falsehood," surely they are sufficient to entitle the press to act on the assumption that she did.[74]

Finally, Marshall raised the issue of whether the Court, having rejected the public interest test in *Rosenbloom* in favor of a public-figure/private-person test in *Gertz*, simply ignored or circumvented the very tests it had just established. The majority in *Firestone* concluded that the subject matter of the alleged defamation, her divorce, was not a "public controversy" as that term was used in *Gertz*. Considering the attention she and her lawsuit had already attracted, it was hard for Marshall to understand what the term "public controversy" means. "The only explanation I can discern from the Court's opinion is that the controversy was not of the sort deemed relevant to the 'affairs of society,' and the public's interest not of the sort deemed 'legitimate' or worthy of judicial recognition."[75] To Marshall, that is precisely what *Gertz* was intended to avoid. The Court did not want to force state and federal judges to decide on an ad hoc basis which issues are of general or public interest and which are not; to determine, in other words, "what information is relevant to self-government." If *Gertz*, therefore, is to have any meaning at all, in Marshall's view, the "focus of the analysis must be on the actions of the individual, and the degree of public attention that had already developed, or that could have been anticipated, before the report in question."[76] For purposes of this case, and following the dictates of *Gertz*, Marshall would hold Mrs. Firestone to be a public figure who must demonstrate actual malice.

If Marshall is correct in suggesting that the Court first made the determination that Mrs. Firestone's divorce was not a matter of public interest, and then secondarily decided that she was not a public figure, then it is apparent that the Court created a public-figure/private-person test from which it was willing to deviate while at the same time pretending that the test was still in effect.

Gertz and *Firestone* seemed to indicate that for someone to be considered a public figure, the controversy in which that person is involved must first pass a now "covert" public interest test, similar to the test so quickly discarded by the Court majority in *Gertz* after its adoption in *Rosenbloom*.

One observer argued that once the Court determined that discussion of Mrs. Firestone's divorce was not deserving of First Amendment protection, it would follow that she would be considered a private and not a public person:

> The result in *Firestone* indicates that the Court actually will not subjugate repu-
> tational interests—even those of arguably public figures—to what is considers
> weak or nonexistent first amendment interests. . . . By defining the con-
> troversy . . . as the divorce itself . . . [and] by carefully categorizing and labeling
> her actions in that controversy, the Court could deny that she had injected her-
> self into it voluntarily.[77]

In the wake of *Gertz* and *Firestone*, it was clear that journalists could no longer tell in advance who would be considered a public figure and who would be a private person. Allowing the courts to define the controversy in terms of its value to self-governance gave them a powerful weapon. Once the controversy is framed in those terms, it is easy to manipulate the determina-tion of whether the plaintiff is a public or private person. It can be argued that defamation plaintiffs deserve more protection from the courts when the con-troversy does not involve a public issue; but when the test is used covertly, and is subject to ad hoc manipulation, no one knows in advance what the de-termination will be as to the status of the plaintiff.

It would be three years before the Supreme Court considered another major libel case, but when it did, the Court did not hesitate to continue down the road of limiting individuals who would be considered public figures.[78] In *Hutchinson v. Proxmire*[79] and *Wolston v. Reader's Digest*,[80] announced the same day in June 1979, the Court held two individuals who might have been considered public figures under previous standards to be private persons.

Ronald Hutchinson, a research behavioral scientist, sued Senator William Proxmire (D-Wisconsin) and his legislative assistant after the federal agency that sponsored his research was given Proxmire's Golden Fleece Award. The senator traditionally gave the award to federal agencies and others who, in his view, had wasted the taxpayers' money. Hutchinson claimed that the award and the nationwide publicity it received damaged him in his "professional and academic standing, and had interfered with his contractual relations."[81]

At the time Hutchinson received the award in April 1975, he was director of research at the Kalamazoo State Mental Hospital. He had received about half a million dollars in research money from several federal agencies during the preceding seven years.[82] Because the key issue in the Court's decision relates to Hutchinson's status, it is necessary to trace his employment history. Before working at the Kalamazoo hospital he had held a similar position at the Ft. Custer State Home:

> Both the hospital and the home are operated by the Michigan State Department of Mental Health; he was therefore a state employee in both positions. During most of the period in question he was also an adjunct professor at Western Michigan University. When the research department at Kalamazoo State Hospital was closed in June 1975, Hutchinson became research director of the Foundation for Behavioral Research, a nonprofit organization. The research funding was transferred from the hospital to the foundation.[83]

Hutchinson mostly studied emotional behavior and characteristics in animals, such as the "clenching of jaws when they were exposed to various aggravating stressful stimuli." The Court noted that NASA and the Navy were interested in the potential of Hutchinson's research for "resolving problems associated with confining humans in close quarters for extended periods of time in space and undersea exploration."[84]

Proxmire's legislative assistant, after examining copies of reports Hutchinson had submitted under grants from NASA, prepared a speech for the senator to be delivered on the floor of the Senate. The text of the speech was incorporated into an advance press release with only minor changes. Copies were sent to a mailing list of 275 members of the news media throughout the United States and abroad.[85] The legislative assistant called Hutchinson to tell him he was the recipient of the award, at which time he protested that the press release contained an "inaccurate and incomplete summary of his research." In the speech Proxmire criticized the spending of federal money on such research:

> The funding of this nonsense makes me almost angry enough to scream and kick or even clench my jaw. It seems to me it is outrageous.
>
> Dr. Hutchinson's studies should make the taxpayers as well as his monkeys grind their teeth. In fact, the good doctor has made a fortune from his monkeys and in the process made a monkey out of the American taxpayer.
>
> It is time for the Federal Government to get out of this "monkey business." In view of the transparent worthlessness of Hutchinson's study of jaw-grinding and biting by angry or hard-drinking monkeys, it is time we put a stop to the bite Hutchinson and the bureaucrats who fund him have been taking of the taxpayer.[86]

A month later Proxmire referred to the Golden Fleece Award in a newsletter sent to about 100,000 people in Wisconsin and other states. The final reference to the award was in a newsletter in early 1976. In April 1976, Hutchinson filed the libel suit in United States District Court in Wisconsin.[87] He argued not only that he had been humiliated by the publicity and suffered a loss of respect in his profession, but he argued that when Proxmire's assistant contacted the federal agencies to "discuss" the award with them, it interfered with his relationship to those who supported his research.

The Supreme Court had to determine if Proxmire's statements were protected by the speech or debate clause of the U.S. Constitution as was decided by the lower courts. For present purposes, those issues are not terribly important. Suffice it to note that the Court ruled, in essense, that Proxmire had waived any right to privilege under the clause by disseminating the information concerning the award in press releases and newsletters outside the Senate chambers:

> The precedents abundantly support the conclusion that a Member may be held liable for republishing defamatory statements originally made in either House. We perceive no basis for departing from that long-established rule. . . . A speech by Proxmire in the Senate would be wholly immune and would be available to other Members of Congress and the public in the Congressional Record. But neither the newsletters nor the press release was "essential to the deliberations of the Senate" and neither was part of the deliberation process.[88]

Of more immediate importance was the status of Hutchinson as a public figure or private person. The district court granted a summary judgment for Proxmire in part because it held Hutchinson to be a public figure and there was no evidence of actual malice:

> Given Dr. Hutchinson's long involvement with publicly-funded research, his active solicitation of federal and state grants, the local press coverage of his research, and the public interest in the expenditure of public funds on the precise activities in which he voluntarily participated, the court concludes that he is a public figure for the purpose of this suit. As he acknowledged in his deposition, "Certainly, any expenditure of public funds is a matter of public interest."[89]

The Supreme Court, in an 8-1 decision written by Chief Justice Warren Burger, rejected the notion that Hutchinson had thrust himself into a public controversy. Burger was not certain that Proxmire had even designated a "public controversy"; at best, it was a concern about general public expenditures:

> But that concern is shared by most and relates to most public expenditures; it is not sufficient to make Hutchinson a public figure. If it were, everyone who received or benefited from the myriad public grants for research could be classified as a public figure—a conclusion that our previous opinions have rejected.[90]

To Burger, Hutchinson had not achieved prominence in the "broad question of concern about expenditures." Neither his application for federal grants nor his publications in professional journals "invited that degree of public attention and comment on his receipt of federal grants essential to meet the public figure level." Burger believed that to whatever extent Hutchinson was a public figure, his notoriety was caused by Proxmire's giving him the award. The Court had said on a number of occasions that the media cannot make someone a public figure by the very statements that are the subject of the libel suit. Burger also believed that Hutchinson did not have the "regular and continuing access to the media that is one of the accoutrements of having become a public figure."[91]

Hutchinson v. Proxmire did not simply continue the Court's efforts to narrow the categories of individuals who would be considered public figures; the opinion also contains the famous footnote 9 in which the chief justice warned lower courts not to grant summary judgments for the defendants in libel suits quickly and deny plaintiffs their chance to prove their case to a jury. The district court, in finding no evidence of actual malice and granting summary judgment for Proxmire, said that in "determining whether a plaintiff had made an adequate showing of 'actual malice,' summary judgment might well be the rule rather than the exception." Summary judgment is one of the media's best friends, for it allows the dismissal of a libel suit before it gets to the trial stage. But Burger warned lower courts not to be hasty: "Considering the nuances of the issues raised here, we are constrained to express some doubt about the so-called 'rule.' The proof of 'actual malice' calls a defendant's state of mind into question and does not readily lend itself to summary disposition."[92]

These issues were considered in some detail in *Herbert v. Lando*, and the effects of Burger's footnote have been the subject of some debate.[93] Nevertheless, *Hutchinson* again demonstrated the Court's willingness to limit the categories of individuals who would be considered public figures. It apparently believed that the spending of federal money on research projects was not a public controversy, and Hutchinson was therefore was not a public figure.

On the same day it announced its decision in *Hutchinson*, the Supreme Court decided *Wolston v. Readers Digest*, which further narrowed the categories of individuals who would be considered public figures. In an 8-1 opinion written by Justice William Rehnquist, the Court even suggested that with the passage of time, someone who could have been considered a public figure some years ago would now be considered a private person.

In 1974 Reader's Digest Association published *KGB: The Secret Work of Soviet Agents*. In telling of Soviet espionage activities in the United States and elsewhere, the book listed more than a dozen names of individuals who were described as "Soviet agents identified in the United States." On the list was petitioner Ilya Wolston, whose index entry read, "Wolston, Ilya, Soviet agent in U.S.'' The book did not claim that the list was complete, but that it ''consists of Soviet agents who were convicted of espionage or falsifying information or perjury and/or contempt charges following espionage indictments, or who fled to the Soviet bloc to avoid prosecution.''[94]

Wolston sued the author of the book and Readers Digest Association for libel in the United States District Court for the District of Columbia, asserting that the passages in the book ''stating that he had been indicted for espionage and had been a Soviet agent were false and defamatory.''[95] The district court granted respondents' request for summary judgment, and also held that Wolston was a ''public figure.'' The court ruled that he could not recover damages unless he proved that the book was published with actual malice. The Supreme Court later noted that the district court had found some inaccuracies in the passages about Wolston, particularly the passages that ''appeared to state falsely that petitioner had been indicted for espionage,'' but the district court ruled that the evidence did not raise a ''genuine issue with respect to the existence of 'actual malice.' ''[96] The United States Court of Appeals for the District of Columbia affirmed.

In reversing the lower courts, the Supreme Court held that Wolston was not a public figure and if he had ever been, he certainly was not one at the time the book was published. In 1957 and 1958 a special federal grand jury in New York investigated the activities of Soviet intelligence agents in the United States. As a result of the investigation, Wolston's aunt and uncle, Myra and Jack Sobel, were arrested and later pleaded guilty to espionage charges. The grand jury's investigation led to participants in a suspected ''Soviet espionage ring'' and resulted in more arrests, convictions, and guilty pleas.[97] As part of the investigation, Wolston was interviewed in Washington, D.C., by FBI agents, was questioned several more times in Washington and New York, and ''traveled to New York on various occasions pursuant to grand jury subpoenas.''

After Wolston failed to appear on July 1, 1958 in response to a grand jury subpoena, a federal judge issued an order to show cause why he should not be held in criminal contempt of court. The Supreme Court noted in its opinion that Wolston had attempted to persuade law enforcement officials not to require him to travel to New York because of his ''state of mental depression.''[98] Wolston's failure to appear before the grand jury attracted some news coverage and at least seven news stories appeared in New York and Washington papers. Wolston did appear on the return date as ordered by the judge as part of the contempt hearing, but he was not allowed to testify:

> A hearing then commenced on the contempt charges. Petitioner's wife, who then was pregnant, was called to testify as to petitioner's mental condition at the time of the return date of the subpoena, but after she became hysterical on the

witness stand, petitioner agreed to plead guilty to the contempt charge. He received a 1-year suspended sentence and was placed on probation for three years, conditioned on his cooperation with the grand jury in any further inquiries regarding Soviet espionage.[99]

The Court noted that during the six-week period between Wolston's failure to appear and his sentencing, fifteen stories in newspapers in Washington and New York discussed the case; after he was sentenced, the publicity subsided and according to the Court, Wolston "succeeded for the most part in returning to the private life he had led prior to issuance of the grand jury subpoena. At no time was petitioner indicted for espionage."[100]

The Supreme Court refused to accept the reasoning of the lower courts that Wolston's failure to appear before the grand jury and his later appearance for the contempt hearing meant he had "become involved in a controversy of a decidedly public nature in a way that invited attention and comment, and thereby created in the public an interest in knowing about his connection with espionage."[101] To Rehnquist, the facts did not justify the conclusion that Wolston had "voluntarily thrust" or "injected" himself into the public controversy:

> It would be more accurate to say that petitioner was dragged unwillingly into the controversy. The Government pursued him in its investigation. Petitioner did fail to respond to a grand jury subpoena, and this failure, as well as his subsequent citation for contempt, did attract media attention. But the mere fact that petitioner voluntarily chose not to appear before the grand jury, knowing that his action might be attended by publicity, is not decisive on the question of public-figure status.[102]

Rehnquist made it clear that the Court was not returning to the public interest test adopted in *Rosenbloom* and discarded in *Gertz*. He argued that a private person is not "automatically transformed" into a public figure "just by becoming involved in or associated with a matter that attracts public attention." Such reasoning would be a return to *Rosenbloom*, which Rehnquist said was "repudiated in *Gertz* and in *Firestone*" and "we reject it again today."[103]

Finally, Rehnquist rejected the argument that any person who engages in criminal conduct automatically becomes a public figure for purposes of comment on a "limited range of issues relating to his conviction." Quoting from the Court's opinion in *Firestone*, Rehnquist argued that, like Mrs. Firestone, Wolston was drawn into a public forum largely against his will.

The Court not only decided that Wolston was not a public figure in 1974 when the book was published, but it seemed to suggest that he may not have been a public figure in 1957 and 1958 during the grand jury and contempt proceedings. In a concurring opinion joined by Justice Marshall, Justice

Blackmun was concerned that the majority had gone farther than it needed in limiting the public figure status, suggesting that his brethren would hold that a person is a public figure only if the person "literally or figuratively 'mounts a rostrum' to advocate a particular view."[104] This, Blackmun believed, adopted a more restrictive definition of public figure than was necessary in the Wolston case. But he also suggested that the passage of time was relevant in considering Wolston's status:

> Assuming... that petitioner gained public-figure status when he become involved in the espionage controversy in 1958, he clearly had lost that distinction by the time respondents published KGB in 1974. Because I believe that the lapse of the intervening 16 years renders consideration of this petitioner's original public-figure status unnecessary, I concur only in the result.[105]

The passage of time, to Blackmun, also affects the ability of the defamed individual to get access to the media for counterargument. During the time of a controversy a plaintiff may have access to channels of communication, but may not have access subsequently; in the case of Wolston, it was unlikely he would have similar access many years later when the book was published. And Blackmun saw in Wolston a conscious effort to return to "anonymity" during the sixteen years following the contempt hearing. Such a view may alarm those who are writing about past events, but Blackmun said there was no need to be concerned:

> This analysis implies, of course, that one may be a public figure for purposes of contemporaneous reporting of a controversial event, yet not be a public figure for purposes of historical commentary on the same occurrence. Historians, consequently, may well run a greater risk of liability for defamation. Yet this result, in my view, does no violence to First Amendment values. While historical analysis is no less vital to the marketplace of ideas than reporting current events, historians work under different conditions than do their media counterparts. A reporter trying to meet a deadline may find it totally impossible to check thoroughly the accuracy of his sources. A historian writing... has both the time for reflection and the opportunity to investigate the veracity of the pronouncements he makes.[106]

Although written in a concurring opinion and not in the Court's majority decision, such a notion should make journalists nervous. It is, of course, not simply historians who are looking at events in the past; journalists also report on past activities and events. It is true that reporters doing such stories may work under less deadline pressure, yet it is often true that with the passage of time, sources and documents may become harder to obtain and to verify, and it may not be possible, as Blackmun suggests, to check the accuracy of every statement in a publication or broadcast. In *Gertz*, *Firestone*, *Hutchinson*, and *Wolston*, the Supreme Court was able to limit severely the protection that media organizations had enjoyed under previous libel decisions; if other members of the Court agreed with Blackmun that public figure status can quickly slip away in the course of time, and express that view in a future case, journalists will find themselves in court facing even more plaintiffs designated as private persons.

The Supreme Court took from 1964 to 1971 to establish standards protective of the First Amendment. It took only five years, from 1974 to 1979, to embark on a campaign to make it easier for those unhappy with the way they have been treated in the media to sue. And in the process, the Court demonstrated an unashamed hostility to the First Amendment claims of journalists. The First Amendment had been around for a long time but, to the Burger Court, it meant something very different in the 1970s from what it had meant in the 1964-1971 period. None of the previous cases had been directly overruled, and the eloquent language of *New York Times v. Sullivan* remained on the books. But certainly the luster was gone from many of those phrases, and people concerned about the First Amendment found little during the Burger Court years about which they could feel positive. Clearly, *Gertz* had some pro-First Amendment provisions, particularly the then-new requirement that states cannot impose liability even for private plaintiffs unless there is some evidence of fault. But the most ominous development from the point of view of journalists was the Court's very successful campaign not only to discard the public interest test in *Rosenbloom*, but to limit the categories of individuals who might be considered public figures and thus have to meet the actual malice standard. And as suggested before, there may be an inherent conflict of interest in allowing state courts to determine plaintiff status, for if they choose private person, state laws, court decisions, and customs apply; if, on the other hand, they choose public figure, then complicated Supreme Court opinions must be followed.

This is not to suggest that state courts are universally hostile to media defendants and anxious to designate libel plaintiffs as private persons. In many of the cases discussed in the preceding three chapters, state and federal courts have found for the media organization, sometimes by granting summary judgment, other times by designating individuals to be public figures. But in the wake of the Supreme Court's determination in the years from 1974 to 1979 not only to limit the use of summary judgment, but to instruct lower courts repeatedly that the cases in which someone is considered to be a public figure will become more and more uncommon, the effect over time must be a corresponding narrowing of the public figure status by lower courts.

The Supreme Court relies on lower courts to comply with its decisions. When those decisions are ambiguous or unpopular, compliance may take a long time. But eventually, lower courts stop fighting, and even those judges who are most sympathetic to the First Amendment claims of journalists cannot forever resist repeated Supreme Court instructions on these issues.

From 1979 to 1983 the Supreme Court declined to review what could be considered a major libel case, but in the fall of 1983 the Court considered three cases that raised a number of important issues. On November 8, 1983 the Court heard oral arguments in a case that could have substantial inipact on the ability of media organizations whose publications or broadcasts are distributed nationally to fight libel suits.[107] In recent years plaintiffs filing libel suits against national media organizations have often looked for the forum most hostile to First Amendment interests. Networks and nationally distributed print organizations have found themselves defending libel suits in distant and sometimes unfriendly environments even if only a fraction of their total circulation is in that particular state or jurisdiction.

An associate publisher of *Penthouse*, Kathy Keeton, sued Larry Flynt and *Hustler* magazine for libel. Because the statute of limitations had expired in every other state, Keeton filed her lawsuit in New Hampshire, which, according to the *New York Times*, accounts for less than 1 percent of *Hustler*'s circulation. Her lawsuit was dismissed by both the federal district court and the United States Court of Appeals for the First Circuit, which argued that "neither the plaintiff nor the magazine had a sufficient connection with New Hampshire to permit the case to be heard in that state."

Keeton's lawyer argued before the Supreme Court that *Hustler* had engaged in "willful, purposeful economic activity" in New Hampshire by circulating copies there. *Hustler*'s lawyer told the Court that "forum shopping presents a real danger to our Federal system."

The Court also heard arguments in a case involving actress Shirley Jones and *National Enquirer*. She sued the magazine, which is based in Florida but has wide distribution in California. The magazine did not fight the decision to hear the case in California, but Jones also sued an *Enquirer* editor and a reporter as individuals. The California Court of Appeals had rejected the editor's and reporter's argument that they should not be forced to defend themselves in a state "with which they had only insubstantial contacts." Neither had entered California while working on the article. Jones's lawyer argued that the *Enquirer* employees "knew their article would be circulated in Calfornia," where Jones lived. "There is no unfairness at subjecting someone who willfully wrongs a resident of a state to the jurisdiction of that state."

On March 20, 1984 the Supreme Court announced its decisions in the *Keeton* and *Jones* cases. A unanimous Court held that Keeton could sue *Hustler* magazine in New Hampshire. Justice William Rehnquist, writing the opinion, held that "the tort of libel is generally held to occur wherever the offending material is circulated. . . . The reputation of the libel victim may suffer harm even in a state in which he has hitherto been anonymous."[108] Rehnquist also argued that *Hustler* should expect to "answer for the contents of that publication wherever a substantial number of copies are sold and distributed."

Rehnquist also wrote the Court's unanimous opinion holding that the reporters for the *National Enquirer* must defend the libel suit in Jones's home state of California. He wrote, "the brunt of the harm, in terms both of respondent's emotional distress and the injury to her professional reputation was suffered in California."[109]

The third case, argued the same day as *Keeton* and *Jones*, could be especially significant for media organizations defending libel suits because so many trial court decisions favorable to the plaintiff are overturned on appeal. At issue was the extent to which a federal appellate court may make an independent review of the evidence in determining whether the actual malice standard has been satisfied. After Bose Corporation, considered by the trial court to be a public figure, won a libel suit against *Consumer Reports*, the United States Court of Appeals for the First Circuit conducted an independent review of the evidence and overturned the judgment.

Bose's lawyer told the Supreme Court that federal rules of civil procedure require the appeals court to accept the trial judge's "factual findings" rather than draw its own conclusions from what he called the "cold, printed record." The lawyer for Consumers Union, publisher of the magazine, argued that forcing an appellate court to accept the trial court's factual finding would make libel judgments essentially "impervious to review."

On April 30, 1984 the Supreme Court, by a vote of 6-3, agreed with the court of appeals that there was inadequate evidence to justify a libel judgment against Consumers Union, and it overturned the $210,000 award. Justice John Paul Stevens, writing the majority opinion, said appellate review was an integral part of the First Amendment principles established by the Court twenty years earlier, and that independent appellate review "reflects a deeply held conviction that judges—and particularly members of this Court—must exercise such review in order to preserve the precious liberties established and ordained by the Constitution."[110]

After almost two decades of involvement in libel, the Supreme Court had drastically altered the previously uninterrupted efforts of the states to develop their own standards. The Court had placed into law thousands of words that the states were bound to follow in striking a balance between reputational and First Amendment interests. The Court did leave one major area of the law to the states: determining the appropriate standard of liability in cases involving private persons. How the states have reacted to and complied with Supreme Court decisions in libel continues to be a subject of much importance. In consideration of the Court's efforts to limit drastically the categories of individuals who could be considered public figures, the states' role in establishing standards in the post-*Gertz* era is especially important.

Notes

1. In a famous concurring opinion in *Ashwander v. Tennesee Valley Authority*, 297 U.S. 288 (1936), Justice Brandeis reviewed the standards the Court had developed to avoid passing on constitutional questions. Among them were the following:

   1. The Court will not anticipate a question of constitutional law in advance of the necessity of deciding it, nor is it the habit of the Court to decide questions of a constitutional nature unless absolutely necessary to a decision of the case.
   2. The Court will not formulate a rule of constitutional law broader than is required by the precise facts to which it is to be applied.
   3. The Court will not pass upon a constitutional question, although properly presented by the record, if there is also present some other ground upon which the case may be disposed of. Thus, if a case can be decided on either of two grounds, one involving a constitutional question, the other a question of statutory construction or general law, the Court will decide only the latter.
   4. When the validity of an act of the Congress is drawn in question, and even if a serious doubt of constitutionality is raised, it is a cardinal principle that the Court will first ascertain whether a construction of the statute is fairly possible by which the question may be avoided. [C. Herman Pritchett, *The American Constitution* (New York: McGraw-Hill, 1977), pp. 136-37.]

2. See discussion of the preferred position theory of the First Amendment in chapter 2.
3. Beginning in 1969 Richard Nixon made four appointments to the Supreme Court: Chief Justice Warren Burger in 1969; Harry Blackmun in 1970; and Lewis Powell and William Rehnquist in 1971. Chief Justice Earl Warren and Justice Abe Fortas left the Court in 1969; Hugo Black and John Harlan, in 1971.
4. 403 U.S. 29 (1971).
5. 418 U.S. 323 (1974).
6. Ibid. at 325.
7. Ibid.
8. Ibid. at 326.
9. Ibid.
10. Ibid.
11. Ibid.
12. Ibid. at 328.
13. Ibid. at 329.
14. Ibid.
15. Ibid.
16. Ibid. at 330.
17. 471 F. 2d 801 (1972) at 805.
18. 418 U.S. at 332.
19. Ibid. at 333.
20. 403 U.S. at 43; 418 U.S. at 337.
21. 418 U.S. at 342.

22. 418 U.S. at 344.
23. Powell recognized that even when a victim of defamation has been given a chance to respond, the damage in most cases has already been done:
    > Of course, an opportunity for rebuttal seldom suffices to undo harm of defamatory falsehood. Indeed, the law of defamation is rooted in our experience that the truth rarely catches up with a lie. But the fact that the self-help remedy of rebuttal, standing alone, is inadequate to its task does not mean that it is irrelevant to our inquiry. [Ibid. at 344 n. 9.]
24. Ibid. at 345.
25. Ibid.
26. Ibid. at 345-46.
27. Ibid. at 346.
28. Ibid. at 347-48.
29. Ibid. at 348.
30. Ibid. at 349.
31. Ibid.
32. Ibid. at 350.
33. Ibid. at 352.
34. Ibid. at 354.
35. Ibid.
36. Ibid. at 363-64.
37. Ibid. at 367.
38. Ibid. at 370.
39. Ibid.
40. Ibid. at 390.
41. Ibid. at 390-91.
42. The author is grateful to Eileen Carroll Prager, who makes some of these points in an incisive article, "Public Figures, Private Figures and Public Interest," 30 *Stanford Law Review* (November 1977): 157-89.
43. See, for example, *Dietemann v. Time, Inc.*, 499 F. 2d 245 (1971), a case in which *Life* magazine lost a privacy suit even though the report was accurate.
44. 424 U.S. 448 (1976).
45. 424 U.S. at 452. The "Milestones" item ran 22 December 1967.
46. Ibid. at 450-51.
47. Ibid. at 451.
48. Ibid. at 452.
49. Ibid. at 453.
50. Ibid. at 453-54.
51. Ibid. at 454-55; from *Gertz*, 418 U.S. at 351.
52. 420 U.S. 469 (1975).
53. 424 U.S. at 455.
54. Ibid. at 455-56.
55. Ibid. at 456.
56. Ibid. at 457.
57. Ibid. at 458.
58. Ibid. at 458-59; emphasis in original.
59. The case is discussed in chapter 4.
60. 424 U.S. at 459.
61. Ibid. at 461.
62. Ibid.
63. Ibid. at 462.

64. Ibid. at 462-63.
65. Ibid. at 463.
66. Ibid. at 470; emphasis in original. Justice Stewart joined this concurring opinion.
67. Ibid. at 476-77.
68. Ibid. at 481.
69. Ibid. at 476.
70. Ibid. at 483-84; emphasis in original.
71. Ibid. at 485.
72. Ibid. Rehnquist rejected the idea that because Mrs. Firestone had held a number of press conferences she had become a public figure:

> Nor do we think the fact that respondent may have held a few press conferences during the divorce proceedings in an attempt to satisfy inquiring reporters converts her into a "public figure." Such interviews should have had no effect upon the merits of the legal dispute between respondent and her husband or the outcome of that trial, and we do not think it can be assumed that any such purpose was intended. Moreover, there is no indication that she sought to use the press conferences as a vehicle by which to thrust herself to the forefront of some unrelated controversy in order to influence its resolution. [Ibid. at 454-55 n. 3.]

73. Ibid. at 485-86.
74. Ibid. at 487.
75. Ibid.
76. Ibid. at 489.
77. Prager, "Public Figures, Private Figures and Public Interest," pp. 175-76.
78. On 18 April 1979, the Court announced its decision in *Herbert v. Lando*, 441 U.S. 153. The case was discussed in chapter 3. Brennan's dissent will be considered in a later chapter.
79. 443 U.S. 111 (1979).
80. 443 U.S. 157 (1979).
81. 443 U.S. at 114.
82. Ibid. Hutchinson had received grants from such agencies as the Office of Naval Research, the National Science Foundation, the National Aeronautics and Space Administration, and the Michigan State Department of Mental Health. [Ibid. at 114-15.]
83. Ibid. at 115.
84. Ibid.
85. 443 U.S. at 116. The Supreme Court noted that Proxmire was not certain that he had ever delivered the speech on the floor of the Senate:

> He said that he might have merely inserted it into the Congressional Record. In light of that uncertainty, the question arises whether a nondelivered speech printed in the Congressional Record is covered by the Speech or Debate Clause. This Court has never passed on that question and neither the District Court nor the Court of Appeals seemed to think it was important. Nevertheless, we assume, without deciding, that a speech printed in the Congressional Record carries immunity under the Speech or Debate Clause as though delivered on the floor. [Ibid. at 116 n. 3.]

86. Ibid. at 116; 121 Cong. Rec. 10803 (1975).
87. 443 U.S. at 118.
88. Ibid. at 127-28, 130.

89. 431 F. Supp. 1325, at 1327; 443 U.S. at 119.
90. 443 U.S. at 135.
91. Ibid. at 136.
92. Ibid. at 120 n. 9.
93. Reaction to Burger's footnote has varied with some state courts continuing to grant summary dismissal in most cases involving public figures who failed to demonstrate convincing evidence of actual malice, while other states have followed Burger's warning more closely.
94. 443 U.S. at 159.
95. Ibid. at 160.
96. Ibid.
97. Ibid. at 161-62.
98. Ibid. at 162.
99. Ibid. at 163.
100. Ibid.
101. Ibid. at 165.
102. Ibid. at 166-67.
103. Ibid. at 167.
104. Ibid. at 169.
105. Ibid. at 170.
106. Ibid. at 171.
107. Linda Greenhouse, "High Court Focuses on 3 Libel Cases," *New York Times*, 9 November 1983, p. B8.
108. Linda Greenhouse, "High Court Rules Libel Suits May Be Filed in Distant Jurisdictions," *New York Times*, 21 March 1984, p. A18.
109. Ibid. On 27 April 1984 the *New York Times* reported that Jones and the Enquirer had settled for an unspecified amount of compensation, and that the magazine had agreed to a retraction of the article that had accused Jones of being too drunk to work on a television series. Aljean Harmetz, "*National Enquirer* Agrees to Settle with Shirley Jones in Libel Suit," *New York Times*, 27 April 1984, p. A17.
110. Linda Greenhouse, "High Court Calls for Special Care in Libel Appeals," *New York Times*, 1 May 1984, p. A18.

6

Broadcasting and Libel: Potential for Trouble

In January 1978, KGO-TV, a station in San Francisco owned by the American Broadcasting Company, aired a series of reports on Synanon Foundation, a nonprofit organization that was founded to rehabilitate alcoholics and drug addicts. Formed in 1958, Synanon by the 1970s had gained an international reputation. But for those who claimed that the organization used threats and violence against neighbors of its northern California headquarters, and against its own members who tried to leave the group, it was no better than the most repressive religious cult.[1] After the group allegedly purchased a large quantity of guns and ammunition, KGO-TV broadcast reports about the group's weapons and alleged that Synanon's head, Charles Dederich, was under investigation for skimming funds from Synanon.[2]

In suing KGO-TV and ABC for libel, Synanon asked for $21 million in damages for the organization, and $21 million for Dederich. By the time the case ended four years later, it proved to be one of the most frightening examples of what happens when a determined organization or individual presses a libel suit, and how poorly suited the courts are to deal with such cases.

According to the *Los Angeles Times*, four months into the trial ABC unexpectedly settled the case for $1.25 million, at the time the largest defamation settlement in the history of American law.[3] And it was reported that defending the lawsuit for four years cost an estimated $7 million.[4]

It is difficult to imagine that legal expenses could amount to that much, and it may be harder to understand why ABC and KGO-TV would settle a lawsuit that they were certain to win. After the suit was filed, the two sides began the slow process of pretrial discovery, where each party requests documents and other information and makes available witnesses for sworn testimony in depositions. ABC sought a great number of documents from Synanon, which had extensive files. As the pretrial procedures continued, ABC eventually

181

won a court order directing Synanon to turn over documents relating to the case. What arrived surprised even ABC's lawyers: Synanon delivered 200,000 documents. Defense attorneys had to hire extra help to examine them and they were eventually microfilmed and indexed by computer. When Dederich finally agreed to give a deposition, his testimony filled twenty volumes of transcribed text.[5]

While ABC's legal expenses mounted, the company heard bad news from Lloyd's of London, the company with whom it had a million-dollar insurance policy. Lloyd's informed ABC that the $1 million mark in legal expenses had been passed and the insurance company was dropping out of the case.[6] ABC then sued Lloyd's, arguing that the policy required it to pay legal fees, settlements, and court judgments. ABC was now on its own to defend the Synanon lawsuit.

After four months of court testimony, ABC unexpectedly informed the judge that it had settled with Synanon in return for Synanon's agreement to drop other suits pending against ABC. The *Los Angeles Times* quoted shocked and bitter employees who believed that vindication of their First Amendment rights required ABC to pursue the lawsuit, and jurors who asserted that ABC would have won a unanimous verdict. ABC did not discuss the case publicly, but the implication is that it settled to avoid having to spend any more on legal expenses.[7]

ABC and KGO-TV survived the libel suit brought by Synanon, but a smaller station with fewer resources may not have been so fortunate. Not all individuals who sue broadcasting organizations pursue their lawsuits with the dedication of Synanon Foundation, and its lawsuit against KGO-TV may not be typical of libel suits against the broadcast media. Yet, for a number of reasons, broadcast news organizations have the potential of being the targets of a multitude of libel suits. In light of the number of people who say that television is their primary source of news, the characteristics of a broadcasting organization that make it susceptible to libel suits and the effects of such suits on news coverage are worthy of examination.[8]

For many years, CBS News has enjoyed a reputation as a first-rate news organization. It program "60 Minutes," for example, which has been at or near the top of the ratings for years, showcases investigative reports by some of television's best-known journalists.[9] The network also features documentaries on important and controversial topics. There are some who believe that one documentary in particular not only cost CBS millions of dollars in legal expenses, but exposed for all to see the techniques some broadcast journalists employ in preparing their stories.

On September 13, 1982 General William Westmoreland, former commander of United States forces in Vietnam, filed a $120 million libel suit against CBS.[10] Westmoreland asserted that the documentary "The Uncounted

Enemy: A Vietnam Deception,'' which was broadcast on January 23, 1982 had damaged his reputation. The documentary said that Westmoreland headed a "conspiracy, at the highest levels of American military intelligence, to suppress and alter critical intelligence on the enemy" during the Vietnam War.[11] Westmoreland explained that his filing of the libel suit had nothing to do with money or vengeance, but was the only way "for me to clear my name, my honor and the honor of the military."[12]

The evidence gathered by CBS and presented in the documentary seemed to prove that Westmoreland and others conspired to deceive President Lyndon Johnson, Congress, and the public about how the war was going. The documentary charged that beginning in 1967 Westmoreland had systematically underreported to his superiors the size and strength of the enemy.[13]

On September 8, 1982 CBS took the unusual step of offering Westmoreland fifteen minutes of unedited time during a proposed one-hour prime-time program as a follow-up of the original documentary.[14] If not a direct violation of CBS news policy, the offer of unedited time was certainly unusual, and it created speculation that CBS was having second thoughts about how fairly it had treated Westmoreland in the documentary.[15] During the summer of 1982 CBS had prepared a sixty-eight-page internal report on the broadcast that concluded that "five violations of CBS News practices had been committed in its preparation," but that CBS stood by the documentary.[16] Westmoreland demanded that CBS apologize for the original documentary and that he be granted access to the internal report. CBS had planned in the new show to follow Westmoreland's fifteen-minute statement with a panel discussion among various individuals knowledgeable in this area, including some who had been involved with or had been interviewed for the original documentary. Instead, in a letter written to Thomas Wyman, president of CBS, Westmoreland asked for a compensatory payment for the harm he had suffered and "a full retraction, of not less than 45 minutes duration," in which CBS would present the "actual facts and methods of preparation, concerning the story you published. The material in this retraction and the production itself must be subject to my complete approval."[17] A few weeks later CBS News President Van Gordon Sauter refused to agree to the conditions, but repeated the invitation to have Westmoreland appear on the follow-up broadcast. Westmoreland declined to accept the offer and filed the libel suit against CBS.[18]

To add to CBS's problems, *TV Guide* published a cover story in its May 29, 1982 issue entitled "Anatomy of a Smear."[19] *TV Guide* argued that CBS began the project already convinced that there had been a conspiracy to mislead the country about the war, and that the producers of the program ignored evidence that suggested otherwise.[20] CBS also paid $25,000 to a consultant for help in researching the documentary, then violated its own news guidelines by coaching the consultant on the questions he would face in the on-camera interview to be used in the broadcast.[21] *TV Guide* also accused CBS of taking quotations out of context, and in one case implying incorrectly that Westmoreland was familiar with a meeting where estimates of the enemy were arbitrarily reduced.[22] The magazine concluded that CBS failed in a number of respects to live up to its reputation as a first-rate news organization:

> Viewers of "The Uncounted Enemy" are left with the memory of a 90-minute documentary misshapen by personal bias and poor supervision. It seems clear that [producer] George Crile began work on the documentary already so firmly convinced of the conspiracy theory that . . . in several instances he failed to include in the documentary information from authoritative sources that cast doubt on [the] theory. . . . The inaccuracies, distortions and violations of journalistic standards . . . suggest that television news' "safeguards" for fairness and accuracy need tightening, if not wholesale revision.[23]

In April 1983, CBS made public the internal report it had prepared on the documentary[24] The report, along with dozens of letters and transcripts of interviews, was released after a federal judge ordered that they be turned over to Westmoreland as he prepared for his libel suit against CBS.[25] CBS had argued that the First Amendment protected the internal document, that its release would inhibit news organizations from initiating studies of work they had produced. The judge ruled, in the words of the *New York Times*, that "CBS had destroyed its right to withhold the report by disclosing portions of it last July to substantiate the points made in the documentary."

The report provided some information beyond the summary that had been released the previous year. It found that there were eleven "principal flaws" in the preparation of the documentary, including "coddling sympathetic witnesses," choosing to interview mostly witnesses who supported the program's overall conclusions, and failing to prove that there had been a "conspiracy" to suppress information about enemy troop strength during the Vietnam War.[26] The report contained portions of unedited transcripts that provided information on material that had been excluded from the broadcast that might have "undermined the documentary's principal conclusions about Westmoreland's actions in the war."[27]

As a public figure, Westmoreland had the responsibility of proving that CBS had acted with actual malice. The Supreme Court had said that in gathering information to prove that an individual who makes a defamatory statement knew it was false or recklessly disregarded whether it was false or not, the plaintiff is entitled to probe the thought processes of the journalists who prepared the statements.[28] In ordering CBS to turn over to Westmoreland the internal report, the judge noted that it "may well lead to evidence of degree of care for accuracy, concern for truthfulness, and possible bias, prejudgment or malice."[29]

In a related development, CBS suspended the producer of the documentary, George Crile, after it became known that he had secretly tape-recorded telephone conversations with former Secretary of Defense Robert S. McNamara and others while preparing the broadcast.[30] CBS said that Crile had violated a written news policy against taping interviews without the consent of the interviewee or "the express permission of the president of CBS News or his designee."[31] In explaining why he had taped McNamara, Crile was quoted as saying, "I was simply trying to get as accurate a record of his remarks as possible." Crile said "it might have been inhibiting" to disclose that he was recording the conversation. He originally told CBS's lawyers that the tapes of the conversation had been lost or erased.[32] McNamara called such a practice "entirely unethical" and said, "I hope that isn't standard CBS practice."[33]

There was widespread speculation as to why Westmoreland would bring a lawsuit against CBS in the first place. Apparently several organizations known for their dislike of the news media "persuaded" Westmoreland to pursue the libel suit against CBS, and the *New York Times* noted that his legal expenses were being paid by several conservative groups.[34]

CBS, in fighting the lawsuit, maintained that it had discovered what its lawyers called a "smoking gun." A 1967 memo written by a CIA official said that "a variety of circumstantial indicators" had led him to the "inescapable conclusion" that Westmoreland had given "instructions tantamount to a direct order" to hold the estimate of Vietcong strength to 300,000.[35] According to the *New York Times*, the author of the memo denies that it was an indictment of Westmoreland and states that it "was jerked out of context."

During the last week of February 1985, and five months into the trial, Westmoreland and his attorneys announced that he was dropping his lawsuit against CBS. Although Westmoreland received no money, no vindication by a jury, and no retraction by CBS, he believed that the joint statement issued by him and CBS was "in essence an apology." The statement read in part: "CBS respects General Westmoreland's long and faithful service to his country and never intended to assert, and does not believe, that General Westmoreland was unpatriotic or disloyal in performing his duties as he saw fit."[36]

Some jurors expressed disappointment at not being allowed to render a verdict just days before they were to receive the case. Several indicated publicly that they were leaning toward CBS. There was widespread speculation that Westmoreland knew he was going to lose after former colleagues testified against him in the days prior to his calling an end to the lawsuit.

Whatever the eventual impact of Westmoreland's suit against CBS, public exposure of the methods the network used in preparing the documentary probably does not add to public confidence in the accuracy and fairness of broadcast news organizations. If nothing else, the Westmoreland suit does indicate how difficult it can be for public figures to win libel suits against media organizations, and that such suits may be very costly in terms of resources and the reputation of the news organization. It is difficult to predict whether Westmoreland's experience will encourage or discourage other public figures from bringing libel suits against major news organizations.

A broadcast news organization whose methods of reporting a story call into question not only its ethics, but its competency, can still suffer damage to its reputation even when successful in defending a libel suit. That is what happened in the view of some observers when CBS and "60 Minutes" successfully defended a libel suit against a Los Angeles doctor in 1983.

On December 9, 1979 "60 Minutes" broadcast a segment reported by correspondent Dan Rather entitled "I's No Accident." It examined an insurance fraud scheme in which a number of individuals at a Los Angeles clinic, including Dr. Carl A. Galloway, allegedly bilked insurance companies through the use of phony medical claims.[37] Rather held before the cameras what he said was a bogus medical report, like those used in the alleged scam, and said that "it was signed by Dr. Carl A. Galloway, M.D." Galloway argued at his slander trial against CBS that his signature had been forged, that he had no knowledge of fraudulent activities, and that he had left the clinic more than a month before the "60 Minutes" report.[38] Galloway sued CBS for $30 million in damages.

On June 6, 1983 a jury, by a vote of 10-2, after three days of deliberations, ruled in favor of CBS.[39] Outside the courtroom, the jury foreman was quoted by the *New York Times* as saying, "We were trying to figure out what was in Dan Rather's mind at the time of the broadcast, and most of us did not feel he had acted in reckless disregard for the truth." And he said of Galloway, "It's a very sad thing for him but we have to do what we think is right."[40]

But to Galloway, the libel laws under which the case was tried never gave him a chance: "I don't know of anyone who could be convicted of defamation under any circumstances, because all they would have to say is 'I never thought about...,'" referring to Rather's testimony that he never had any doubt about the authenticity of the doctor's signature on the bogus medical report.[41]

Between the time the report was filmed and the time it was aired, Rather, according to his testimony, left several messages for Galloway at the clinic and producer Steve Glauber subsequently left several more messages. Rather considered Galloway's failure to return those messages to be an admission of guilt, an attitude described by Galloway's attorney as "arrogant."[42] That view may have been encouraged by Rather himself during the three days he spent testifying in the trial. Although he admitted that he never met or talked to Galloway during the preparation of the report, he told the jury that "if it looks like a duck, walks like a duck and quacks like a duck, you've got a duck.''[43] He also had several other comments that suggested that he was not taking seriously Galloway's efforts to vindicate his reputation.[44]

CBS won the case, but its reputation as a news organization did not emerge unscathed. One observer, noting that there was time to check the story out more carefully before it was aired, criticized such methods:

> With so much at stake for everyone involved, the failure to have the [Galloway's] signature checked by a handwriting expert can only be attributed to the rush to air the story. An expert called to court testified that it was a forgery. The best CBS could muster were claims of followup phone calls, with their authenticity disputed in court as well. Hunkered down behind a ''nobody ever called back'' defense, the network may have presented the more convincing version for jurors. For a company with the resources and impact of CBS it seemed lame to cite undocumented phone calls when a copy of a registered letter clearly spelling out the accusation to be made and an invitation to respond would certainly be a far more credible sign of acting ''in good faith.''[45]

Even those relieved that CBS had won were afraid that the publicity generated by the case would lead to more libel suits. A well-known First Amendment attorney, Floyd Abrams, expressed such a concern: ''Probably the very fact of widespread coverage may bring some more people to court than might otherwise have been the case.''[46] At the time of the Galloway case, CBS had fifty-seven libel suits pending against it, a number comparable to other recent years, according to a CBS executive.[47] CBS did suffer some embarrassment when the ''outtakes'' from the report were shown to the jury. The ''outtakes,'' filmed segments not shown on the air, were ordered turned over to Galloway. In the outtakes, a woman is being questioned by an investigator, later described on the air as ''tough questioning.'' The outtakes reveal, however, that the woman had already admitted she had filed a false claim, and the outtakes indicated that the interview was shot many times.[48] In another portion of the outtakes not shown on the air, Rather pursues a clinic employee into the parking lot and when he refuses to talk, Rather says, ''Adios, see you on television.'' There were some, such as Fred W. Friendly, former president of CBS News and now professor at the Columbia School of Journalism, who thought such examinations of the media were positive: ''All libel has a chilling effect . . . but we dish it out. We put our cameras on an awful lot of people. I think the fact that we are accountable that way can't help but be good for all of us. The fact that CBS was willing to defend itself is an indication that they believe in their own product.''[49]

The *Synanon, Westmoreland,* and *Galloway* cases provide some indication of the problems broadcasters face in defending libel suits. Although the development of libel laws has centered largely on cases involving newspapers and other print media outlets, broadcast organizations, because of their impact, visibility, and the nature of the journalism they practice, are tempting targets of those anxious to recover damages in libel suits. With some exceptions, to be discussed below, libel laws do not distinguish between print and broadcast journalists; however, the circumstances leading to libel litigation reflect institutional differences between the media. In addition, juries contribute an additional element by reacting to television's high visibility and impact.

Some of the evidence for such a theory is gleaned from direct observation within the broadcasting industry and may be anecdotal in nature. Other evidence comes from studying libel cases involving broadcasting organizations, and from observing the final products of broadcast journalists, namely newscasts, public affairs shows, and other programs that could lead to libel litigation. Initially, the discussion is limited to television, the medium that most Americans identify as their primary source of news. Because of the way news is gathered and reported on television, there is the potential for increased libel litigation and thus, increased self-censorship on the part of broadcast journalists. The nature of television news and the potential for libel trouble created by it are worthy of serious examination.

Working within a visual medium, television news organizations need to provide pictures to go with their news stories. Yet it is much easier to photograph and interview individuals than issues. Television is most adept at transmitting emotion, and people, not issues, emote. Television news can be most personal, sometimes to a fault. As an audience, we feel great sympathy for the parents who have just learned that their son has died in fighting abroad, but we may have mixed feelings about the interview. We can be curious about the reaction of people in such a situation, we can also believe that the showing of such an interview on television is a clear invasion of privacy, which may make us feel both uncomfortable and worried that if we were to be involved in such a story, the camera could be pointed at us. It is much easier for broadcast journalists to film parents who have just been informed that their son was killed in battle than it is to explain the war in which he gave his life.[50]

When a television camera is turned on, it cannot record pictures of an "issue" such as the economy, or unemployment, or corruption in local government. Instead, it captures a reporter talking to individuals waiting in the unemployment line, or trying to get a public official to admit taking kickbacks. Many issues of importance in today's society, and thus worthy of news coverage, are immensely complicated. Newspaper articles can explain the history and details of an issue in a way that is almost impossible in television, and print reporters can devote a significant amount of time to the issue itself. Television, because of the need to treat an issue visually within a short period, concentrates instead on persons associated with it.

There is substantial pressure in television news to "personalize" each story. The pressure sometimes comes from those convinced that such techniques help with ratings; sometimes from those who think the audience will simply be better able to understand the significance or context of the story. Whatever the reason, the personalization of television news distinguishes it somewhat from print and presents an almost endless variety of potential libel suits.

Television personalizes by demonstrating to the audience how an issue or circumstance would affect an ordinary individual. It has been a year since the state's new drunk driving law has gone into effect. The newspaper concentrates on statistics—the number of arrests and convictions now as opposed to last year—and interviews with police officers who discuss telltale signs of drunk drivers. But a television news report of a minute and a half's duration cannot dwell on statistics. It needs pictures of someone's being stopped by police on suspicion of drunk drinking and being given a sobriety test. The camera captures the police removing an empty liquor bottle from the car and the suspect being taken away in the police car. We may never learn whether the alcohol level in the suspect's blood is above the legal limit.

A city council is deciding whether to approve a zoning change that would allow a five-story, low-rent apartment building in what had been a largely residential neighborhood. The newspaper reporter may interview various residents who object to the construction of the building, and is likely to use comments that are mostly representative of the views of the majority of residents. The television reporter is drawn not to soft-spoken, thoughtful individuals whose comments may reflect the sentiments of the neighbors, but to the persons who are the most animated or lively in interviews. Such persons are especially appealing to the television reporter because they introduce the additional element that their objections may be racist in nature, and not just that the apartment building would change the makeup of the neighborhood. The viewpoint may not just be unrepresentative; those holding it may constitute a very small minority. Nevertheless, if they are visually interesting, they are more likely to be chosen for the television interview than the less colorful, less outspoken residents whose attitudes may be more representative. When the interview is shown, the others strenuously take exception to the use of pictures of their demonstration in a story that "suggests" residents are racists by objecting to the new apartment building. Yet, the story has been personalized because the audience knows how this story "affects" people like them.

A new study has come out with evidence indicating that violence and vandalism are becoming increasingly serious problems in public schools. The newspaper article discusses in detail the scope of the problem: how much vandalism there is; how much the repairs cost; how many assaults against teachers there are; how many arrests. Although the television reporter's narration includes some of the above information, and that narration can be shown over pictures of the outside of the school, or the broken windows, eventually the report will show pictures of the students. There may be the unavoidable impression that the students shown during the report are either guilty of such acts or capable of them. Yet without such pictures of the students, the report would not be personalized.

The differences between print and broadcast media are seen in the very stories that are chosen. As the above discussion suggests, television needs to cover stories that either automatically lend themselves to a visual presentation or have an aspect that can be visualized. Both media may be attracted to a story on abuse of the food stamp program; the television camera shows a person at the grocery checkout using food stamps. Even a disclaimer in the narration that the individual shown is not an abuser of food stamps does not totally erase the implication that the person is doing something wrong. Why else would the person be on camera?

Local television in particular spends a substantial amount of time covering stories that are appealing because they have visual elements and can be covered quickly. Fires, automobile accidents, demonstrations, press conferences, and government meetings are prominently featured on local newscasts for those reasons. They also allow a reporter to cover and report on them within the same day. Other stories that may be more important to a community are more scarce because they require a time commitment that may last several days or more. There is not only little time to show a television news story on the air, but often little time to gather the information and put the story together.

If there is an inherent bias in television news, it is haste. Few reporters, whether working for print or broadcast organizations, intentionally set out to damage someone's reputation. But under the time pressures of producing a daily newscast or daily newspaper, mistakes are easily made. It is not unusual, in many television stations, for a reporter to be responsible for more than one story in a day. A reporter who cannot stay with a story for very long may rely on others for information that may or may not be reliable. In some cases, the reporter relies on a newsmaker or those with a personal interest in the story for information. A news director, producer, or assignment editor clamoring for a reporter to produce several stories that day will not be very understanding if the reporter stays so long at the first story to double-check all the facts that the press conference across town is not covered. The reporter may then end up relying on others for information in situations where, if there were more time, he or she would have checked everything personally. It is true, of course, that print reporters also must sometimes cover more than one story the same day and rely on others for information that then is not personally verified. The differences, however, are several: a print reporter can track down information over the phone back at the office while the television reporter must personally appear at the next story to shoot a "stand-up" or interview or a "live" remote that places the reporter, in the view of the audience, at the scene of the story. In addition, with television's impact and visibility, there is always the possibility that the victim of a defamatory statement may perceive the harm to be magnified beyond its actual scope because of the size of the audience and the fanfare that often accompanies television news reports.

Decisions relating to the actual stories chosen for a television newscast have been affected by several trends in recent years, a number of which suggest the potential for more libel suits against broadcasters. There are indications that more and more local television stations are experimenting with "investigative reporting." Investigative Reporters and Editors, a national organization of print and broadcast journalists, defines such reporting as:

- A matter that some person(s) would rather not see publicly revealed
- Substantially the work-product of the reporter(s)
- A matter of importance (usually significant improprieties or wrong-doing)
- Directed to the public good.[51]

A survey by a former news executive asked television journalists in the top hundred markets about their commitment to such reporting.[52] Of the 299 stations contacted, 175 (59 percent) responded.[53] The survey found that the average number of full-time reporters at the 175 stations was 10.5, and of those, 3.14 (30 percent) were said to do investigative reporting "at least periodically." In other words, 58 (33 percent) of the 175 stations had at least one full-time investigative reporter.[54] Thirty-six percent of the news directors said that they planned to increase their commitment to investigative reporting.[55] The survey also reported that "libel suits were visited on 37 (24 percent) of stations doing investigating reporting. 'Privacy' suits preoccupied 16 (11 percent). Nine (6 percent) were cited for alleged 'trespass.'"[56]

Television investigative reporting requires specialized skills that are highly rewarded in most television markets.[57] Perhaps the most difficult challenge that television reporters doing investigative pieces face is how to capture on camera evildoing that is rarely committed in the open. Some have used hidden cameras or microphones, although recording conversations without the consent of all parties is prohibited in a number of states.[58] Other television investigative reporters have gone undercover, usually by representing themselves as other than journalists.[59] Although usually not specifically prohibited by law, such deception can certainly be considered by a jury when deciding whether to award damages to the unwitting victim of the defamation. While undercover methods of both print and broadcast journalists raise serious ethical questions inside and outside journalism, some argue they are justified if the story is important and can be covered in no other way.[60]

Investigative reporting, by its very nature, is a portrayal of evil that most likely focuses on the transgressions of an individual or several individuals. Yet except in the most unusual cases, wrongdoers are not likely to make it easy to show their misdeeds on camera, which often requires catching them "in the act." The techniques for doing so can be interesting and sometimes very exciting for the viewer to watch, but may leave the viewer, or the jury, feeling some sympathy for the alleged wrongdoer. There are indications that the use of hidden cameras and "ambush" interviews may be waning in television news. Even some reporters fond of such methods seem to be more and more committed to asking the subject of the story to sit down for an interview before deciding to leap from behind the bushes with microphone in hand.

Nevertheless, a principle of journalism that provides an almost irresistible lure to all reporters is especially dangerous in television: the more sinister the evildoer looks, the better the story. A city council member who had not realized that his or her family owned a part of the land being considered for a zoning change is a lot less appealing in terms of news value than the doctor who knowingly performed abortions on women who are not pregnant. When the doctor is confronted by the news crew and begins to smash the equipment and assault the reporter, the doctor becomes an "ideal" subject for a television investigative piece.[61] A state legislator who calmly admits to driving a state-provided car for personal use and charging the taxpayers for the gas is a lot less interesting than the legislator who curses at the reporter and takes off in a huff down the street.[62] A real estate developer who tries to run down a determined reporter with a car provides more exciting film than one who sits in an office calmly denying the allegations.

This is not to suggest that the reporters involved in the stories cited above were guilty of exaggerating the dimensions of the wrongdoing; it is true, however, that television investigative reporting becomes increasingly interesting and involving for the audience if the "villain" can be shown doing something "visual" on camera. It is very difficult for even the most innocent subject to appear that way when confronted by a reporter demanding answers to questions. A "no comment" can be placed within almost any context in the story and may be used in a way that suggests the person has something to hide. Even an individual's refusal to comment can be amplified to appear as an admission of guilt by a determined reporter. If mistakes are made in the story, the individual may fight back with a libel suit.

One cannot assume that even an experienced television reporter can resist the temptation to make someone's wrongdoing seem more sinister than is in fact the case. An investigative piece for television can take many weeks or months to put together. Once it is finished, those associated with it become its strongest advocates. They lobby to convince station managers and lawyers that the report is accurate and fair. There is often the feeling that management has to be satisfied that the time and resources given to the investigative team are worth it, that the result is something as triumphant as the exposure of a corrupt public official, a dangerous product, a polluted water system, or other stories of the highest public interest.

Those producing such television news pieces become their strongest advocates; they want to prove the station's financial commitment was justified, but further, because changing a completed report in television is substantially more difficult than in print. The process, though, also gives television reporters substantial discretion to shape stories to reflect their own perceptions.

The editing of videotape, the means by which raw "footage" is turned into a completed "package," provides tremendous flexibility. Videotape is divided into a certain number of frames per second, usually thirty. Each frame represents a tiny portion of the interview. Videotape editing systems allow a reporter to interrupt the interview at the end of almost any word, then connect it with a later statement. If left in that form, the audience would see the picture "jump" and would know that a portion of the interview was cut. However, because the audio and video are recorded on separate parts of the videotape, the reporter can insert a quick "cutaway"—usually a shot of the reporter listening to the subject—then return quickly to the face of the interviewee. If done correctly, the audience has no way of knowing that audio has been cut out.

The implications of skillful misleading editing are somewhat frightening. A reporter determined to make someone look bad can match question A with answer B. Comment A can be connected to comment C. The issue is not so much whether reporters routinely employ such methods to make the subjects of their news stories appear to be more sinister than they actually are, it is that the technology is available. With many television stations trying to do investigative reporting, there is the potential for some persons to take advantage of the editing process. They may later find themselves on the witness stand explaining to a skeptical jury why they edited the material that way.[63]

To change an already completed video report may require reshooting in the field and rerecording narration. The camera crew must be pulled away from another story and the reporter must be available. Changes may be required when the investigative unit is weary of the current story and ready to move on to something new. The new parts must then be edited and integrated with the earlier footage. All in all it is far more time consuming and involves more people than is required to change a newspaper story on a video display terminal.

Finally, there is the difference in the impact that a television piece has compared with other media. It is certainly true that a hard-hitting investigative piece in a newspaper can have substantial impact: a corrupt official resigns, or is indicted; the polluted river is cleaned up; the public does not buy cars from the dealer who turns back odometers, and so on. But there is something about an investigative report on television: it can build excitement as the viewers anticipate the coming confrontation with the wrongdoer and they are treated to what one observer has called a "polygraph" test.[64] When the television camera comes in for a tight shot of someone's face, the audience may come to its own conclusions as to guilt or innocence if, say, the individual sweats, has shifting eyes, or changes expression. The transmitting of such "clues" is rarely possible in print. It is important to note that some individuals who are entirely innocent of the "charges" may appear not so because the camera makes them nervous. Nevertheless, the audience sees a sweaty face and quivering lip as it plays the role of armchair jurors.

The impact of a television investigative report is also related to audience size. In a large television market, hundreds of thousands of viewers may see an investigative series, sometimes several times the number who would read a detailed investigative story in a newspaper. There are numerous examples of television investigative reports that brought about *immediate* changes in some situation.[65] There are times, however, when a television report exposing some wrongdoing or unfairness has, to the surprise of those who put it together, little impact.[66]

The power of television to effect some changes in society by shaping public opinion has negative consequences as well. Persons defamed in television news reports that they know are seen by many thousands of people may believe that the allegations, if left unchallenged, will have such a devasting effect on their personal or business reputations that they cannot remain silent and hope that the defamatory statements will soon be forgotten. Such a perception may or may not be accurate, but persons seeking to vindicate damaged reputations may find some comfort in the publicity given to their efforts to sue for libel. A suit may ultimately be unsuccessful, but the opportunity for counterargument may provide some personal satisfaction. There is also the possibility that a suit will lead a television station to think more carefully about doing a similar story in the future.

The decision to sue a television station for libel even when the chances of success are minimal seems ill-considered, yet an aggrieved party can inflict harm to a station because it needs to protect something very valuable to it: its reputation. After its license, the most precious possession of a station is its reputation. A substantial part of its revenue is generated by its news operation. Its news department requires the trust and commitment of its viewers. If there is evidence of poor reporting or a conflict of interest, and the audience feels the reporters are no longer acting as neutral observers, or carefully exercising their tremendous power, the news team will lose credibility and most likely ratings will drop.[67] It can take many years to convince an audience that the news staff has changed its ways or is deserving of another chance. Reputations, good or bad, are difficult for news organizations to change. Sloppy or unfair reporting brought to the public's attention in even unsuccessful libel suits can be very damaging. Such harm to reputation may greatly outweigh in the long run the cost of defending or settling a libel suit.

Other trends in television news suggest at least the potential for more libel activity. Many television stations now broadcast several hours of local news daily. In some of the largest television markets, for example, it is not unusual for a local newscast to run from 4:00 or 4:30 in the afternoon until 6:30 or 7:00 at night. Yet the expansion from a half-hour or hour news period to several hours has not always been matched by a corresponding increase in the number of staff members who put the newscast together. Resources that were formerly sufficient are stretched thin when news time doubles. With more stories on the air, there is the increased potential for mistakes to be made. More stories mean more interviews, more chances that defamatory statements will be made, more opportunities for reporters to make accusations that turn out later to be false.

The situation is aggravated by one of television's inherent problems. In a newspaper newsroom, a variety of editors see *everything* that will run before it is printed. But a television producer, particularly in a large market with many crews and reporters putting stories together throughout the day, probably cannot view them all before they run on the air. A producer may be able to examine all the scripts but there is not likely to be enough time to view all the video. The video could include shots of an individual that are reputationally damaging, yet a reading of the script would not be enlightening in that regard. A producer in such a situation must rely on reporters to call attention to potential legal problems in the story. However, relying on a reporter who has a personal interest in seeing that the story gets on the air, and who may possess very little knowledge of libel and other legal issues, may lead to potential problems. As the producer sees the completed piece for the first time on the air, he or she may realize that it has harmed someone's reputation in a way that invites libel litigation. By then it is too late.

It will be recalled that the *Alton Telegraph* lost a libel suit in 1980 after a developer sued the newspaper over a memo written by two reporters that was never published, but that damaged his reputation after it wound up in the hands of federal officials.[68] Because the memo was not written for publication, it did not undergo the normal review by editors who might well have prevented its dissemination. A similar situation is present in many television newsrooms; those who may be the most knowledgeable about legal issues may not see completed reports until they are run on the air. Reporters who hesitate about informing producers or news directors that they included possibly defamatory statements in their stories do not want the pieces they have labored over shelved or perhaps barred from the airwaves. They may hope that their superiors or the subjects of the defamation do not notice when a story of that nature is broadcast. The subsequent "explanation" that too much time had been devoted to a story not to run it would probably not be a very convincing defense in court.

The nature of careers in television news also creates the potential of increased libel activity. Few industries can claim a more transient population than broadcasting.[69] Broadcasting careers are usually pursued hierarchically. A broadcast journalist usually begins in a relatively small market, then moves to a larger city and a station that offers a bigger salary, more opportunity to pursue specialized areas of interest, better equipment, more staff to help with various aspects of putting a news story or show together, and other advantages. Salaries in the largest markets can be huge, and those making substantially less in smaller markets are likely to consider a move to a bigger city and a higher standard of living to be an important goal.[70] Nomadic careers have consequences relating to libel litigation.

Most news stories featured on a local television station are on subjects that are not new. Zoning or transportation or housing decisions are city hall topics of long standing. The board of education may have debated for many sessions whether to close a school that has low enrollment, and that decision is related to a court decree handed down years ago after a discrimination suit was filed. A new television reporter assigned to cover the city council or board of education is not likely to have for some time a grasp of the history of the issues nor on the workings of the municipality. If the reporter plans to move to a larger market for career advancement in a year or two, the incentive to acquire knowledge of those issues may not be present. There may in fact be few rewards for doing so. Stories of the kind mentioned above are important to a community, but do not lend themselves to a visual presentation. A television reporter who sends an audition tape to the news director in the larger city, knows the competition is with dozens of others who are also sending tapes. If the video is almost entirely of meetings, some of the least visual of news events, the likelihood of being hired is thereby diminished. Some news consultants who advise television stations on how to improve ratings, strongly suggest that meeting footage never be shown. They believe that it bores viewers, who will eventually turn to the local station with the "action news" format. The reporter also knows that because stories on city hall or the school board usually run a minute and a half at the most, there is little time to include the background and history of an issue.

If, however, a reporter tries to cover city hall without understanding the issues, the report could become an open invitation for a libel suit. It will be recalled in *Time, Inc. v. Firestone*, for example, that the Supreme Court thought that *Time*'s stringer should have understood Florida divorce law in such detail that he would have known that those judged guilty of adultery cannot be granted alimony.[71] The Court showed no sympathy with the argument that the divorce decree was very confusing, and that a stringer covering the long trial could not be expected to have mastered every relevant aspect of Florida divorce law.

When a reporter covers city government without the benefit of knowing the history of an issue, there is an almost unlimited number of circumstances that could lead to libel trouble. For example, just deciding whom to believe may be very troublesome. A source within city hall tells our intrepid reporter that there is waste, mismanagement, and corruption in the water department, and the head of the department is trying to cover up. The source has a responsible position in city government, and by citing several examples, seems to be knowledgeable about the activities of the water department. He demands and is granted confidentiality. It is getting close to the time of the evening newscast and the reporter is rushing to get the story on the air. The reporter, refusing to name the source, confronts the head of the water department, who vigorously denies the allegations. The reporter goes with the story of the allegations and the denial. What the reporter did not know at the time is that the source, whose identity is known only to the reporter, was ousted from his job in the water department by its current head, and they have been political and bureaucratic enemies for years. In addition, veteran city hall reporters know that the · person providing the information has a propensity for greatly exaggerating and therefore is not very reliable. Even with the denial by the water department head, the charges, announced in a live report from the steps of city hall, leave the impression of truth. A reporter familiar with the department and the people, and who understood the history of the dispute, may not have gone with the story, at least not without more thorough checking. Our reporter, who also covered two other stories that day, wanted to get the "scoop" on the air. The water department head, although a public official, may choose to sue. The problems are obviously compounded if the story involves a private person, and many stories reported from city hall involve in some way private individuals.

There is also the possibility that a reporter looking for a solid investigative piece for a tape—one that may impress the news director in the next city, as would a report that exposes corrupt officials in city government—may not be very concerned about the libel suit brought against a former employer. The reporter by then has moved on to a new job in a larger market. In many libel suits brought against news organizations, the reporter or producer of the story is eventually dropped from the suit, leaving the news organization as the sole defendant. While our peripatetic reporter may guess wrong and have return to the scene of the "crime" to defend the suit, most libel plaintiffs do not go after reporters who have limited assets and are unlikely to have personal libel insurance. Instead, the target is the organization, which is better able to pay if it loses.

It also must be said that broadcast journalists seem remarkably uninformed about legal issues, especially libel. For example, even though about half the states have laws that specifically prohibit conversations from being recorded without the consent of all parties, some news reporters in those states employ such "undercover" techniques and explain later that they did not know it was illegal to do so.[72] Few reporters were schooled in libel law while receiving their education and training. Many broadcast journalists not only do not understand libel, but may think it is unlikely they would ever be sued.[73]

Finally, consultants, or "news doctors" as they are known, provide at least the potential for increased libel activity. Although consultants have been around for quite a few years, they continue to be criticized for emphasizing style over journalistic substance. Hundreds of television stations get advice, for which they pay a substantial amount of money, from consultants on how to improve their ratings.[74] But some critics allege that consultants are searching for people whose talent will generate larger audiences, and whose journalistic skills are of secondary importance. Ron Powers, a Pulitzer Prize-winning television critic, charges that in a blind quest for ratings, broadcasters violate the public's trust:

> When local stations create and choreograph entire news programs along guidelines supplied by researchers—toward the end of gratifying the audience's surface whims, not supplying its deeper informational needs—an insidious and corrosive hoax is being perpetrated on American viewers through a system that implicitly asks, and has been granted, their trust.[75]

Consultants received a substantial amount of publicity in connection with the Christine Craft case in late 1983 and early 1984. Craft, a news anchor at KMBC-TV in Kansas City, was dismissed because she could not be shaped so as to create the type of image that the station wanted for its woman anchor. In January 1984, a jury awarded her $325,000 in damages after the trial judge had set aside the first jury's verdict.[76] It became apparent during the trials that the consultants who persuaded the station to fire her were not concerned in the least with her journalistic skills; the question was merely one of entertainment or show business: could she get the station higher ratings?[77]

There is a almost endless debate in television news over the role that "cosmetics" play in deciding whom to hire. Because audience perception of news anchors and reporters can have a lot to do with which newscasts have the largest ratings, television stations are under tremendous pressure to hire those who will generate ratings, and they may worry less about their journalistic skills. The audience, which watches attractive news people with great commitment, shares part of the blame for the emphasis on show business and entertainment in television news.[78] Nevertheless, television news people are charged with the responsibility of informing the public about important issues in their communities and elsewhere. When the best, most thorough journalists can find themselves defending libel suits, newscasters and reporters whose foremost qualification is appearance render their employers particularly susceptible to legal problems.

It can be argued that because news consultants have been active for almost two decades, and if their clients have diligently followed their advice and hired news personnel without regard for their journalistic skills, there would have been a rash of libel suits that would have dampened the journalistic fervor of many television stations. But it can also be argued that the publicity surrounding libel suits in which juries have awarded huge sums of money, that now take place in a changing legal environment in which it is easier to be designated a private person, are relatively recent developments. It may be too early to tell whether television stations that continue to hire on-air talent with undeveloped journalistic skills so as to increase ratings will bring upon themselves increased libel litigation. This is not to suggest, of course, that all news directors hire attractive people without regard to their journalistic skills. Nor does it suggest that the hiring of such individuals always results in higher ratings. Yet a news director whose newscast is journalistically solid, but has poor ratings, should not make any long-term financial plans; arriving at work one day, he or she may find the lock on the door has been changed.[79]

The type of journalism practiced by television news organizations does present the potential for more libel suits, although they face such problems with the benefit of some history. Radio and television stations have been the objects of libel and privacy suits for many years, and an examination of those suits may yield relatively clear patterns that suggest the pace of libel activity may pick up in the years ahead.

One of the earliest cases of defamation arising out of statements made on radio occurred in 1939 in *Summit Hotel v. National Broadcasting Company*.[80] NBC had rented its facilities to an advertising company that had sponsored a series of radio programs over one of its networks. Comedian Al Jolson, who along with all other performers was paid by the advertising corporation, was the principal performer. A script for each program was prepared in advance, submitted to NBC, and followed exactly by the performers at rehearsals.[81] The script for June 15, 1935 called for an interview by Jolson with the winner of an annual golf tournament. When the live program was about half over, Jolson interjected an extemporaneous remark that led to the lawsuit. In response to the winner's statement that he secured his first job at the Summit Hotel in Uniontown, Pennsylvania, Jolson said, "That's a rotten hotel."[82]

The Supreme Court of Pennsylvania noted that the remark was made without warning; it did not appear in the script, had not been made at rehearsal, and NBC did not know that the words were going to be used. Present in the studio were officials of NBC and the advertising firm, none of whom had an opportunity to prevent Jolson's remark.[83]

The hotel brought an action in trespass for defamation against NBC and won $15,000. The Pennsylvania court said the key issue was whether "a radio broadcasting company which leases its facilities is liable for an impromptu defamatory statement . . . by a person not in the employ of the broadcasting company, the words being carried to the radio listeners by its facilities."[84] The court noted that it was the first time such a question had been presented to an appellate court in the United States or England.[85]

In discussing NBC's liability, the court considered issues that are very much related to modern broadcasting. Broadcasters no longer turn their facilities over to paid sponsors, but in the course of covering news events, they do interview individuals or provide live coverage of events where inadvertent defamatory statements can be made. The court in *Summit* considered whether NBC should be responsible for the remark:

> There was no power or means possessed by the broadcasting company that enabled it to prevent the transmission of the defamatory remark. It was physically impossible for the monitor or program director to have intervened, as the performer, without notice, interjected his terse defamatory remark so quickly that no one in appellant's employ was able to prevent its transmission.[86]

In the *Summit* opinion the court devoted considerable attention to the applicability of strict liability, or some form of liability without fault.[87] It rejected the hotel's argument that NBC was liable under such a standard, which had been applied to cases involving newspapers:

> In these circumstances the analogy between the radio broadcaster and the newspaper publisher is demonstrably weak, considering not only the practical differences between the two media of communication, but the different conditions under which the industries operate. Newspaper matter is prepared in advance, reviewed by members of the various staffs, set into type, printed, proof read and then "run off" by employes of the publisher; at all times opportunity is afforded the owner to prevent the publication of the defamatory statement up to the time of delivery of the paper to the news-vendor. The defamation thus may be said to be an intentional publication, or at least one published without due care.[88]

In reversing the judgment, the court suggested that victims of defamation by radio need not be as concerned that actual damage to their reputation took place as they would be if the defamation had appeared in print: "Newspaper defamations possess possibilities for real harm far greater than defamations by radio, as they constitute permanent, continuing records, which, through circulation, are constantly republished. The radio word is quickly spoken and, generally, as quickly forgotten."[89]

Although admitting the law regarding defamation by broadcasters was in its early stages, the court expressed concern that state standards of liability without fault, which may be appropriate in cases involving newspapers, may impose too heavy a burden on radio. Newspapers, the "freest medium of communication in the country today," in the words of the court, should be subject to a rule of civil liability for libel, considering their opportunity for "correction and control." But because broadcasters are regulated by the federal government and subject to numerous restrictions, courts need not impose strict standards in libel cases because of regulatory sanctions available to punish irresponsible broadcasters:

> Radio is a governmentally-regulated industry.... The... Communications Commission is given broad powers to formulate rules for the conduct of radio stations; severe penalties are imposed for violations. A broadcasting company that oversteps these rules may have its license revoked and lose the value of its entire plant; this, in the realm of radio, is capital punishment. And, the publication by a broadcasting station of defamatory matter... may, if persisted in, result in the revocation of the license of the station.[90]

Summit involved a broadcasting station that leased its facilities to an advertiser who sponsored and produced the program, but the issues in *Summit* are related to modern libel problems faced by broadcasters. The court noted that if a broadcasting station's "employe or agent makes the defamatory remark, it is liable, unless the remarks are privileged and there is no malice."[91] There is, however, another class of individuals who do not work for the broadcasting station or the advertiser who may be in a position to utter defamatory statements that the broadcaster would be helpless to prevent: those within range of the television camera.

Hundreds of television stations today have the capability of going live from the field, and in fact many do live remotes just to demonstrate that they have such a capability.[92] In all but the biggest stories, the live event must be shown sometime during the newscast; yet many events either have taken place before or will take place after the newscast. Usually, a camera set up for a live report cannot be moved once the report is on the air; that means that for the live shot to be a success, there has to be some action taking place that is captured by the camera and transmitted to the audience. If there is no action during the time the live shot is scheduled, it often means that the reporter must find at least one of the protagonists involved in some controversy who can provide the action through animated and sometimes disputatious statements. A live shot with a calm, soft-spoken interviewee is likely to provoke criticism from the news director, who has been told by consultants that the audience demands action pictures, or at a minimum, controversy. In such a situation, the station is vulnerable not only to those who are interviewed and in a position to make defamatory statements, but to individuals standing nearby who may react in untoward ways to the presence of a television camera.[93] Whether a court would apply the *Summit* precedent to a case involving an interviewee who made live defamatory statements would depend on how strictly liable a broadcasting station should be held for statements over which it may or may not have control.

In the years following *Summit*, courts were faced with a number of difficult issues in cases involving defamation by radio. In *Howser v. Pearson*,[94] a 1951 case decided by the United States District Court in the District of Columbia, truth was held to be an absolute defense to a libel suit brought against Drew Pearson, the well-known columnist and radio commentator. But the court was faced with a more difficult issue of jurisdiction and applicability of various state laws, an issue that faces judges today in libel cases involving national media organizations.

Fred Howser, a former California attorney general, was accused by Pearson in a radio broadcast of having accepted a bribe of $1,200 in exchange for protecting an accused gambler from criminal prosecution.[95] The jury found for Pearson, and Howser filed a motion for a new trial. There was conflicting testimony about the accuracy of Pearson's statements in the broadcast, yet the jury reached the conclusion that the truthfulness of the statements had been established.[96] To the trial judge, "this finding was a complete defense to the action and alone necessitated judgment for the defendant."[97] Pearson had also asserted a defense of qualified privilege, but in the judge's view, such an issue became "insignificant" once truth was shown.

Of more importance, however, was the decision facing the judge as to which state law applied in the case. The broadcast originated in Washington, D.C., and was carried by radio stations in California and nine other western states.[98] California law included a qualified privilege to criticize public officials that was more protective of the defendant's rights than were the laws of the other states. It said, in effect, that a defamatory statement concerning a public official or candidate for public office is privileged even if the statement is untrue, provided it was uttered in good faith and without malice.[99] The judge observed that California's qualified privilege is "far broader than that generally prevailing at common law, for ordinarily privilege in respect to attacks on public officials and candidates for public office is limited to fair comment and criticism and does not extend to untrue statements of fact."[100]

It was therefore necessary for the judge to determine which state laws would govern the rights of the parties in the case. Pearson argued that California law should apply because the plaintiff was a resident of the state, and that "by far the greater part of the dissemination of the defamatory statement took place in California," and that the "injury to the plaintiff, if any, occurred principally in the state." Howser contended that the "law of each state to which the defamatory matter had been transmitted should govern as to so much of its distribution as took place within its borders."[101]

It was a decision of much significance because the law in Nevada, for example, followed the common-law privilege and would have afforded a defendant less protection. To the judge, it made no sense to ignore the Nevada law just because the broadcast was also heard in California:

> It appeared illogical and unreasonable to hold that because the material was disseminated in two or more States, say in Nevada and California, the Nevada rule should no longer apply to so much of the circulation as took place in that State and that the law of California, which is more favorable to the defendant, should regulate the rights and liabilities of the parties throughout. . . . It seemed fallacious to evolve a doctrine that the law of the place where the defamatory statement was published should govern only if the circulation took place solely in a single State, but the law of the plaintiff's domicile should rule if the publication occurred in two or more States.[102]

Despite the obvious problems that such a ruling would present to a jury, the judge held that the law in all the states in which the broadcast was heard would apply:

> The substantive law of each of the States in which the defamatory matter was circulated should govern . . . in respect to so much of the circulation of the offending material took place in that State. The . . . defendant was not entitled to the benefits of the broad California rule as to privilege, except as the dissemination that took place in that State and the other States in which the same doctrine prevailed.[103]

The defense counsel argued that such a conclusion would make it difficult for a jury to decide the issues in the case: "It would certainly be an unworkable procedure to tell a jury that they should award damages, so far as they were suffered in State X, according to one measure, and, so far was they were suffered in State Y, according to another."[104] The judge dismissed the argument, saying trial judges could develop procedures that would allow a jury to consider the substantive issues:

> It would be unfortunate if practical obstacles were to stand in the way of applying a correct rule of law. Trial judges are under a duty to develop devices that would minimize such difficulty. In any event this hurdle did not appear insurmountable in this instance. Although the defamatory statement was heard in ten States, actually there were only two rules of law as to privilege to be applied, each of the ten States falling into one or the other of these two categories.[105]

It seems unreasonable to expect a jury to apply the laws of different states in a case involving a national media organization. The Supreme Court solved the problem with respect to public officials and public figures by establishing national standards, but left to the states the appropriate standard of liability in cases involving private persons. It is conceivable that a private person defamed in a national radio and television broadcast could argue that the jury should determine the extent to which the broadcast was heard or seen in a given state, and thus the extent to which the law of that state would be applied in assessing damages. The Supreme Court has begun to consider various issues related to jurisdiction, but many questions remain about which laws apply in cases involving media organizations that disseminate information in several states.

Six years later another U.S. district court judge encountered jurisidictional and other issues in a libel suit filed by a county attorney against a television station. In *Gerhart v. WSAZ*,[106] the station, on five occasions over a period of three days during its newscasts, said that the plaintiff was guilty of corrupt, unethical, and criminal practices as an attorney and a county official. The broadcasts also accused him of collaborating with known criminals "in the organization of a vicious and corrupt political machine for the purpose of exploiting his constitutency and corrupting his community."[107] After first considering the jurisdictional issues, the judge held that because the television station was seen in several states, it was appropriate to hold the trial, in which the plaintiff was awarded $5,000, in federal court under its diversity jurisdiction.[108]

The judge then turned to the question of the defamation itself. He was especially concerned that the broadcast had been repeated five times and, unlike the Pennsylvania Supreme Court in *Summit*, believed that defamation by broadcast can be harmful:

> While there may be no distinction in the law as a general proposition, I believe it is proper to point out a distinction in this case between a broadcast or telecast read from a manuscript and libelous matter printed in a newspaper or publication. A written statement in its full context with proper punctuation may appear to the public in one light. The same matter read in a telecast by a trained individual, whose profession requires him to make the news interesting, by emphasis and accent may leave an entirely different impression. . . . Those who make money out of attracting a listening public to news broadcasts should not be permitted to also sell the good name, standing and integrity of honorable, conscientious officials on the uncorroborated word of criminals.[109]

In upholding the jury's award of damages, the judge noted that defamatory remarks made by a television station were to be governed by the laws of libel and not slander, and in any event, "the record discloses that the remarks were read from a transcript of notes and has been held to be libel."[110]

The Supreme Court had been largely silent on the question of defamation by broadcast, but two years later in *Farmers Educational & Cooperative Union of America v. WDAY*,[111] it considered whether radio and television stations that provide time to political candidates under section 315 of the Communications Act are liable for damage to reputation caused by those broadcasts. The issues caused much disagreement as the Court divided 5-4. Justice

Black, who wrote the majority opinion, held that section 315 provided immunity from libel suits. Section 315 reads:

> If any licensee shall permit any person who is a legally qualified candidate for any public office to use a broadcasting station, he shall afford equal opportunities to all other such candidates for that office in the use of such broadcasting station: *Provided,* That such licensee shall have no power of censorship over the material broadcast under the provisions of this section. No obligation is imposed upon any licensee to allow the use of its station by any such candidate.[112]

A candidate for the U.S. Senate from North Dakota, A.C. Townley, made a speech that was broadcast over the radio and television facilities of WDAY in which he accused his opponents and the Farmers Educational and Cooperative Union of America of conspiring to "establish a Communist Farmers Union Soviet right here in North Dakota."[113] The station had believed itself compelled to broadcast Townley's remarks by the requirements of section 315 as a reply to previous speeches made over WDAY by two other senatorial candidates.

Farmers Union sued Townley and WDAY for libel. The district court dismissed the complaint against the station and the North Dakota Supreme Court affirmed. In the words of the North Dakota Supreme Court, WDAY was unable to censor the broadcast and therefore could not be held liable for its content:

> Section 315 imposes a mandatory duty upon broadcasting stations to permit all candidates for the same office to use their facilities if they have permitted one candidate to use them. Since power of censorship of political broadcasts is prohibited it must follow as a corollary that the mandate prohibiting censorship includes the privilege of immunity from liability for defamatory statements made by the speakers.[114]

The U.S. Supreme Court rejected the plaintiff's view that Congress intended to give broadcasters the right to delete libelous materials from programs aired under section 315.[115] The Federal Communications Commission and the courts, in the Supreme Court's view, had interpreted the section to mean that no censorship of such broadcasts would be permitted. The purpose of section 315 was "full and unrestricted discussion of political issues by legally qualified candidates." Allowing a broadcasting station to censor such discussion would undermine the basic purpose of section 315:

> Recognizing radio's potential importance as a medium of communication of political ideas, Congress sought to foster its broadest possible utilization by encouraging broadcasting stations to make their facilities available to candidates for office without discrimination, and by insuring that these candidates when broadcasting were not to be hampered by censorship of the issues they could discuss.[116]

In the Court's view, it would be very difficult for a broadcasting station to decide, in the heat of a political campaign, which statements were potentially libelous and ought to be censored and which were not. Noting that it is rarely clear whether a statement is defamatory, the Court expressed concern that if a station were held responsible for the broadcast of libelous material, "all remarks even faintly objectionable would be excluded out of an excess of caution."[117] Moreoever, a station determined to censor the remarks of a candidate could "inhibit a candidate's legitimate presentation under the guise of lawful censorship of libelous matter." If statements were improperly excluded from a broadcast, the courts probably could not act quickly enough to restore the deleted remarks before the end of the campaign.[118]

The plaintiff also argued that section 315 does not grant a broadcasting station immunity from liability for defamatory statements made during a political broadcast even though the law prohibits the licensee from censoring the allegedly libelous matter. The Court rejected such a view, reasoning that interpreting section 315 that way "would sanction the unconscionable result of permitting civil and perhaps criminal liablity to be imposed for the very conduct the statute demands of the licensee."[119] There was also the complicated question of whether state libel law applied to broadcasts required by federal law. Black determined that whatever North Dakota may do in interpreting state law, the "question for us is whether Congress intended to subject a federal licensee to possible liability under the law of some or all of the 49 states for broadcasting in a way required by federal law."[120] Black recognized that some persons may interpret such a ruling as interfering with a state's ability to compensate victims of defamation:

> We are aware that causes of action for libel are widely recognized throughout the states. But we have not hesitated to abrogate state law where satisfied that its enforcement would stand "as an obstacle to the accomplishment and execution of the full purposes and objectives of Congress." Here, petitioner is asking us to attribute to [section] 315 a meaning which would either frustrate the underlying purposes for which it was enacted, or alternatively impose unreasonable burdens on the parties governed by that legislation. In the absence of clear expression by Congress we will not assume that it desired such a result.[121]

Justice Frankfurter, joined by Justices Harlan, Whittaker and Stewart, dissented. They argued that the Court majority had interfered with the right of North Dakota to apply state libel law in the case:

> The claim that WDAY cannot be held liable under constitutionally enacted state libel laws must be tested not by inquiring whether a particular result would be "unconscionable" but whether the result is or is not barred by federal legislation as construed and applied in accordance with settled principles of statutory and constitutional adjudication.[122]

The dissenters argued that Congress did not intend to grant such immunity, for if it had, it would have said so specifically. They also disputed Black's interpretation that the FCC had consistently interpreted section 315 to mean that broadcast licensees were immune from such libel suits.[123] Thus, it is incorrect to assume that Congress, by inaction, had acquiesced in the FCC's interpretation:

> Thus, it may well be urged that repeated refusal [by Congress] to relieve from state libel laws amounted to an affirmance that the state laws of defamation should continue in operation since the Congress debated the issue in terms of erecting a defense to these laws, and then declined to do so. In any event, the legislative history emphatically does not support the affirmative conclusion that Congress intended preclusion of state law. Congress can speak with drastic clarity when it so intends. It has not so spoken here; it has refused to speak with drastic clarity.[124]

The dissenters would have reversed the North Dakota Supreme Court with the instructions that section 315 "has left to the States the power to determine the nature and extent of liability, if any, of broadcasters to third persons."[125]

Courts have sometimes found classifying libel by radio or television stations to be difficult. In some states defamation uttered over broadcasting facilities is considered libelous if it is read from a script, and slander if it is extemporaneous. Other states may call such defamation slander, but apply libel standards to it. In a 1962 case, an appeals court in Georgia chose a new name for defamation by broadcasting: "defamacast."

American Broadcasting-Paramount Theatres, Inc. v. E.L. Simpson[126] involved entertainment and not news programming, but gave the Court of Appeals of Georgia the opportunity to discuss broadcast defamation. In considering the common-law development of libel and slander, the court suggested that a new type of defamation had emerged:

> When the common law first recognized a right of action for defamatory remarks the only action was for slander. Then the development of a new media—the printing press—led to the development of an action for printed defamation called libel. May not the common law of Georgia develop a new classification to deal with these new [radio and television] media?[127]

Although the court did not specifically indicate how "defamacast" legally differs from libel or slander, it seemed to hold that because defamatory statements transmitted by broadcasters can pose substantial harm to reputation, victims of such defamation are entitled to sue as if the statements are disseminated in a more permanent form:

> The genius of the common law has been its ability to meet the challenges posed by changing circumstances. Can there be any doubt that this situation poses one

of those challenges?.... That defamation by radio, in the absence of a script or transcription, lacks the measure of durability possessed by written libel, in nowise lessens its *capacity for harm*. Since the element of damage is, historically, the basis of the common-law action for defamation, and since it is reasonable to presume damage from the nature of the medium employed when a slander is broadcast by radio as when published by writing, both logic and policy point the conclusion that defamation by radio should be actionable per se.[128]

The appeals court invited courts deciding future cases to expand the concept of "defamacast," although it appears few have chosen to do so. Most states treat statements made over broadcasting facilities as libel and apply the comprehensive and complex standards developed in libel cases over the years. Nevertheless, the Georgia court's invitation to develop separate standards for broadcast defamation raises a number of interesting questions.[129]

The potential for harm to reputation that follows a defamatory broadcast concerned the Pennsylvania Supreme Court a year later in *Purcell v. Westinghouse Broadcasting Co.*[130] A radio station in Philadelphia had broadcast a news documentary about the plaintiff's alleged involvement in "towing car rackets." The program was broadcast after his indictment but before trial. The indictments were dismissed and he was never convicted of charges in connection with the car-towing scheme.[131] The court held that the radio station had acted irresponsibly in accusing the plaintiff of wrongdoing, holding that the broadcast contained "exaggerated additions" and brought "embellishments to the account."[132] In language that is unusually colorful for a judicial opinion, Justice Musmanno discussed the need to protection one's reputation from such reporting:

> A man's good name is as much his possession as his physical property. It is more than property, it is his guardian angel of safety and security; it is his lifesaver in the sea of adversity, it is his parachute when he falls out of the sky of good fortune, it is his plank of rescue in the quicksands of personal disaster.... The defendant treated the plaintiff's name with reckless unconcern, culpable indifference and palpable irresponsibility.[133]

In the documentary the station reported on an official investigation into the car-towing racket, and discussed the hearing before a district magistrate following the indictments. The Pennsylvania Supreme Court was particularly critical of the way the issues were reported in the documentary:

> The defendant could have done an excellent public service by telling its audience truthfully what it had discovered in its investigation.... The fault lay in breaking the egg of the extra-judicial "investigation" and the egg of the judicial hearing into one omelet and seasoning it with comment and observations which made the parentage of either original egg impossible of ascertainment as to taste, color, shape or form.[134]

Finally, the state supreme court suggested that any citizen's reputation is vulnerable to a broadcasting station that, in its view, is determined to be irresponsible:

> The highlighting of *Purcell* in the broadcast could not be attributed to his being of public importance or even one at all known to the general public. In the vast panorama of the population of Philadelphia he was only a blur in the picture. This blur KYW proceeded to enlarge under the magnifying glass of exaggeration, it was then sharpened with the pencil and keen knife of purpose, colored to meet the design of the defendant, until what was a gray, meaningless dot of anonymity became the portrait of an enemy of society. . . . If this can be done with impunity, no one can be assured of immunity from defamation, no matter how pure his life or honest his intentions.[135]

Purcell had been awarded $10,000 in compensatory damages and $50,000 in punitive damages. The state supreme court agreed with the jury's verdict, but it reduced the punitive damages to $30,000, sustaining an award of $40,000.[136]

The Pennsylvania Supreme Court in Purcell recognized the potential of radio to damage one's reputation, but the potential of television, as a visual medium, to cause reputational injury is significantly greater. In the past decade, various courts have expressed concern over television's ability to inflict serious harm. In *Green Valley School v. Cowles Florida Broadcasting*,[137] a Florida television station broadcast a report about a not-for-profit school that received federal funds and on whose campus about sixty-five students lived.[138]

Law enforcement officials invited a reporter and a photographer from the station to accompany them on a midnight raid of Green Valley School. According to the news report that was shown twice on the air, the school allegedly maintained filthy conditions and the school administrators physically and sexually abused the students.[139] In reversing the trial judge's decision to grant summary judgment for the television station, the District Court of Appeal of Florida's First District focused on statements by students and school officials that contradicted the allegations made in the news report.[140]

A most interesting aspect of the case was the fact that the state attorney, who had investigated conditions in the school and who was involved in planning the raid, invited the television news crew to accompany law enforcement officials and provided opportunities for the newspeople to record pictures of the conditions and interviews with the students. The appeals court rejected the station's argument that such an invitation entitled its personnel to be on the premises, and expressed concern about the privacy rights of school officials:

> To uphold appellees' assertion that their entry upon appellant's property at the time, manner, and circumstances as reflected by this record was as a *matter of*

law sanctioned by "the request of and with the consent of the State Attorney" and within the "common usage and custom in Florida" could well bring to the citizenry of this state the hobnail boots of a nazi stormtrooper equipped with glaring lights invading a couple's bedroom, at midnight with the wife hovering in her nightgown in an attempt to shield herself from the scanning TV camera. In this jurisdiction, a law enforcement officer is not *as a matter of law* endowed with the right or authority to invite people of his choosing to invade private property and participate in a midnight raid of the premises.[141]

Television news departments do not always wait to be invited before staging their own "raids," although courts have recently looked upon such activities with impatience. In what one judge called a "precedent-setting" opinion, the Appellate Division of the New York Supreme Court in *Le Mistral v. CBS*[142] upheld a trespassing civil suit against WCBS-TV in New York.

At about 2:00 p.m. on July 6, 1972 a reporter and camera crew entered Le Mistral, one of a number of restaurants that had been cited for health code violations.[143] The camera crew was apparently instructed to enter the restaurant with cameras rolling and lights on. After the entry, the owner of the restaurant ordered the camera crew to leave. In a footnote the court discussed the effect of the crew's visit:

> The defendant's employees burst into plaintiff's restaurant in a noisy and obtrusive fashion and following the loud commands of the reporter . . . to photograph the patrons dining, turned their lights and camera upon the dining room. Consternation, the jury was informed, followed. Patrons waiting to be seated left the restaurant. Others who had finished eating, left without waiting for their checks. Still others hid their faces behind napkins or table cloths or hid themselves beneath tables.[144]

The court especially noted the reluctance of crew members to leave when ordered to do so, and observed that the record indicated they had to be "pushed" from the premises.[145] The jury held that the WCBS-TV crew had been guilty of trespass and awarded $1,200 in compensatory damages and $250,000 in punitive damages. The trial court, on defendant CBS's motion, upheld the jury verdict in finding that the conduct of the defendant constituted a trespass, but set aside the damage awards.[146] The court demonstrated much impatience with CBS's claim that the First Amendment provided news organizations with immunity from damage awards in such cases:

> The First Amendment is not a shibboleth before which all other rights must succumb. This Court "recognizes that the exercise of the right of free speech and free press demands and even mandates the observance of the co-equal duty not to abuse such right, but to utilize it with right reason and dignity. Vain lip service to 'duties' in a vacuous reality wherein 'rights' exist, sovereign and independent of any balancing moral or social factor creates a semantical mockery of the very foundation of our laws and legal system."[147]

The court restored the jury's award of compensatory damages, but re-manded the matter for a trial on the issue of the punitive damage award. The court based its decision on the grounds that exclusion of a certain testimony by a defense witness denied CBS the opportunity to prove that its motives were not "evil or wrongful" or that there was no "willful and intentional misdoing or a reckless indifference equivalent thereto."[148]

Judge Murphy, who dissented in part, held that CBS should pay compen-satory damages, but punitive damages should not be permitted. Although the judge forgave the station because it was "merely pursuing a newsworthy item in the overly aggressive but good faith manner that characterizes the operation of the news media today,"[149] he wanted news organizations to know such be-havior in the future would not be tolerated: "In this sensitive and evolving First Amendment area, I would permit this precedent-setting opinion to stand as a warning to all news gatherers that future trespasses may well be met with an award of punitive damages."[150]

The efforts of the courts to grapple with the privacy issues raised by *Green Valley* and *Le Mistral* are indicative of the problems courts face when deter-mining standards of privacy. Privacy has long been part of our legal vocabu-lary, but unlike libel it has not evolved into the detailed standards derived from many decisions over the years.[151] The four privacy torts have been recognized for some time, yet only recently have they been applied to news organiza-tions. When struggling to fit historical notions of privacy with modern news-gathering technology, courts have not always looked favorably on assertions that the First Amendment provides substantial protection from such litigation.

In *Dietemann v. Time, Inc.*,[152] a 1971 case that caused much concern among news organizations, the United States Court of Appeals for the Ninth Circuit upheld an invasion of privacy suit against *Life* magazine. The plain-tiff, A.A. Dietemann, described by the trial court as a "disabled veteran with little education," was said to engage in the "practice of healing with clay, minerals and herbs—as practiced, simple quackery."[153] In an effort to expose the plaintiff as a quack, two employees of *Life* arranged with the district attor-ney's office to visit Dietemann to gather information and take pictures. One employee posed as a patient while the other took photographs. Once inside Dietemann's office, one of the magazine employees took his picture with a hidden camera without his consent, and one such picture later appeared in *Life*. While Dietemann was examining his "patient," an examination that was apparently quite bizarre, their conversation was transmitted by radio trans-mitter hidden in her purse to a tape recorder in a parked car.[154] In the car another *Life* employee and officials of the district attorney's office and State Department of Public Health listened to the conversation. The recorded con-versation was not quoted in the article in *Life*, but it was mentioned that the *Life* correspondent was "making notes of what was being received via the radio transmitter, and such information was at least referred to in the article.''[155]

The plaintiff was subsequently arrested for practicing medicine without a license. At the time of the arrest, a *Life* photographer was there to take pictures, as were newspaper reporters invited by the law enforcement officials. Dietemann eventually pleaded nolo contendere to misdemeanor violations of the California Business and Professions Code and the California Health and Safety Code.

Dietemann sued *Life* for invasion of privacy and was awarded $1,000 in damages "for injury to [his] feelings and peace of mind.''[156] At the outset, the court was critical of the way the *Life* employees had gained entrance to Dietemann's property:

> Defendant's claim that the plaintiff's house was open to the public is not sustained by the evidence. The plaintiff was administering his so-called treatments to people who visited him. He was not a medical man of any type. He did not advertise. He did not have a phone. He did have a lock on his gate. To obtain entrance it was necessary to ring a bell. He conducted his activities in a building which was his home. The employees of the defendant gained entrance by subterfuge.[157]

The court recognized that California law was somewhat unsettled on this issue, but had "little difficulty concluding that clandestine photography of the plaintiff in his den and the recordation and transmission of his conversation without his consent resulting in his emotional distress warrants recovery for invasion of privacy in California.''[158] The court argued that although an individual takes a risk that the "visitor may not be what he seems, and that the visitor may repeat all he hears and observes when he leaves," he should not be required to take the risk that what is heard and seen will be "transmitted by photograph or recording, or in our modern world, in full living color and hi-fi to the public at large.''[159]

The court also rejected *Time*'s contention that the First Amendment provides immunity from such an invasion of privacy suit because *Life* employees were gathering news and it was using "indispensable tools of investigative reporting":

> We agree that newsgathering is an integral part of news dissemination. We strongly disagree, however, that the hidden mechanical contrivances are "indispensable tools" of newsgathering. Investigative reporting is an ancient art; its successful practice long antecedes the invention of miniature cameras and electronic devices. The First Amendment has never been construed to accord newsmen immunity from torts or crimes committed during the course of newsgathering. The First Amendment is not a license to trespass, to steal, or to intrude by electronic means into the precincts of another's home or office. It does not become such a license simply because the person subjected to the intrusion is reasonably suspected of committing a crime.[160]

Finally, the court held that publication of the statements is not "an essential element of plaintiff's cause of action." That the publication resulting from an invasion privacy may be truthful, or may provide information of public interest, was not persuasive to the court. The truth may be a defense in libel but not, the court appeared to say, in an invasion of privacy suit. In fact, the mere fact of publication can be considered when assessing damages for emotional harm:

> No interest protected by the First Amendment is adversely affected by permitting damages for intrusion to be enhanced by the fact of later publication of the information that the publisher improperly acquired. Assessing damages for the additional emotional distress suffered by a plaintiff when the wrongfully acquired data are purveyed to the multitude chills intrusive acts. It does not chill freedom of expression guaranteed by the First Amendment.[161]

Journalists not only must be concerned about intrusion, but also must be careful, in the wake of *Zacchini v. Scripps-Howard Broadcasting*[162] in 1977, not to infringe upon a person's right to be compensated for the commercial use of the person's name or likeness. Hugo Zacchini called himself "the human cannonball" and in his act, which was shown at fairs and other exhibitions, he was shot from a cannon into a net. After a television station, over his objections, took pictures of and had shown the act during its newscast, he sued for invasion of privacy. The Ohio Supreme Court said the First Amendment precluded any recovery because the newscast covered a matter of "legitimate public interest."

The Supreme Court reversed, arguing that there was no constitutional exemption to being sued if the state courts wanted to hear such a suit. In distinguishing *Zacchini* from other invasion of privacy suits, Justice White held that Zacchini was entitled to maintain control over the publicity given to his performance: "The effect of a public broadcast of the performance is similar to preventing petitioner from charging an admission fee. . . . No social purpose is served by having defendant get for free some aspect of the plaintiff that would have market value and for which he would normally pay."[163] The case was returned to the Ohio courts and Zacchini eventually won his lawsuit.[164]

Justice Powell, whose dissenting opinion was joined by Brennan and Marshall, was concerned that the *Zacchini* case could lead to a "degree of self-censorship."[165] Instead of focusing on a "quantitative analysis" of Zacchini's act—was it the entire act?—the court should have considered actions of the news media. Because the film was used for a routine portion of a regular news program, Powell would hold that the First Amendment protects the station from a "right of publicity" or "appropriation" suit, unless there was a strong showing by the plaintiff that the news broadcast was a "subterfuge or cover for private or commercial exploitation."[166]

Powell expressed concern about efforts by the subjects of news stories to influence the way they are presented:

> The plaintiff does not complain about the fact of exposure to the public, but rather about its timing and manner. He welcomes some publicity, but seeks to retain control over means and manner as a way to maximize for himself the monetary benefits that flow from such publication. But having made the matter public—having chosen, in essence, to make it newsworthy—he cannot, consistent with the First Amendment, complain of routine news coverage.[167]

It is difficult to predict the eventual effect of well-publicized libel suits brought against broadcast news organizations. Television in particular seems to be a medium of communication with which the public has a love/hate relationship. The public watches television news in large numbers and sometimes with great intensity, yet it is quick to criticize the way broadcast journalists cover news events and the individuals caught up in them. Juries will continue to have the opportunity to punish broadcasters who they believe have irresponsibly injured personal reputations, or who have simply grown too pleased with their own importance and success. Broadcast technology may change in the years ahead, but the nature of the journalism practiced by broadcasters will continue to provide opportunities for persons seeking redress for reputational harm to make their case before a jury of their peers, many of whom feel it is appropriate to punish the messenger for bringing bad news. Appellate courts will continue to be called upon to separate cases of actual harm resulting from grossly irresponsible reporting from those where juries have awarded huge sums of money to persons simply unhappy with the way they have been portrayed in news stories. As will be discussed in the final chapter, whether the media defendant is a print or broadcasting organization, current libel laws inadequately protect the First Amendment and at the same time fail to provide a reasonable method by which those harmed can successfully vindicate their reputations.

Notes

1. Synanon has been accused of violence against neighbors, visitors, and its own members. After Los Angeles lawer Paul Morantz won a civil judgment against Synanon in October, 1978, he was bitten by a rattlesnake that had been placed in his mailbox. He was rushed to a hospital, and later recovered. Two members of Synanon's "Imperial Marines" pleaded no contest to charges of conspiracy to commit murder and assault with a deadly weapon in the attack. Charles P. Wallace, "ABC Payoff: Unanswered Questions," *Los Angeles Times*, 3 July 1982, p. 22.
2. Ibid.
3. Ibid., p. 1. Developer James Green and the *Alton Telegraph* eventually settled in 1983 for $1.4 million.
4. Ibid. Other news organizations have found themselves defending libel suits

brought by Synanon. In 1972 the *San Francisco Examiner* published an exposé about Synanon that, according to the *Los Angeles Times*, contained a number of errors. Synanon sued for libel and won an out-of-court settlement from the paper's parent company, Hearst Corporation, of $600,000. The *Times* reported that Hearst later paid Synanon a reported $2 million to settle another suit in which it was alleged that men hired by Hearst had broken into Dederich's office and taken some of his tape recordings.

In December 1977, *Time* magazine ran an article about Synanon. After reportedly spending $2 million in legal fees to defend a libel suit brought by Synanon, the magazine was, according to the *Times*, able to have most of the charges thrown out of court. It was reported that Synanon later dropped the suit against *Time* and reportedly paid the magazine a large settlement. Ibid., pp. 22-23.

5. Ibid., p. 24.
6. Ibid.
7. Ibid., p. 1. The *Los Angeles Times* quoted Norman E. Isaacs, chairman of the National News Council, as saying, "To hear of a media organization as rich as ABC settling a Synanon case by 'mutual agreement' and refusing to comment further, cannot help but raise questions about the network's commitment to ruggedly independent journalism." A number of jurors were quoted as saying that ABC would have won the case if they had been allowed to decide it. An ABC staff member, who asked not to be identified, was also critical of the way the organization handled the suit: "As an amoral business decision it [settling the case] really made sense . . . ABC got out of an expensive suit. The First Amendment issues were absolutely secondary to ABC executives." Ibid., p. 23.
8. A number of national polling organizations report that between 60 and 70 percent of the American people claim that television is their primary source of news.
9. "60 Minutes," however, has been the subject of much criticism and has been sued for libel on a number of occasions. A suit against "60 Minutes" will be discussed in this chapter.
10. Sally Bedell, "Westmoreland Files Libel Suit against CBS," *New York Times*, 14 September 1982, p. C9.
11. Ibid.
12. Ibid. Westmoreland was quoted as saying that if he won his suit against the network, he would donate the money to charity.
13. Don Kowet and Sally Bedell, "Anatomy of a Smear: How CBS News Broke the Rules and 'Got' Gen. Westmoreland," *TV Guide*, 29 May 1982, p. 3.
14. Sally Bedell, "CBS Reportedly Offers Time to Westmoreland," *New York Times*, 11 September 1982, p. 45.
15. While the CBS offer of unedited time to Westmoreland was unusual, it was not unprecedented in network television. According to the *New York Times*, in July 1981 the Kaiser Aluminum and Chemical Corporation was given four unedited minutes on ABC's "Viewpoint" program in which it complained about its treatment in an ABC News report. Ibid., p. 45.
16. Ibid.
17. Bedell, "Westmoreland Files Libel Suit Against CBS," p. C9. Westmoreland's letter to Wyman was dated 10 August 1982.
18. Westmoreland asked for $120 million in compensatory and punitive damages. Named in the suit, which was originally filed in South Carolina, Westmoreland's home state, were Van Gordon Sauter, president of CBS News; George Crile, producer of the documentary; Mike Wallace, the program's narrator and inter-

viewer; and Samuel A. Adams, a consultant paid by CBS who helped with the program. The case was later moved to New York City.

19. The report, running almost eleven pages, was extremely critical of CBS and the way the documentary was prepared.

20. Kowet and Bedell, "Anatomy of a Smear," p. 4.

21. Ibid., p. 9. *TV Guide* quoted (p. 9) an unnamed source who described the way Adams was prepared for the interview: "Literally, they did a mock interview . . . George [Crile] and Alex [Alben, the researcher] ran through the questions in chronological order—the ones basically used by Wallace. Not only did they do a run-through—they gave Sam [Adams] definite feedback on his answers. It was a conscious effort to rehearse the whole interview, from top to bottom."

22. Ibid., p. 4.

23. Ibid., p. 15.

24. Richard Bernstein, "CBS Releases Its Study of Vietnam Documentary," *New York Times*, 27 April 1983, p. C24.

25. Ibid. A senior executive producer, Burton Benjamin, in preparing the report, interviewed thirty-two people, including twelve CBS News employees. Benjamin also reviewed unedited transcripts of interviews for the broadcast. CBS issued a statement saying Benjamin had promised confidentiality to many of those he interviewed. Jonathan Friendly, "CBS Is Told to Give Westmoreland Internal Study on Vietnam Report," *New York Times*, 22 April 1983, p. C32.

26. Bernstein, "CBS Releases Its Study of Vietnam Documentary." p. C24.

27. Ibid.

28. *Herbert v. Lando*, 441 U.S. 153 (1979).

29. Friendly, "CBS Is Told to Give Westmoreland Internal Study on Vietnam Report," p. C32.

30. Stuart Taylor, Jr., "CBS Producer Suspended For Secret Taping," *New York Times*, 16 June 1983, p. C27.

31. Ibid.

32. Ibid.

33. Stuart Taylor, Jr., "McNamara Criticizes CBS on Taping of Call," *New York Times*, 14 June 1983, p. C15. Attorneys for CBS denied the allegation that Crile had secretly recorded an in-person conversation with McNamara by concealing a tape recorder. Such tactics, according to an attorney representing CBS, would be against the law.

34. John Corry, "Weighing the Facts in Westmoreland vs. CBS," *New York Times*, 4 September 1983, p. H19. See also Jonathan Z. Larsen, "The Battle of Black Rock," *New York Magazine*, 24 October 1983, pp. 40-53; Anthony Lewis, "Libel and Politics," *New York Times*, 18 August 1983, p. A27.

35. John Corry, "Westmoreland Suit Data Released," *New York Times*, 25 August 1983, p. C24.

36. Ibid.

37. "Jury Finds for CBS and Rather in Slander Case," *New York Times*, 7 June 1983, p. C11.

38. Ibid.

39. Under California law, a nine-vote majority is required for a decision in a civil case.

40. "Jury Finds for CBS and Rather in Slander Case," p. C11.

41. Ibid.

42. Ibid.
43. "Rather Again Defends CBS in Suit," *New York Times*, 1 June 1983, p. C23.
44. In September 1983, Steve Wilson, an investigative reporter for "Breakaway," a syndicated program shown in approximately seventy television markets, did a series of reports on Galloway's suit against CBS and Dan Rather. He included comments from Rather on the witness stand that to some observers could only be described as "arrogant." In preparing his report, Wilson tried several times to arrange an interview with Rather. When he finally confronted him outside CBS News headquarters, Rather directed a four-letter word at him that while bleeped out in Wilson's report, was clearly discernible to the audience. Rather later apologized but still refused to be interviewed by Wilson about the case.
45. Tom Girard, "Not in the Murrow Tradition," *Variety*, 15 June 1983, p. 39.
46. Sally Bedell Smith, "Decision's Effect on CBS, '60 Minutes,' and Rather," *New York Times*, 7 June 1983, p. C11. Some observers are becoming concerned about the role that organizations openly hostile to the media are playing in libel suits. Galloway, according to the *New York Times*, received a $5,000 contribution from Reed Irvine, chairman of Accuracy in Media (AIM). AIM is described by the *Times* as a "conservative group that publishes a biweekly newsletter criticizing what it says is bias in various press reports." AIM has played a significant role in a number of cases involving individuals who have sued or brought complaints against media organizations. See, for example, *National Broadcasting Company v. FCC*, 516 F. 2d 1101 (1974).
47. Smith, "Decision's Effect on CBS, '60 Minutes,' and Rather," p. C11. The executive was Gene Mater, a senior vice-president of CBS News. Mater was quoted in the *Times* as saying that CBS News has settled only one libel suit out of court, a case several years ago involving a "60 Minutes" report about the cocaine trade. Mater said, "It was a nuisance suit and CBS settled for $5,000." Mater is referring to the network, but two television stations owned by CBS settled libel suits out of court for substantial sums in 1982. See note 67 below.
48. On the witness stand Rather was reminded by Galloway's attorney that in pretrial depositions, he admitted that the investigator's interview with the woman could not be described as "tough questioning." The audience was not told, however, that the woman had already confessed several days earlier that she had filed a false claim.
49. Smith, "Decision's Effect on CBS, '60 Minutes,' and Rather," p. C11.
50. It was reported in *Time* magazine that when military officers visited the families of those killed in the 1983 Beirut bombing of the U.S. compound, television news photographers and reporters followed so they could capture on film the reaction of family members to the news of a son's or brother's death. *Time* discussed several instances of such behavior by the media:

> When word came over the wires that Private First Class Michael Devlin of Westwood, Mass., was the first confirmed casualty from that state, reporters besieged his mother. Recalls Christine Devlin, "They are on top of you before you have a chance to get the family together. Why should people have to know how you look or feel under those circumstances?" At Camp Lejeune, N.C., a TV crew reportedly paid children to go door to door in areas closed to the press to find out which families were awaiting word. ... In perhaps the most tasteless single snippet of this deathwatch footage, a CBS News crew taped the actual

moment when Marine officials arrived to report to his family that Corporal Timothy Giblin... had been killed. ["Journalism Under Fire," *Time*, 12 December 1983, pp. 83-84.]

51. Charles Burke, "Sleuthing on Local TV: How Much? How Good?" *Columbia Journalism Review* (January/February, 1984): 43

52. Ibid., pp. 43-45.

53. Burke noted one organization that did not respond. CBS headquarters sent him a note that dismissed questionnaires as "onerous and time-consuming." Thus, WCBS-TV, the CBS-owned station in New York City, and one that does a substantial amount of investigative reporting, was not included in Burke's study. Burke notes that the NBC-owned and ABC-owned television stations in New York City also did not respond. Burke, "Sleuthing on Local TV."

54. Ibid., p. 44. Seven (30 percent) of the twenty-three stations in Burke's study doing no investigative work considered such "likely" in the "foreseeable future."

55. It is interesting to note that Burke's study reported that over half (51 percent) of the news directors at the stations doing investigative reporting remained unconvinced that it "means higher ratings." Ibid.

56. Ibid.

57. It is not unusual for an investigative reporter in a large television market to earn $50,000 to $100,000 or sometimes more. Burke quoted a number of print investigative reporters who now work in television who cited the higher salaries as one reason they made the change. Ibid., p. 45.

58. It is interesting to note that although it may be illegal to record a conversation without the consent of all parties, it is usually legal to record pictures of someone without his or her consent, particularly in any "public" place.

59. Burke's study suggests that the use of such "undercover" techniques or the use of hidden cameras, is relatively limited. Forty (27 percent) reported going "undercover" at some point in the previous two years; thirty-one of those (78 percent) did so in only one or two stories. Burke, "Sleuthing on Local TV," p. 44.

60. Particularly in television, where pictures must be recorded with the use of a camera, it is sometimes necessary for a reporter to mislead the subject of an investigation as to the actual purpose of a story to gain access to premises where the events or conditions can be photographed. Many reporters try to avoid outright lying, but they obviously do not always explain the entire focus of their story in advance.

61. This was an actual story in which the doctor was confronted by a television news reporter. The reporter's research assistant had posed as a woman seeking an abortion. Although she was not pregnant, the doctor had planned to perform an abortion on her. Her discussions with the doctor were recorded on tape with a hidden camera, after which the reporter confronted the doctor in his outer office.

62. In this series, which won local awards for best investigative reporting, there were a number of instances where angry state legislators had heated conversations with the reporter after being asked about their use of the state-provided vehicles.

63. In the "Breakaway" series on Galloway's lawsuit against "60 Minutes," there were allegations that during the editing process "60 Minutes" substituted answers from different questions without informing the audience that they had done so. Westmoreland, in his libel suit against CBS, charged that the editing process was used to distort answers that would have helped exonerate him of the charges.

64. Clarence Jones, *How to Speak TV: A Self-Defense Manual When You're the News* (Miami: Kukar & Company, 1983). Jones, a former print and now television investigative reporter, describes the camera's ability to discover "truth": "The camera is an excellent lie detector. Like the polygraph, it can sometimes be fooled. But if you're caught in an on-camera lie, television will never forget. It will be played over and over again. You can't say you were misquoted. The lie is there, on tape, to haunt you forever. The audience is also smart enough to know when you're evading a question" (p. 102).

65. In December 1983, "60 Minutes" broadcast a story about an engineer in Texas who had been sentenced to life imprisonment for a robbery that his co-workers said he could not have committed. The widespread attention caused by the "60 Minutes" piece resulted in his release from prison and a few months later, the charging of another man with the crime.

66. It is, of course, often difficult to measure impact. Some stories bring about immediate changes; others contribute to the public's knowledge of a subject in a more general way that later results in changes.

67. In October 1982, the CBS-owned television station in Philadelphia, WCAU-TV, settled out of court a libel suit filed by the city's Democratic mayor, William Green. The station had broadcast a report that Green was being investigated for involvement in corruption, including accepting bribes and participating in kickback schemes. The station later apologized but Green sued for $5.1 million. Even though Green was a public official and would have had to prove actual malice, CBS settled for a reported $250,000 to $400,000. A number of observers attributed WCAU-TV's subsequent decline in the ratings to the damage to its credibility caused by the severe criticism directed toward it following the Green case. The same week that CBS settled the Green case, it settled out of court for a reported $100,000 a case involving two police officials in Gary, Indiana, who claimed the CBS-owned station in Chicago, WBBM-TV, had libeled them in a series of reports aired in 1979. Jonathan Friendly, "CBS Agrees to Pay in Two Libel Suits," *New York Times*, 21 October 1982, p. A18.

68. See John Curley, "How Libel Suit Sapped the Crusading Spirit of a Small Newspaper," *Wall Street Journal*, 29 September 1983, p. 1.

69. Some of the effects of such transcience are also discussed in chapter 1.

70. Some broadcast journalists become very attached to the communities in which they work and voluntarily choose to spend their careers in a small city; they do so, however, at some sacrifice, particularly in terms of income.

71. See chapter 5.

72. Jones notes that although half the states have made it a crime to record conversations secretly, federal law, "simply stated, says if you participate in a conversation, you may record it." But Jones also notes that "if you plant a microphone, tape recorder or 'bug' to intercept a conversation that you cannot hear, then you have committed a serious federal crime." *How to Speak TV*, p. 134.

73. See chapter 7 for a discussion of the effect of libel suits on both print and broadcast journalists. There is the possibility that as more libel suits are filed against broadcast news organizations, more broadcast journalists will begin to think it could happen to them.

74. Bob Marich, "Consulting the 'News Doctors,'" *Electronic Media*, 2 February 1984, p. 15. Consultant fees typically range from $20,000 to $50,000 annually, depending on the market size (p. 52).

75. Ron Powers, *The Newscasters* (New York: St. Martin's Press, 1977), p. 234.

76. Marich, "Consulting the 'News Doctors,'" p. 15.

77. A consultant who had worked with Christine Craft commented on the nature of television news after she filed her lawsuit: "Ideally, credibility is based on journalism, not wardrobe . . . but that is not the reality of what TV news is today. The reality is that TV news is contained in an entertainment medium and the criteria used to judge TV news people are the same ones used to judge people in soap operas and talk shows." Howard Rosenberg, "Sour Saga of a Woman TV Anchor," *Los Angeles Times*, 12 April 1982, part VI, p. 3.

78. Such news programs are often near or at the top of the ratings. See Powers, *The Newscasters*, pp. 33-45.

79. Some news directors have successfully resisted pressures to hire newspeople for cosmetic or other nonjournalistic reasons. One such news director is Ralph Renick of WTVJ-TV in Miami, who thinks that the "consultant period" may have peaked: "They took what was a fledgling business that in many respects operated in an almost amateurish way and brought it to a sort of *National Enquirer* level. . . . Then the dust settled and, between the peaks and valleys, it's a pretty good product now." Marich, "Consulting the 'News Doctors,'" p. 52.

80. 8 A. 2d 301 (1939).

81. Ibid. at 303.

82. Ibid.

83. Ibid.

84. Ibid.

85. Ibid.

86. Ibid. at 308.

87. Ibid. at 304.

88. Ibid. at 308-9.

89. Ibid. at 310.

90. Ibid. at 311.

91. Ibid. at 312.

92. See Bob Teague, *Live and Off-Color: News Biz* (New York: A & W Publishers, 1982), especially his discussion of "silly live remotes."

93. It is not likely that a television station would be held liable for a defamatory statement made by someone shouting into a live microphone, but there still remains the possibility that a judge or jury would hold a station completely responsible for anything broadcast over its facilities.

94. 95 F. Supp. 936 (1951).

95. Ibid. at 940.

96. Ibid. at 939-40.

97. Ibid. at 940.

98. The states were Oregon, Washington, Nevada, Idaho, Colorado, Texas, New Mexico, Arizona, and Utah.

99. 95 F. Supp. at 938-39.

100. Ibid. at 938.

101. Ibid.

102. Ibid. at 939.

103. Ibid.

104. Ibid.

105. Ibid.

106. 150 F. Supp. 98 (1957).

107. Ibid. at 108.

108. Ibid. at 101-4.
109. Ibid. at 108-9.
110. Ibid. at 112.
111. 360 U.S. 525 (1959).
112. 48 Stat. 1088, 47 U.S.C. sec. 315 (a); emphasis in original.
113. 360 U.S. at 526-27.
114. Ibid. at 527.
115. Ibid. at 527-28.
116. Ibid. at 529.
117. Ibid. at 530.
118. Ibid.
119. Ibid. at 531.
120. Ibid. at 534 n. 16.
121. Ibid. at 535.
122. Ibid. at 536.
123. Ibid. at 538.
124. Ibid. at 541.
125. Ibid. at 547.
126. 126 S.E. 2d 873 (1962).
127. Ibid. at 878.
128. Ibid. at 879.
129. Some of these issues will be considered in the final chapter.
130. 191 A. 2d 662 (1963).
131. Ibid. at 664-65.
132. Ibid. at 668.
133. Ibid. at 665.
134. Ibid. at 668.
135. Ibid.
136. Ibid. at 673.
137. 327 So. 2d 810 (1976).
138. Ibid. at 810-11.
139. Ibid. at 811-12.
140. Ibid. at 813-16.
141. Ibid. at 819.
142. 3 Med. L. Rptr. 1913 (1978).
143. Ibid. at 1913.
144. Ibid. at 1913 n. 1.
145. Ibid.
146. Ibid. at 1913.
147. Ibid. at 1914.
148. Ibid.
149. Ibid. at 1915.
150. Ibid.
151. See, for example, Donald L. Smith, "Privacy: The Right That Failed," in *Mass Media and the Supreme Court*, 3d ed., edited by Kenneth S. DeVol (New York: Hastings House, 1982), pp. 373-76.
152. 449 F. 2d 245 (1971).
153. Ibid. at 245.
154. Ibid. at 246. One of the pictures taken of the examination that appeared in *Life* showed Dietemann with "his hand on the upper portion of Mrs. Metcalf's (one

of the *Life* employees) breast while he was looking at some gadgets and holding what appeared to be a wand in his right hand. Mrs. Metcalf had told plaintiff that she had a lump in her breast. Plaintiff concluded that she had eaten some rancid butter 11 years, 9 months, and 7 days prior to that time.''

155. Ibid.
156. 449 F. 2d at 247.
157. Ibid.
158. Ibid. at 248.
159. Ibid. at 249.
160. Ibid.
161. Ibid. at 250.
162. 443 U.S. 562 (1977).
163. Ibid. at 575-76.
164. Wayne Overbeck and Rick D. Pullen, *Major Principles of Media Law* (New York: Holt, Rinehart & Winston, 1982), p. 126.
165. 443 U.S. at 580.
166. Ibid. at 581.
167. Ibid. at 582.

7

Getting Out of the Libel Morass

Libel has become immensely important and complicated, yet debate the past two decades over what standards should apply in what cases has not always reflected its importance or its complexity. Libel suits have been viewed by some simply as a method to punish media organizations who either bring news we would rather not hear, or fail to live up to standards that allow no innocent error. Efforts to be compensated for harm to reputation are to some persons no different from suing a company that has manufactured an unsafe product.

Debate in libel has often centered on the motives and responsibilities of the defendant. The extent to which news organizations enjoy a privilege to publish or broadcast false statements has depended on the status of the subject of the news story and the "thought processes" or motives of journalists as they prepared the news report. The right to vindicate one's reputation has been pitted against glowing references to freedom of speech and press and arguments that the defamatory statements reflected haste and innocent error, not known or reckless falsehood.

But those who publish or broadcast are in no ordinary business and when perched on a scale opposite reputational interests, they bring heavy baggage: the First Amendment. Freedom of speech and press occupy a position of unparalleled reverence in our constitutional system. Courts have tolerated obnoxious, offensive, and even dangerous communication in order to protect speech that helps us, even indirectly, to govern ourselves. The theory that inhibiting any form of speech poses a threat to all forms of speech has been largely untarnished by decades of litigation. There have been cases of prior restraint, individuals were sentenced to jail and fined for publishing obscene materials, and some demonstrations have been curtailed because of time, place, and manner restrictions. But courts have shown substantial tolerance for protecting speech of any social value.

223

In the past decade the Supreme Court and some lower courts have not demonstrated such tolerance in libel suits. They have either viewed the craft of journalists as relating only indirectly to the ideals suggested in the First Amendment, or they have held that when such interests are balanced against those of reputation, they are to be given equal weight in a battle that either side is entitled to win.

Part of the genius of the Constitution is its creation of a complex system of competing interests, none of which is supposed to be strong enough to overwhelm the others. At the core of the system lies communication. When citizens are denied access to information they need to govern themselves by controlling their agents, they dangerously surrender a portion of their sovereignty to players who participate in political battles from which the strongest emerge. Lack of information converts the people from "governors" to sideline observers. Abuse of power, including threats to precious constitutional rights, necessarily follows when the "servants" of the people know no one is watching.

Modern mass media have become the means by which we watch. Courts and others have long understood the indispensable role of the mass media in informing citizens in a democratic society; they also understand the potential of the media to abuse its special position. Out of concern for the very substantial power of the media to injure reputation have emerged libel laws seeking to provide guidelines under which both First Amendment and reputational interests can be protected.

Yet those guidelines and standards have evolved in a way that neither side seems satisfied. Plaintiffs in libel suits wait many years for their day in court and often spend large sums of money just to get there. Juries award huge judgments that seem to media organizations not only disproportionate to the alleged harm, but threatening to news-gathering and reporting. Meritless suits cost only slightly less to defend because summary dismissal seems more difficult to obtain. Trial judges or astonished appellate courts overturn jury awards in a large percentage of cases. By that time each side has wasted precious monetary and personal resources. Much depends on the initial decision as to the public or private status of the plaintiff.

It is difficult to measure the impact of libel suits on media organizations, but it is clear that the threat posed by libel suits requires an examination of the standards that have evolved, and suggestions for improving the situation. Because the filing of libel suits in substantial numbers and the large judgments awarded by juries are relatively recent phenomena, very little has been written about the effects of libel suits. Initial evidence suggests that libel has begun to affect the news-gathering and news-reporting process.

"Chilling Effect" of Libel Suits:
A Preliminary Study

Every year Investigative Reporters and Editors (IRE), an organization founded in 1975, holds a national convention. In 1983, approximately 1,300 reporters, editors, producers, and other journalists from both print and broadcasting belonged to the organization. A survey of thirty-nine open-ended questions was distributed at the convention held in St. Louis in June 1983, attended by about 500 IRE members.[1] Eighty completed questionnaires were returned. Questions relating to a variety of topics were asked, such as demographics, psychological perceptions of the legal environment in which investigative reporters work, commitment in terms of time and resources in investigative reporting, and most important for present purposes, any self-censorship or inhibiting effect of libel suits.[2]

Obviously a self-selected group, the convention probably represented the largest concentration of journalists involved in investigative reporting gathered in one place at one time.[3] Investigative reporting has become an increasingly important part of print and broadcast journalism. And because of the nature of investigative reporting, it often involves defamatory statements that may lead to libel suits.

Sample Characteristics

Most of the participants in the survey identified themselves as either reporters (51 percent) or investigative reporters (19 percent). The remainder were divided among producers (9 percent), editors (4 percent), and a few other miscellaneous categories.

The survey has implications for other types of reporting because a substantial number of those responding to the survey did not do full-time investigative reporting; two-thirds (64.5 percent) said they spent no more than half their time doing such reporting. A quarter said they were employed as investigative reporters on a full-time basis.[4]

The vast majority (76 percent) of the subjects were male. The overwhelming majority were also quite young: 80 percent were thirty-five or younger; 53 percent were thirty or younger. Similarly, most had very few years of experience, with half having six or fewer years. Most of those surveyed were quite well educated: over 96 percent had at least a college degree, and one-fifth had an advanced degree, perhaps reflecting a growing level of specialization among reporters, especially investigative reporters.[5]

Over half the respondents worked for print organizations (60 percent), with most of the rest working for commercial broadcasting organizations (36 percent). The remainder (4 percent) worked in public broadcasting. The respondents came from a relatively diverse cross section of small- to large-sized media organizations and markets. Those working for newspapers reported circulations from 3,000 to 1,000,000; the average was about 170,000, with a third having a circulation of 45,000 or less, a third between 46,000 and 150,000, and a third between 151,000 and 1,000,000. Among those working for broadcasting organizations, a third were from the top ten markets, a third were from markets size 11-30, and a third were from markets 31-104.[6]

Results

Although the data gathered in this survey are not generalizable in any statistical sense because of the self-selected nature of the sample, the results do suggest possible trends or patterns and indicate growing concern about libel.

Over 80 percent of those surveyed indicated that there was at their organizations at least a moderate level of concern about being sued for libel. Half of these said the concern was at "a very high level." Such concern no doubt contributed to the lopsided response to the following question:

> Richard Salant, the former president of CBS News, wrote recently that in newsrooms across the country, stories are not being covered that ought to be covered because of recent libel judgments. Do you agree with this statement?

Almost two-thirds (65 percent) of those answering this question (seventeen did not answer it) said they agreed at least in part with Salant's statement. Perhaps more important, the results strongly suggested that for at least some journalists, the fear of being sued has had a significant effect on the reporting of news. For example, one-fifth (19.7 percent) of those surveyed indicated that there had been at least one occasion in which their readers or viewers were not informed about something important because the reporter or the news organization was worried about being sued for libel. Furthermore, over half reported that the concern at their organization about being sued has had some effect on their decision to cover certain stories, or the manner in which they are presented.

The basis for this observed level of concern about libel is also reflected in the number of lawsuits that were lost, settled out of court, or were still pending. According to those surveyed, almost 10 percent (seven) said their news organization had lost at least one libel suit; the amounts paid ranged from $5,000 to $800,000. Over 25 percent (twenty-two) indicated that their organization had at least one (up to six) suit pending against it. It is important to note that many respondents simply did not know if any suits were pending—thus the number may actually be higher. Almost a third (32 percent) had settled at least one libel suit out of court, for amounts ranging from $500 to $70,000.

Contributing to the overall problem in regard to libel may be a lack of knowledge about libel laws among those who work in newsrooms. Most of those surveyed said they believed that they themselves were well informed (70 percent), but they felt that their supervisors—those persons responsible for approving stories—were not so well informed. In fact, only about half (49 percent) said their supervisors were well informed; almost one-fifth (16.4 percent) said their supervisors were poorly informed. This represents a significant burden for some reporters because, as the data indicate, almost half (43 percent) do not have direct access to legal staff when libel questions arise. Rather, they must go through their supervisors and rely on their advice.

In addition to inadequate access to legal advice is the substantial pressure investigative reporters are under to "produce." Almost two-thirds (63 percent) of those surveyed said they felt at least some pressure to come up with results, with one in five (18 percent) indicating they felt a great deal of pressure. A quarter (26 percent) also indicated that their supervisors had very little, if any, understanding for stories that fail to "pan out."

Most of those surveyed indicated an understanding of the need for reporters to be trained in libel—90 percent said reporters should be given some kind of training. They also generally recognized the need for continuing education—over two-thirds (69 percent) of those answering (nineteen did not answer this question) said they needed a refresher course in libel or media law. Unfortunately, for many, the opportunities to learn may be scarce. Fewer than half (47 percent) said their news organization had ever sponsored a workshop or seminar on the subject.

If the results of the survey are at all representative, journalists in both print and broadcasting have a real concern about being sued for libel. Their very substantial agreement with Salant's statement suggests that libel judgments against media organizations in recent years have begun to take their toll. There appears to be both the attitude that some stories should not be pursued because they could lead to legal trouble and some evidence, as shown by the survey, that such stories are actually not being covered.

Changing Court Procedures

In many cases, the process by which a libel suit is brought and defended is sheer madness for those involved. The Synanon case discussed in the previous chapter indicated the cost and time required in just getting to trial. Other cases such as General Westmoreland's and Colonel Herbert's libel suits against CBS also show how pretrial motions and the discovery process in particular can last for years.[7] Subsequent appeals can take many additional years.

Judges must do a better job limiting pretrial discovery. Only those documents, notes, and other materials directly bearing on the case should be part of

the discovery process. It must not be used to exhaust the opposing party finan-
cially or emotionally. Judges must allow each side to learn what evidence and
information the other side has, but must bar pretrial maneuvering mostly designed to prevent the case from ever getting to trial.

It will be recalled that Justice White, writing the majority opinion in *Herbert v. Lando*, a case that went to the Supreme Court on a largely procedural
issue related to discovery, expressed concern over the cost and delay resulting
from pretrial activities. But he clearly rejected the argument that news organizations need constitutional protection from the burdens related to the discovery process in order to perform their task:

> Creating a constitutional privilege foreclosing direct inquiry into the editorial
> process, however, would not cure this problem for the press. Only complete
> immunity from liability for defamation would effect this result, and the Court
> has regularly found this to be an untenable construction of the First Amendment.
> Furthermore, mushrooming litigation costs, much of it due to pretrial discovery,
> are not peculiar to the libel and slander area. There have been repeated expres-
> sions of concern about undue and uncontrolled discovery and voices from this
> Court have joined the chorus. But until and unless there are major changes in the
> present Rules of Civil Procedure, reliance must be had on what in fact and in
> law are ample powers of the district judge to prevent abuse.[8]

Federal judges, as noted by White, already have the power to curtail abuse
of the discovery process. The Federal Rules of Civil Procedure require that
they "be construed to secure the just, *speedy*, and *inexpensive* determination
of every action."[9] In addition, the requirement of Rule 26(b)(1), that the
material sought in discovery be "relevant," should be—in the words of the
Supreme Court—"firmly applied," and the district courts should, according
to Rule 26(c), protect a party or person from "annoyance, embarrassment,
oppression, or undue burden or expense." The Court added, "With this authority at hand, judges should not hesitate to exercise appropriate control over
the discovery process."[10]

One problem related to the discovery process that is especially troublesome
when a news organization is a party in a lawsuit is the public release of sensitive information that has been obtained through discovery. Some litigants
energetically resist discovery motions for fear that secrets that would be
helpful to their competitors or harmful in some way would be released. Struggle over providing such information to the opposing side can prolong the pretrial process.

Both sides engage in such activities. In the Westmoreland libel suit against
CBS, Westmoreland's attorney released an internal report prepared by a
senior news executive that demonstrated, in the view of the attorney, that CBS
was guilty of actual malice. The attorney also later released a tape recording
of phone conversations between the author of a book critical of CBS and a

CBS news executive who oversaw the Westmoreland documentary that was potentially damaging to CBS's case.[11] CBS, meanwhile, released documents that it claimed showed Westmoreland had in fact conspired to alter enemy troop estimates to mislead the president, Congress, and the public during the Vietnam war.[12]

On May 21, 1984 the Supreme Court, in a unanimous ruling, issued an opinion that may reduce the possibility that the discovery process will be used to fight a separate battle in the court of "public opinion." In *Seattle Times v. Rhinehart*,[13] the Court held that a judge may bar a news organization from releasing information it obtained during discovery if the judge has "good cause" for issuing such a protective order. Justice Powell, writing for the Court, said such an order did not involve prior restraint: "An order prohibiting dissemination of discovered information before trial is not the kind of classic prior restraint that requires exacting First Amendment scrutiny. . . . A litigant has no First Amendment right of access to information made available only for purposes of trying his suit."[14] News organizations could argue that such a ruling is an impermissible abridgment of their First Amendment rights, but Powell noted that they are free to publish the information if they obtained it independently. In addition, any information that is introduced in open court can also be published, even if it was obtained through the discovery process.[15]

The Court's ruling in *Seattle Times* may cut down on the length of time needed to complete pretrial procedures. If one side can be assured by a judge's protective order that the opposing party will not publish or release the information, it may be less reluctant to turn over such documents and may not, as in the case of KGO-TV and Synanon, hand over hundreds of thousands of documents to obscure the ones that contain the information being sought.[16]

Despite Chief Justice Burger's warning in *Hutchinson v. Proxmire* that trial judges should not hastily grant summary judgments in favor of media defendants, judges should continue to watch closely for cases that lack merit. Individuals have many reasons for bringing libel suits. Judges must remain vigilant in dismissing those that are brought to harass the news media, or merely for the purpose of attracting publicity. News organizations should consider malicious prosecution suits against those who continually bring meritless suits against them, although in many states it is difficult to win such cases.

A libel plaintiff seeking to vindicate his or her reputation is entitled to a fair hearing, but it is consistent with the principles of the First Amendment for a judge to determine whether the case should go to trial and be presented to a jury. Clearly it is difficult for a judge hearing pretrial motions to know whether the case will subsequently be reversed on appeal. Yet something is wrong with the process when approximately 70 percent of the judgments won by plaintiffs are reversed on appeal. If judges had dismissed those suits before the trial, it would have saved both sides much trouble and expense, and cumulative harm to the First Amendment. That is not to suggest that persons with legitimate suits should be denied their day in court. But if, for example, the suit is brought by a public official or a public figure, and there is no evidence of actual malice, the judge should grant summary judgment in favor of the media organization. If the plaintiff is a private person and there is no evidence that would satisfy the minimum fault requirement because the publishing or broadcasting of the false statement was innocent error, the case should also be dismissed before it goes to trial. If a jury gets the opportunity to award large damages, it will most likely do so.[17] Appeals courts are also likely to reverse the verdict or at least reduce the damages awarded. In many cases, the only winners may be the lawyers who brought or defended the lawsuit.

Fact-Finding: Juries or Judges?

The jury has been a sacred part of our legal system for centuries. It has proved to be an indispensable element in a democratic society that treasures personal freedom. But unfortunately, juries have demonstrated that they are often unable to understand and fairly apply complex libel laws and standards. Appellate courts, in reversing jury decisions to award huge sums unrelated to any actual harm, have sometimes sharply criticized the jury's inability to set aside dislike for the news media or other prejudice and apply appropriate standards.

In a very important case, *Bose Corporation v. Consumers Union*,[18] the Supreme Court on April 30, 1984 held that appellate courts can make an independent review of the evidence in a libel case even though appellate review in most areas of the law has traditionally been limited to an examination of court procedure. Bose Corporation had won $210,000 from Consumers Union, publisher of *Consumer Reports*, after the magazine wrote a critical review of one of the company's stereo speakers. When the United States Court of Appeals for the First Circuit reversed the jury's verdict, Bose appealed on the grounds that an appeals court must accept the facts established at trial unless it can show that the trial court's findings were "clearly erroneous."[19] Justice Stevens, writing for the Court's majority, rejected the contention that an appeals court could not conduct an independent review. The Court, beginning in *New York Times v. Sullivan*, intended for appellate review in cases relating to the First Amendment to be exacting:

> The requirement of independent appellate review . . . reflects a deeply held conviction that judges—and particularly members of this Court—must exercise such review in order to preserve the precious liberties established and ordained by the Constitution. The question whether the evidence in the record in a defamation case is of the convincing clarity required to strip the utterance of First Amendment protection is not merely a question for the trier of fact. Judges, as

expositors of the Constitution, must independently decide whether the evidence in the record is sufficient to cross the constitutional threshold that bars entry of any judgment that is not supported by clear and convincing proof of "actual malice."[20]

Appellate judges should not exercise the power to conduct independent review arbitrarily, but must be encouraged to review actively both before and after the trial the merits of cases that touch vital First Amendment interests. And in cases that are to be decided by juries, trial court judges must find ways of explaining to them what their responsibilities are and if they fail to fulfill them, the judges must overturn the decisions.

In one major libel case, the trial judge used a method of jury instruction that is likely to serve as a model for other cases in which public figures sue media organizations. On February 21, 1983, *Time* in its cover story accused Israeli Defense Minister Ariel Sharon of not taking steps to prevent the massacre of hundreds of Palestinians in two refugee camps in 1982.

The judge in *Ariel Sharon v. Time, Inc.*, Abraham Sofaer, divided the jury's verdict into three parts, and allowed the jurors to announce them separately. Such a method allowed both Sharon and *Time* to claim victory in the case, although Sharon won no monetary damages. Three days after beginning deliberations, the jury announced that the disputed paragraph in the *Time* article had, in fact, been defamatory. Two days later the jurors returned to the courtroom to announce that the paragraph in question was false. Sharon was able to stand on the steps of the federal courthouse and claim that *Time* had lied about him, and that the jury's first two verdicts had been the vindication he was seeking.

On the third, and most difficult issue, whether *Time* was guilty of actual malice, the jurors said that the magazine had not acted maliciously, but the jury foreman read a statement that was very critical of the magazine's reporting methods: "Certain *Time* employees, particularly Correspondent David Halevy, acted negligently and carelessly in reporting and verifying the information which ultimately found its way into the published paragraph of interest in this case."[21]

By dividing the verdict into three parts, the jury was able to distinguish among several key issues that often confuse juries in libel suits involving public officials or public figures. The question of falsity and the defamatory nature of the statement was separated from the question of actual malice. Judge Sofaer's method not only allowed the jury to focus separately on the key issues, but allowed Sharon to claim victory while not winning any money in damages. Such a step-by-step approach to jury verdicts in libel suits received much attention in the days following the trial, and it appears to be a way to keep juries focused on the key issues in libel cases.

As an alternative to going to court, those concerned about the effects of libel suits should explore the possibility of establishing arbitration panels made up of citizens from a variety of professions and organizations—law, journalism, universities—and lay citizens. Both sides would agree to be bound by the decision of an arbitration panel, although a limited right of appeal to actual courts should probably be available. Arbitration panels as a replacement for courts are not likely to happen quickly or easily. Because the mechanism is already in place, the best short-run solution may be the enhanced role of the judge before, during, and after trial.

The Court's very strong endorsement of the role of the judge in conducting an independent review of evidence in libel cases provides some justification for a corresponding diminution of the jury's role. It is probably not feasible in the short run formally to exclude juries from all libel cases and replace them with a judge sitting alone, or some type of arbitration panel. That may not be wise no matter how such a proposal would be implemented. At the same time there is nothing to limit an enhanced role for the judge, an idea that the Supreme Court, in light of its *Bose Corporation* decision, may welcome.

When a judge overturns a jury's award to a libel plaintiff, it may reduce the chances of successful appeal. Appellate courts, recognizing the need for careful review in areas affecting fundamental First Amendment interests, understand that the trial judge not only sits through the presentation of evidence and testimony of witnesses, but conducts his or her own preliminary "appellate" review. In such a case, the trial judge is convinced that the evidence did not support the jury's verdict or that the jury was moved by passion or prejudice unrelated to the facts in the case. If the trial judge only reduces the amount of the award, the assumption may be that the monetary damages were wholly disproportionate to the harm suffered.

Judges exercise awesome power in our constitutional system and there must be controls to curb abuse. But when fundamental constitutional issues are at stake, and when juries have demonstrated an inability to separate their dislike or distrust of the press from the facts in the case at hand, judges must play a more active role. Such a role should include a greater willingness to dismiss at the summary stage, as discussed before, and more exacting scrutiny of a jury's verdict before the long battle through appellate courts begins.[22]

One can sympathize with the libel plaintiff seeking to vindicate personal reputation who has waited for years for the case to get to trial, then wages a difficult courtroom battle and wins a jury award, only to have the trial judge reverse the jury's decision after the trial has ended. The plaintiff then faces the prospect of another trial or the slim chance that an appeals court will reverse the judge. Yet, our system cannot survive if the press is inhibited, or easily dragged into court to prove that everything published or broadcast is true. It may seem fundamentally unfair to the victim of the defamation, but the harm to society when the press stops covering stories of importance because of fears of being sued is likely to be significant. In a system that relies heavily on the right to speak and write freely, individual reputation must sometimes be sacrificed.

Legislative Solutions

Absent from much of our experience with libel is action by state legislatures. Although all states have libel statutes, court activities over the past few decades have greatly modified, and in some cases outright nullified, legislative pronouncements on libel. It will be recalled that in *Gertz* the Supreme Court discussed at great length the importance of state autonomy over some aspects of libel. There are areas in which legislative action may provide partial solutions.

Legislatures could pass laws either severely limiting or prohibiting punitive damages in libel suits involving media organizations. The Supreme Court has refused to take such action itself, yet has stated that it would allow substantial state discretion in determining when punitive damages should be awarded. The Court has expressed concern about punitive damages that have been assessed in amounts wholly unrelated to actual harm. Many states do not allow punitive damages if a retraction or reply has been published or broadcast, although the statutes or case law dealing with retractions are often outdated and confusing.[23]

Punitive damages are assessed to punish the losing party and to deter others from committing similar acts. Such punishment seems inappropriate when First Amendment interests are involved. News organizations, which serve such a vital function in our society, are likely to be particularly sensitive to the deterrent effect of punitive damages. Any self-censorship is especially ominous not only because it may deprive readers and viewers of important information about their community, but because it is virtually impossible to detect. Journalists themselves may not know why they did not pursue a particular story. Punitive damages seem better suited to product liability cases or, say, when chemical companies pollute water or air; they do not square with First Amendment principles.

When legislatures are changing laws relating to punitive damages, they may also consider defining more clearly what constitutes compensatory damages. The Supreme Court has declined to explain what compensatory damages should be for, except to say they should not be limited to out-of-pocket expenses. General pain and suffering caused by harm to one's reputation, although difficult to measure, have been included. Compensatory damages should probably include, at a minimum, legal expenses for the winning side, reimbursement for loss of income, and some reasonable compensation for the humiliation or suffering caused by the libelous statements. But they should be strictly controlled and should bear a strong relationship to the actual harm.

The Supreme Court in *Gertz* clearly stated that punitive damages will be awarded only in cases where actual malice has been proved, whether the plaintiff is a public figure or private person. Juries, however, have difficulty understanding the Court's ruling on punitive damages, and seem routinely to award punitive damages even in the absence of actual malice. State statutes ending or severely limiting punitive damages would help to alleviate some of the problems.

It is conceivable that eliminating punitive damages could have unintended effects hostile to the First Amendment. Appellate judges, alarmed by outrageous punitive damages, may feel compelled to overturn a jury's verdict on the theory that if the jury irresponsibly awarded such an enormous sum in punitive damages, it may have mishandled the entire case. Without punitive damages as a red flag, it is possible that appellate courts would routinely sustain more jury verdicts if the compensatory damages seemed reasonable. Compensatory damages are usually tied more directly to evidence introduced at the trial demonstrating actual loss of income or some other measurable harm. Overturning the award of compensatory damages would, therefore, require independent review of the evidence. Despite the Supreme Court's holding in *Bose Corporation* that appellate courts may review the evidence, those courts with already crushing case loads cannot welcome the prospect of doing so in every libel case. While it is obviously speculation, cases with compensatory awards that appear to be reasonable may win appellate court approval in higher percentages than those with punitive damages, regardless of the merits of the cases.

State legislatures could also preempt courts and actions by deciding the appropriate standard of liability in cases involving private persons. The Supreme Court held in *Gertz* that as long as states do not impose liability without fault, they may choose for themselves the appropriate standard in private person libel cases. The Court did not say such rules must be promulgated by courts. A state legislature could, for example, choose New York's standard of "gross negligence," a compromise between negligence and actual malice, in cases involving private persons. Such a statute would be subject to review by state and federal courts, but it is possible they would sustain it on the basis that libel standards can be grounded in both statutory and common law, and that legislators should play some role in balancing First Amendment and reputational interests. Granted, legislators are not always understanding or appreciative of a free and vigorous press, particularly when it is critical of them. Nevertheless, legislatures do not need to grant to the courts unlimited discretion to determine standards of liability in libel cases. If they enact legislation that either fails to provide a proper balance, or is threatening to vital First Amendment interests, courts can quickly invalidate or modify such laws.

In states where libel statutes are clearly out of date, legislatures should revise them; some state statutes, for example, predate the growth and importance of modern electronic media, particularly television. In the revision process, confusing language relating to defamatory statements can be cleared up, for many state laws discuss the standards in vague and contradictory terms. What constitutes defamation, and whether the judge or the jury makes the determination should be unambiguously set out. If a statement is held by a judge to be incapable of defamatory meaning, he or she should be able to grant summary dismissal on those grounds.

Legislatures should also consider shortening the period of time covered by the statute of limitations. The *Keeton* case clearly demonstrated the chaos caused by state variance in the time period in which a suit can be filed. Considering the transience of journalists who often move from one news organization to another, it is especially burdensome for them to fight libel suits filed years after they have left the newspaper or broadcasting station that disseminated the statements alleged to be defamatory. A one-year statute seems reasonable. Whatever harm to reputation resulted from the publication or broadcast of the defamatory statements should have become apparent by that time.

There is also a substantial need for legislatures to clarify further the extent to which certain privileges limit liability for news organizations in libel suits. All states, whether or not they have demonstrated a commitment to open government with ''sunshine'' or open-meeting laws, should grant substantial privilege to news organizations to cover individuals who conduct the ''public's business.'' If the privilege enunciated by statute is insufficient to protect news media access, courts can modify the laws. States that have shown less appreciation for the importance of public scrutiny of government meetings should make efforts to open such proceedings to the press and provide a clear statement of privilege.[24]

Those concerned about the First Amendment often resist legislative action on the grounds that the principles of the amendment should stand on their own. They fear that any ''elaboration'' or modification of the provisions of the amendment dilutes their vitality. Such an attitude was demonstrated when, in the wake of *Branzburg v. Hayes*, congressional efforts to pass a federal shield law failed to gain much support from the journalism community.[25] More recently, the inability of Senator Robert Packwood (R-Oregon) to gain support for a constitutional amendment to grant broadcasters full First Amendment rights demonstrates an uneasiness over ''tampering'' with such fundamental principles.[26] Concern over legislative incursions into the area of freedom of speech and press is often justified; still, legislatures can make a positive contribution to getting out the libel morass. If it appears they are creating more problems than they solve, courts should closely monitor their activities and stand ready to invalidate the newly passed laws.

Right to Reply

The Supreme Court made it clear in *Miami Herald v. Tornillo*[27] that it would not tolerate state laws requiring newspapers to provide space to reply for those who were the subjects of critical articles or editorials. The Court also held in *Red Lion Broadcasting v. FCC*[28] that because of the unique nature of broadcasting, a right to reply to a personal attack can be provided without abridging broadcasters' First Amendment rights.

Journalists, whether working for print or broadcast organizations, tirelessly fight any suggestion that victims of defamation ought to have some type of mandated access to newspaper columns or broadcast airwaves to counteract harmful statements. They argue that journalism and debate are not the same, and under the First Amendment, journalists alone must decide what is to be published or broadcast.

In a society that places great value on fairness to the individual, an argument for some type of access seems to have merit. Yet, such a right to reply creates many problems. It will be recalled, for example, that before Westmoreland filed his $120 million libel suit, CBS offered him fifteen minutes of unedited time that would be broadcast as part of a follow-up program. Although an unusual departure from CBS news policy, it was not the first time a broadcast news organization had offered an individual unhappy with the way he or she had been portrayed in a news program time to reply. Westmoreland declined the offer and filed the libel suit, saying that fifteen minutes of unedited time would not be enough to counteract the very serious charges made in the original documentary.

And that is part of the problem. The subjects of defamatory statements usually feel that no forum within the news organization will provide the necessary exposure to challenge thoroughly the original allegations. A small correction box buried in the newspaper hardly gets the attention the original story did on the front page with large headlines. If the reply were mandated and as prominent as the original story, the news organization would be forced to turn over control of its facilities to nonjournalists. A requirement that a newspaper prominently feature a reply it was unable to edit would be viewed as an intolerable infringement of its First Amendment rights. In the view of many journalists, it is one thing to allow an aggrieved party to write a letter to the editor refuting charges; it is quite another requiring the paper to run a front-page story with the headline "Newspaper Lies: Irresponsible Reporting Destroys Reputation."

A partial solution may be found in current procedures used in a number of states. If a news organization has made a mistake and prominently features a correction or retraction, the individual defamed should be prevented from collecting punitive damages. In most states juries can consider such actions as evidence to refute charges that the news organization acted with malice. Such a limitation should be uniform in all states. The problem, of course, would be in deciding whether the reply or retraction was "prominently" featured.

Such a system needs to provide the libel plaintiff with some incentive for choosing the reply. It could be argued that no plaintiff would surrender the right to pursue punitive damages or the libel suit itself in return for a reply or retraction that may not counteract the harm done by the original article or broadcast. But the solution lies not in increased litigation, but in the dissemination of more ideas and information.

The key to such a system of reply may depend on expanding the notion of "innocent error." Under current libel laws in most states, a private person may collect compensatory damages, which can be substantial, if he or she proves the defamatory statements were negligently published or broadcast. Even though the Supreme Court has stated that some minimal level of fault must be demonstrated, news organizations that make innocent errors are punished along with those who were clearly irresponsible. Mrs. Firestone's successful libel suit against *Time*, whose reporter was unable to understand the trial judge's decree, is an example of punishment for innocent error. He did not intend to injure Mrs. Firestone's reputation; he read a poorly written, extremely confusing decree and misunderstood the grounds for the divorce.

If news organizations could be reasonably assured that a full confession that they were in error would provide either immunity or substantial protection from libel suits, they would be less likely to resist right-to-reply or retraction proposals. Errors are always going to be made in journalism, particularly when a news organization is responsible for a daily newspaper or newscast. If the news organization is able to say it was wrong, and feature the admission of guilt in a prominent way, it should enjoy substantial if not complete immunity from libel suits. Under present standards such an admission may not only harm the reputation of the news organization, but also provide ammunition for the aggrieved party to use at the libel trial. Current laws necessarily make news organizations defensive when they are charged with printing or broadcasting false statements. The natural reaction, partially out of arrogance and partially because the news organization's reputation is at stake, is to fight the allegations. The public, which already holds news organizations in relatively low esteem, would probably welcome candid and prominent discussion of such mistakes.[29] Whatever the effect such retractions or apologies would have, it cannot be any worse than the publicity generated by a libel suit.

Details as to which party would write the reply, and where in the newspaper or in the broadcast day it would be disseminated, remain to be worked out. The virtually automatic, defensive reaction of news organizations to libel suits is motivated in part by the theory that their most precious possession is their reputation. There is substantial truth in such a statement. Yet libel suits that are brought when news organizations make mistakes, but when they are not so careless that their actions constitute gross irresponsibility, could be handled through a reply or retraction procedure.

Clearly, if the news report is substantially correct, and especially if it involves a public official or public figure, the news organization should fight the libel suit with all its resources. But a fair number of libel suits brought against journalists whose crime is haste and not malice could be prevented if a reply procedure were in place.

In a case where the defense is innocent error, it would obviously be necessary to require the plaintiff to participate in the retraction or reply procedure. At a minimum, a plaintiff refusing to participate would be deprived of the opportunity to sue for pain or suffering, or "general" harm to reputation. Such sanctions forcing participation may seem harsh, but in a society that relies heavily on communication, the goal of any plaintiff should be to vindicate his or her reputation in the "court of public opinion," and to be reasonably compensated for the expense of bringing about such vindication. If there was loss of income or some other clearly demonstrated harm, that too should be awarded. Compensating libel plaintiffs in amounts so disproportionate to the actual harm is antithetical to a society that highly values press freedom. The answer is not monetary damages offered by jurors skeptical of the press; it is more communication.

There is no assumption here that any of these suggestions would automatically provide an appropriate balance between First Amendment and reputational interests, or that any of the proposals could be easily implemented. But they might help eliminate lawsuits brought by victims of innocent error. The First Amendment must provide enough breathing space to allow such error even when the subject of the news story is a private person.

The Supreme Court has eloquently argued that private persons must be able to win a libel suit with a lesser standard of liability because they, unlike public officials and public figures, do not have access to channels of communication to refute the charges. It is certainly arguable that few public officials or public figures have automatic access to such channels that would provide the necessary forum to counteract the original charges. The reply proposal would provide such access for both public and private persons.

Broadcasters have long argued that personal-attack rules enforced by the Federal Communications Commission, and ultimately the courts, violate their First Amendment rights. The rules require that when the integrity of an individual has been attacked over the airwaves, the individual is to be notified of the attack and given time to respond. The constitutionality of the personal-attack rules and the fairness doctrine was sustained by the Supreme Court in *Red Lion*. Personal-attack rules, however, are infrequently invoked. Part of the reason may be that the subject of the attack is not notified, or the subject believes that responding to the attack would cause additional attention to be focused on the original critical statements. Others probably do not use the personal-attack rules because it may prevent a libel plaintiff from suing for punitive damages.

Broadcasters claim the rules are onerous and difficult to implement, and a clear example of their "second-rate" First Amendment status. But the rules, which have been in effect since 1967, have not prevented broadcasters from aggressively covering newsworthy events and individuals, and while the rules may occasionally be a nuisance, most broadcasters have not found them to be especially burdensome.

The rules clearly raise important First Amendment issues because they are applicable to broadcasters only, and force them to abide by a government-enforced policy of reply. Yet it would be difficult to argue that broadcasters have been intimidated or inhibited as a result of their compliance. The fairness doctrine, of which the rules are a part, create substantially more problems for broadcasters.[30]

Setting aside the constitutional questions for a moment, if broadcasters can "live" with the right-to-reply requirements of the personal-attack rules, it is possible that newspapers, if the choice were between compliance and defending a libel suit, could also "live" with some type of reply procedure. Such an idea is not an argument for reversing *Miami Herald*, which includes very eloquent language about the importance of leaving the decision as to what to publish in the hands of editors. Yet a right-to-reply procedure that does not remove all control from journalists, but could reduce the number of libel suits, is worth exploring.

This notion should not be interpreted as arguing that because broadcasters do not enjoy full First Amendment rights, it is appropriate to abridge to a certain degree the rights of print journalists by instituting some type of right-to-reply procedure. Those concerned about the First Amendment rights of all journalists would argue that such a move heads in the wrong direction. But it is true that broadcast journalists have lived with right-to-reply procedures enunciated in the personal attack rules. Whatever damage such a rule would do to the First Amendment rights of print journalists could hardly be more serious than the growing number of libel suits against all news organizations.

Other Solutions

There is something especially pathetic about demands that the Supreme Court reverse itself in a particular area of the law. With lifetime tenure and a determination not to "tamper" too often with important provisions of the Constitution, it can take many years and a change in membership before the Court changes direction or reverses a previous set of rulings. When the Court has struggled for so long to reach consensus, as in libel, it seems unlikely it would change course anytime soon.

Nevertheless, the Court must eventually turn away from the public-figure/private-person distinction in libel. The initital decision as to the status of the plaintiff carries such importance that it sets the tone and likely outcome in many libel cases. So much is at stake in the decision, almost always made by a judge, as to who will have to prove malice and who will need only to demonstrate negligence. The public-figure/private-person test is too thin a ledge on which to place fundamental First Amendment interests.

The public interest test, developed by the Court plurality in *Rosenbloom* and rejected by the Court three years later in *Gertz*, focuses attention on the news event and not the status of those involved. The Court's argument that judges are unqualified to decide which issues are of general or public importance but are able, almost miraculously, to determine who is a public figure and who is a private person, defies reason. As the Court minority has protested in libel cases the last ten years, the public's most compelling interest is in the importance of the news story, not the individuals involved. Many persons can obtain notoriety in areas unrelated to the article or broadcast leading to the libel suit.

Justice Brennan argued, for example, that the public's interest in the *Walker* case was in the event, namely the riot at the University of Mississippi. General Walker had, in fact, obtained fame for reasons unrelated to those events. Brennan contended that the public's interest in efforts to desegregate a university would in no way be diminished if a previously unknown individual and not someone famous had been involved. The First Amendment protected coverage of what was clearly an event of the highest public importance.

The effect of the public-figure/private-person test has been to grant wide latitude to discuss the private activities of public figures while severely limiting the privilege to discuss the public activities of private persons. It has also forced judges to make an essentially artificial determination as to the extent to which the individual's participation in public issues was voluntary.

Such an argument mangles many decades of First Amendment history and practice. As Meiklejohn eloquently argued, the First Amendment extends protection to any statements or ideas, no matter how seemingly insignificant, that provide information that helps us govern. He tried to distinguish between public and private libel, the latter in his view falling outside the First Amendment, but argued that the ''governors,'' namely, the people, were entitled to access to anything that is relevant. His view of what was relevant was very broad.

When the Court determines how much First Amendment protection will be extended to discussion of events or issues by first considering the status of those involved, it in effect allows irresponsible coverage of individuals who are clearly public figures, and penalizes coverage of private persons who may be very influential in public affairs without holding public office or being prominent. If private persons in such cases did not "thrust" themselves into the "vortex" of a public controversy, the statements about their activities enjoy substantially diminished First Amendment protection.

The First Amendment protects ideas and communication; protection of reputation is found elsewhere in the Constitution. The First Amendment does not grant journalists license to destroy reputation, but the scope of its protection should not be limited by the actions of individuals subjected to discussion in the media. Individuals harmed by irresponsible reporting must have some method by which they can be vindicated, but news organizations must be allowed to perform their vital function. It may be a high price to pay for those who are innocent victims of press irresponsibility, but the harm to society caused by an overly cautious press is much greater.

Journalists, even though clothed with the sacred principles of the First Amendment, are not all angels. Much could be done within journalistic organizations to reduce the number of mistakes they make. Special care and discretion could be exercised in stories involving private individuals who, through no fault of their own, get caught up in matters of public interest. Journalists could make a conscious effort to control their most pervasive bias: haste. Fewer mistakes might be made if reporters, editors, producers, and others had a little more time to spend on each story. Even though the public may suffer from less exposure to other stories, journalism and personal reputation may be better served.

Libel gives every indication that it will get worse before it gets better. Short-term solutions such as libel insurance will not provide long-term answers. As juries continue to award large judgments, those who believe they have been wronged will hire lawyers and go to court. Insurance premiums will rise as the cost of defending such suits continues upward. If current trends continue, news organizations will eventually be afraid to cover news stories that they fear will lead to legal trouble. Self-censorship on the part of the media serves neither the interests of the press nor society. That is because in a self-governing society like ours, those interests are often the same.

Notes

1. IRE officials indicated that the overwhelming majority of individuals attending the IRE national convention were IRE members, but it is possible that some who completed the survey were not members of the organization.
2. The data were analyzed with the help of John V. Pavlik, assistant professor of journalism, Pennsylvania State University. See "The Legal Environment of Investigative Reporters: A Pilot Study," *Newspaper Research Journal*, Spring, 1985.

3. Subsequent IRE national conventions may have attracted more people.
4. It is interesting to note that over half (57.3 percent) said that they had been at least occasionally prevented from doing an investigative story because they had to cover a more routine assignment.
5. Some of the advanced degrees were in journalism or communications. Many graduate programs allow some kind of specialization, although they often require a broad liberal arts emphasis.
6. Broadcasting markets are generally measured by size, what is called the Area of Dominant Influence (ADI). There are approximately 209 television markets in this country; New York is the largest (number 1), and Glendive, Montana, the smallest (number 209).
7. Months before the trial, the law firm that represented CBS had already billed the company for over $1 million. The Capital Legal Foundation, the organization that paid for Westmoreland's defense, had at that point reportedly spent $900,000. The two sides had taken depositions from fifty witnesses and reviewed 200,000 pages of government documents. Jonathan Friendly, "CBS Moves to Halt Westmoreland Suit," *New York Times*, 24 May 1984, p. C26.
8. 441 U.S. at 176-77. Justice White noted some of the effort involved in discovery in the *Herbert* case:

> It is urged that the large costs of defending lawsuits will intimidate the press and lead to self-censorship, particularly where smaller newspapers and broadcasters are involved. It is noted that [CBS producer] Lando's deposition alone continued intermittently for over a year and filled 26 volumes containing nearly 3,000 pages and 240 exhibits. As well as out-of-pocket expenses of the deposition, there were substantial legal fees, and Lando and his associates were diverted from news gathering and reporting for a significant amount of time [441 U.S. at 176 n. 25].

9. Ibid. at 177; emphasis added by Justice White.
10. Ibid.
11. "Smoking Guns, Secret Tapes," *Time*, 21 May 1984, p. 86. A number of journalists both inside and outside CBS were very critical of Don Kowet, the author of *A Matter of Honor*, for turning the tapes over to Westmoreland's attorneys without a fight. See Jonathan Friendly, "Critic of CBS Yields Tapes to Westmoreland Lawyers," *New York Times*, 15 May 1984, p. C21.
12. See Jonathan Friendly, "Libel Litigants Can Gain From Disclosure," *New York Times*, 22 May 1984, p. A19; Friendly, "CBS Moves to Halt Westmoreland Suit."
13. 104 S. Ct. 2199 (1984).
14. 104 S. Ct. at 2207.
15. Linda Greenhouse, "High Court Backs Trial Data Curb," *New York Times*, 22 May 1984, p. A19.
16. See chapter 6 for a discussion of the case.
17. See chapter 1 for a discussion of the study by the Libel Defense Resource Center.
18. 104 S. Ct. 1949 (1984).
19. Linda Greenhouse, "High Court Calls for Special Care in Libel Appeals," *New York Times*, 1 May 1984, p. A1. 104 S. Ct. at 1955.
20. 104 S. Ct. at 1965. The trial court had held Bose to be a public figure and thus Bose had to prove actual malice.
21. Arnold H. Lubasch, "Time Cleared of Libeling Sharon But Jurors Criticize Its Reporting," *New York Times*, 25 January 1985, p. A1.

22. There are cases where appellate courts have not been satisfied with a trial judge's reversal of a jury verdict in a libel case. In *Tavoulareas v. Washington Post*, Judge Oliver Gasch overturned a $2.05 million libel judgment awarded to William Tavoulareas, the president of Mobil Oil Corporation. 567 F. Supp. 651 (1983). In rejecting the jury's finding, Gasch said: "The article in question falls far short of being a model of fair, unbiased investigative journalism. There is no evidence in the record, however, to show that it contained knowing lies or statements made in reckless disregard of the truth." Stuart Taylor Jr., "Court Overturns Libel Verdict Against the Washington Post," *New York Times*, 3 May 1983, p. A1. The United States Court of Appeals for the District of Columbia reversed. In a decision announced 9 April 1985 the court held that the *Post*'s reputation for hard-hitting investigative reporting could be considered when deciding whether the newspaper is guilty of malice: "It certainly is relevant to the inquiry of whether a newspaper's employees acted in reckless disregard of whether a statement was false or not." 11 Med. L. Rptr. 1777 (1985) at 1798. Journalist Anthony Lewis commented after the court of appeals decision, "the opinion, if it stands, will effectively warn editors to be timid, or else." Anthony Lewis, "Libel: What the Courts Could Do," *Columbia Journalism Review*, (May/June, 1985), p. 20.

23. At the end of 1982 thirty-five states had provisions in statute or common law that made it more difficult for a libel plaintiff to collect punitive damages if a retraction were published or broadcast. But many of the standards are vague and can easily be viewed by journalists as hostile to their interests.

24. Such privilege should be extended when public officials discuss the public's business away from city hall. In 1979, WKBS-TV in Philadelphia broadcast a talk show in which an assistant district attorney criticized a local judge for declaring a mistrial in a case he was prosecuting. The judge sued the station over the remarks. A trial court dismissed the case, but it was reinstated by the Pennsylvania Superior Court. When a television station is fulfilling its public trustee responsibilities by broadcasting public affairs programming about important community issues, it should not be held strictly liable for statements made by public officials about other public officials. It may have been appropriate for the judge in this case to pursue a personal lawsuit against the prosecutor, but it is unfair to force the television station to defend actions of this type in a libel suit.

25. See C. Herman Pritchett, *The American Constitution* (New York: McGraw-Hill, 1977), p. 341.

26. The amendment, "The Freedom of Expression Act of 1983," was discussed at length by Packwood in "The Fifth Estate's Freedom Fighter," *Broadcasting*, 13 February 1984, p. 188.

27. 418 U.S. 241 (1974).

28. 395 U.S. 367 (1969).

29. In the spring of 1984, the *Wall Street Journal* published a series of articles revealing that one of its reporters had leaked information from a column in advance of publication that allegedly allowed some individuals to gain huge investment profits. See Raymond Bonner, "U.S. Charges 5 with Stock Fraud in Use of Wall St. Journal Articles," *New York Times*, 18 May 1984, p. A1.

30. See, for example, Richard E. Labunski, *The First Amendment Under Siege: The Politics of Broadcast Regulation* (Westport, Conn: Greenwood Press, 1982).

Index